EDDIE BARKER'S NOTEBOOK

EDDIE BARKER'S NOTEBOOK

Stories that made the news
(and some better ones that didn't!)

. . . .

Eddie Barker

and

John Mark Dempsey

JOHN M. HARDY PUBLISHING

ALPINE & HOUSTON

2006

First Printing: March 2006

1 3 5 7 9 10 8 6 4 2

ISBN 0-9717667-6-2

Printed and Bound in the United States of America

Cover Design - David Wilgus
Dallas, Texas
Oswald murder photo by Bob Jackson
Oswald and Ruby mug shots courtesy of the *Dallas Morning News*
Barker photo by Juan Garcia
Microphone icon by Karen Boudreaux

John M. Hardy Publishing Company
Houston, Texas
www.johnmhardy.com

Dedication

To Jane, for all she has meant to me for over fifty years, and for being the kind of mother kids only dream about.

To Allan, Susan, Leslie, Ben, and Jeanne.

To grandchildren Paul, Ben, Julie, and Christian Munguia; Laura, Jack, Sam, and Claire Wilgus; and Charlie Garcia.

Jane understands that I'm using this page to remember and say thanks to that great KRLD newsroom staff of our glory days. Some have gone on: Henk deWitt, Frank Gleiber, Jay Hogan, Buster McGregor, Steve Pieringer, George "Sandy" Sanderson, Joe Dave Scott, Jim Underwood. The others know who they are and know how much they meant and still mean to me. I'm thankful for what they did then and the great memories we look back on today. Thanks guys. It was a blast.

Table of Contents

Foreword

By Walter Cronkite

I'm a traditionalist. That's a fancy word for "old-fashioned." Perhaps it is not wise to live in the past, but, frankly, I liked a lot of things from my youthful years, things that have been lost in the name of progress.

Now right there is an example of my problem: I think that "journalist" is far too high blown for what most people in the news business do for a living. No intention here to denigrate their importance in the machinery that serves one of the most vital functions of our democracy—the production and maintenance of a free press, accurate and impartial. It is a noble calling, but I liked the old designation of "newspaperman" to encompass all of us who work in the profession. And I have long maintained that it is a profession, since it has an important ethic, perhaps not as exacting as that of doctors or lawyers but comparable. The newsperson's ethic is that of fairness and impartiality in reporting, editing, publishing, and, now, broadcasting.

Obviously, "newspaperman" hardly fits those in radio and television news. Therefore, it hardly fits Eddie Barker, who has spent a very long career solely in broadcasting. But in my book (as you will find in his) he warrants my definition of a real newspaperman, that is, someone who is totally dedicated to gathering and reporting the news of the day, in print or on the air. He (or she) has what the great CBS news producer Fred Friendly called "fire in the belly."

Eddie has fire in the belly—a five-alarmer burning in his gut. When a good story breaks, Eddie becomes inspired. He leaves no stone unturned until he or members of his staff have mined the territory for every nugget of information. He remains doggedly at the story until his highly developed news sense tells him there is nothing left uncovered.

His success is built on the fundamental of having good and reliable sources. As nearly as I have been able to determine, he knows every cop, fire fighter, emergency room doctor, and ambulance attendant in Dallas and surrounding counties. That, of course, is besides the city, county, state, and federal officials whom he taps for information when required.

It takes a certain toughness to do that job as well as he does it. The saving grace there is a cheerful graciousness that is his—excepting only when the clock is racing toward the broadcast deadline and his newsroom's story isn't complete to Eddie's satisfaction. But that is excusable for a guy with his gut on fire.

Eddie's television station, KRLD, was an affiliate of CBS at the time of President Kennedy's assassination, and Eddie's sources proved invaluable to the network.

But I'm encroaching now on Eddie's own book. Let me conclude by simply emphasizing that he meets all the requirements to go on my list as the complete newspaperman—the highest accolade I can express for the consummate news reporter, writer, and director, even if his career has been mostly, as has mine, in the broadcast world.

Prelude: "What's the Real Story?"

Writing a book, especially one about yourself, can be a monu-
mental task, since it is so easy to fall back on that old bugaboo,
procrastination—you'll get around to it in due time, you tell yourself.
I was fortunate to meet Texas A&M University–Commerce professor
John Mark Dempsey, who was "practicing what he preaches" at the
Texas State Network (TSN). I was working Saturdays at my alma
mater, KRLD, and Professor Dempsey was across the divider at TSN.
He kept telling me, "You've got a story to tell," and I kept telling him
I'd get around to it in time. When he reminded me that none of us live
forever, I took heed and looked at the clock. I agreed to do it, but only
if he would be along for the ride. He said okay, and the pages that
follow are the result.

Gary Mack's infinite knowledge of every facet of the JFK story led
me to seek his advice and counsel. The curator of the Sixth Floor
Museum graciously agreed. I am in his debt.

When you've been on the scene as long as I have, people think
you've got some pretty good stories to tell, and I think I do. And you
get a lot of questions, such as, "What's the real story of November 22,
1963?" In these pages you'll find out what really happened, and 'tis
not the same as you'll find in most of the umpteen books written on
the subject.

"Hey, you didn't really throw Dan Rather out of your newsroom,
did you?" As a matter of fact, I did.

"Well, why?" Read on and you'll find out.

"How did you end up being the first reporter to interview Marina
Oswald?" Interesting how easy it was.

"Did she think Lee Harvey shot the president?" I'll tell you about
it.

"Did you ever pay for a story?" I'll let you be the judge of whether
or not I'm guilty.

"Did your bosses ever tell you to drop a story you were
covering?" With a heavy heart I tell you yes. And you'll be surprised

whom and what the story was about. It never made the news before this because of who is involved.

"Have you ever been fired?" Once, and at the time I was so crushed I wanted to disappear. But like so many times when one door closes, another one opened, and that's what happened in my case. See if you don't agree.

"Did you ever meet Edward R. Murrow?" Well, sort of, but under, shall we say, unusual circumstances.

Reporters meet all types along the way, which gives us a realistic view of humanity. As the poet Sam Walter Foss writes:

Let me live in a house by the side of the road,
Where the race of men go by—
The men who are good and the men who are bad,
As good and as bad as I.

So true, too, is the Book of Daniel's warning about false gods with "feet of clay." You may be surprised by who has clay feet.

I hope there's a story or two here that will catch your fancy and that you'll say the read has been a good one.

1

"It Is True . . ."

Lives of great men all remind us
We can make our lives sublime
And departing leave behind us
Footprints on the sands of time
— Henry Wadsworth Longfellow, "A Psalm of Life"

I begin with these lines from Longfellow for a couple of reasons.
First, I'll be talking about some of the greats I've known—of course,
"great" is relative. Some are great only in their mothers' eyes. And
speaking of mothers, they're the second reason for the lines from "A
Psalm of Life." Before I learned that b came after a and y preceded z,
my mother was reading poetry to me, and it's been a big part of my
life. Since this is the only book I'll ever write, it's a way of remembering her, too.

But let's move on. In my years as news director of KRLD-TV and
radio in Dallas, I was part of a lot of stories, none bigger, of course,
than what happened on November 22, 1963. And that may be the
principal reason you bought the book: to get my slant on what
"really" happened. I certainly have some definite reasons for
believing what I do about why Lee Harvey Oswald shot John F.
Kennedy, and I'm going to share them with you. And there are some

other stories I think will hold your attention as well. But you want to know about the assassination, so let's begin there.

"Eddie, he's dead."

It was a long time ago, but I remember hearing those chilling words as though it were yesterday. As I mentioned, I was news director of Channel 4, KRLD-TV and KRLD-AM, the CBS affiliates in Dallas, having held those positions for nearly fifteen years. In those days we didn't have as many television stations as we have now, and television was still in its infancy. Communications were much less sophisticated, and the three major networks relied more than they do today on their local stations.

Channel 4 was part of a three-station pool covering the president's visit to Dallas. KRLD was responsible for coverage of the luncheon at the Trade Mart. I was there to say whatever needed to be said before and after the speech. The people who would be there to hear the speech were, for the most part, people who voted against Kennedy in 1960 when Richard Nixon ran against him. These were the "movers and shakers" of Dallas, a lot of Republicans and a lot of conservative Democrats who disagreed with the president and felt he was too liberal. In fact, the split between the conservatives and the liberals in the Texas Democratic Party is the main reason why Kennedy came to Texas—to heal the rift between the two factions.

The Dallas conservatives may not have liked the president's political philosophy, but he was their president, too. Kennedy was a master at winning over his opponents, and he saw this speech in Dallas as a rare opportunity to do it again. So it was that I was at the Trade Mart to cover the activities surrounding the speech. As it turned out, my being at the Trade Mart commenced the coverage of a story that, it seems, will never end.

It was shortly before one o'clock central time. President Kennedy's arrival at Dallas's Trade Mart had been delayed. Something had happened in the motorcade. Rumors were rampant that the president had been shot in downtown Dallas, about two miles from the luncheon site.

Suddenly, sirens were audible as the president's car and a parade of accompanying vehicles sped by the Trade Mart. We knew where they were headed: Parkland Hospital, where the most serious trauma cases were treated. Its outline was visible in the distance some two miles away.

I was getting ready to report on the president's speech for KRLD-TV and radio and the other local stations that were part of our pool coverage. When the cars raced by without stopping, I went on the air, relaying what little I knew about what had happened and describing what was happening in the Trade Mart. In New York, CBS, like all of the networks and wire services, was frantically trying to get something from Dallas. Unbeknownst to me, CBS had picked up our broadcast and was airing it on the network to the vast audience that every afternoon tuned in to the soap opera *As the World Turns*.

We hear a lot these days about news sources, the good ones, the bad ones, and those you'd just as soon didn't have your phone number. There's a lot of talk now about how many sources you should have to go on the air with a story. I wonder how many of those who profess to not using a story with only one source practice what they preach. I'm afraid I wouldn't do well with today's requirement for multiple sources before using a story. But I always made it a point to know my source. That way I didn't get into trouble.

I knew a doctor who was a member of the staff at Parkland Hospital and who happened to be at the Trade Mart for the president's speech. Like the rest of us, the doctor realized something wasn't right, went to a pay phone, and calmly placed a call at 12:35. An acquaintance in the emergency room matter-of-factly told the doctor that the president was dead when they brought him through the door. Of course, the president was not officially pronounced dead until 1:00 p.m., but the information my doctor acquaintance received more closely reflected the reality of the situation.

My friend saw me struggling to maintain a coherent broadcast with the limited information available, walked over, and whispered in my ear words that would shock the world and stay with me for a lifetime: "Eddie, he's dead." Those words sent a cold chill running down my spine. I didn't want to believe them, but the source was too good.

I then made a decision that has caused a lot of comment in the years since that strangely brilliant Friday afternoon. I told an audience that included the whole CBS network that a reliable source had confirmed to me that President Kennedy was dead. What I didn't know was that my shocking report caused a lot of anxiety at CBS News headquarters in New York. Walter Cronkite, holding the story at arm's length, repeatedly gave me, the local newsman, credit for saying the president was dead. As the minutes went by, Walter was generous in crediting me with the story, making sure the local reporter was given the credit he deserved. And the history books take note of the fact that it was CBS News that stuck with the story of a reporter they knew and trusted.

CBS Evening News editor Ed Bliss was in the newsroom. Here's how he describes what happened in his fascinating insider's look at broadcast journalism, *Now the News*:

> Eddie Barker reported on CBS Television that President Kennedy was dead. The network had aired rumors to that effect. Cronkite had responsibly labeled them as rumors. But, now, reporting from the Trade Mart, Barker had something that was more than a rumor. He said: "The word we have is that President Kennedy is dead. . . . "
>
> The doctor was a friend of Barker's. What he had told the newsman was "Eddie, he's dead." In reporting his television exclusive, Barker thought his words were being carried only on KRLD. Instead, millions of people had heard.
>
> A minute later, Cronkite, who was now on camera at his anchor desk, said, "We just had a report from our correspondent, Dan Rather, in Dallas that he has confirmed that President Kennedy is dead. He emphasized there was still no official confirmation."
>
> At 2:37 [Eastern time], as news editor, I handed Cronkite a piece of paper from the AP wire. He read it carefully to himself, then looking up into the camera and said, his voice breaking, "From Dallas, Texas, a flash, apparently official. President Kennedy died at 1 p.m., Central Standard Time, 2 o'clock, Eastern Standard Time." He looked at the studio clock and added, "Some 38 minutes ago."[1]

The videotape of the report from the Trade Mart is powerful. The cameras in the great room convey the images of the stunned would-be audience for the president, a black waiter wiping away tears, a worker removing the presidential seal from the dais. My doctor friend interrupted me in mid-sentence as I was struggling to ad lib a coherent report. Here is the announcement I made of the president's death, word for word:

BARKER: The Texas School Book Depository, which is a building about eight floors in height. . . .Yes? [Pause of seven seconds]. And who are you, sir?
DOCTOR: I don't want to be identified.
BARKER: We have just been told by a member of the staff at Parkland Hospital the president is dead. What is the governor's condition?
DOCTOR: He's been shot in the chest.
BARKER: Do you have any report on that?
DOCTOR: No.
BARKER: Thank you, sir. This is the report of a doctor at Parkland Hospital who was here for the luncheon. He says that the president is dead. We do not have a confirmation on this. We only pass it along as the word of a man who we take to be a good source at this time. The word we have is that President Kennedy is dead. [Woman's cries can be heard in the background]. This we do not know for a fact. . . . The word we have is from a doctor on the staff at Parkland Hospital who says that it is true. He was in tears when he told me just a moment ago.

I knew who the doctor was, but in the excitement of the moment, I couldn't remember his name. Anyway, he asked not to be identified.

Several publications commented on my "beat." A 1965 article by Richard Van der Karr in the scholarly publication, *Journalism Quarterly* notes: "In the absence of official confirmation, [this] may be the most important journalistic event of the [Kennedy assassination] period; it will certainly be one of the greatest snap evaluations of a source in the history of broadcast journalism."[2] An article in *Broadcasting*, then as now, the radio-TV industry's best-known trade publication, notes that Cronkite frequently referred to KRLD's report of Kennedy's death and, because of my instantaneous decision to report the tip from my doctor acquaintance, "CBS had a beat of several minutes that Mr. Kennedy had died of his wounds."[3]

Of course, had my doctor acquaintance been mistaken, it would have been a very different story. The bouquets would have been brickbats. But I was so certain of my source, I didn't hesitate to report the news, although you'll notice as you read the transcription above that I was careful to say we didn't have official confirmation.

To be fair, my old friend Dan Rather, who was in Dallas covering Kennedy's trip, also received recognition for reporting the president's death first—but on radio.

As described in Ed Bliss's book, Dan was talking simultaneously by phone with the CBS Radio editor and me. Rather heard me say Kennedy had died. "Yes, that's what I hear, too. That he's dead," Dan told his editor. The editor mistakenly thought Rather was giving him independent confirmation of Kennedy's death and put the report on CBS Radio, as announced by anchorman Allan Jackson. I don't know where in the world Dan came up with this telephone thing; I was nowhere near a phone.

In fact, many books credit Dan as the first to report the president's death. University of Pennsylvania Annenberg School of Communication professor Dr. Barbie Zelizer, in her 1992 book, *Covering the Body*, observes that my role in covering the assassination—indeed, the role of many Dallas reporters—has been overlooked: "In most current chronicles, however, Barker's role in the story has shrunk to near omission. Today it is mentioned in only the most extensive and detailed accounts. . . . The role of the local reporter has been consistently understated alongside the more extensive accounts accorded of his better-known and more prestigious national counterpart."[4]

A few years ago, I faxed Dan the account of our joint coverage of the Kennedy assassination in *Covering the Body*. He called me on my cell phone. "I'm so glad we finally got this straightened out," he said generously.

Certainly, I never covered a bigger story than the assassination of John F. Kennedy. I don't suppose anyone else has, either. But how I came to be standing there in front of a camera with a microphone in my hand that historic Friday afternoon also makes quite a story.

As far back as I can remember, radio has appealed to me. As a kid,

I always listened to Bill Stern, the colorful sportscaster, on Friday night. "Bill Stern—the Colgate shave cream man—is on the air!" I listened to newscasters H. V. Kaltenborn, Gabriel Heatter, and Elmer Davis. And, of course, I always listened to Edward R. Murrow's London broadcasts during World War II. I knew that somewhere down the road, I wanted to do what they were doing.

In 1944, when I was a high school student in San Antonio, I was working at Sommers' Drug Store as a delivery boy. One day I thought, "Well, my voice has changed—I don't have to worry anymore about squeaking." So I decided I would go to a radio station and apply for a job, just to see what would happen. The big station—then as now—was WOAI. But I was scared to go there. I was sure I wasn't ready.

KONO was another San Antonio station. It was kind of a "blood-and-guts" station and covered all the accidents and shootings. It was located out on the edge of town and, because I didn't have a car, it would have been hard for me to go there. So I figured, well, there's KMAC. It was a Mutual Broadcasting System station. Mutual was the third major radio network in those days, behind NBC and CBS, and it served mostly smaller stations. One day, I told myself, I'm going to go down there and apply for a job. Finally, I did.

The station was on the tenth floor of the National Bank of Commerce building in downtown San Antonio. I went up the elevator, and down at the end of the hall was the radio station. Well, I froze. I couldn't go in. I saw the door to the staircase and I went in there and prepared myself. Cleared my throat a lot. I must have stayed in there half an hour. Finally, I came back out and went into the office. First time I'd ever been in a radio station. "Whom would you like to see?" the receptionist asked. "I want to see someone about a job," I managed to tell her. "Well, I'll ask Mr. Davis if he'll see you," she kindly replied.

The man who owned the radio station was Howard W. Davis. The receptionist beckoned for me to come into Mr. Davis's office. It was a long, rectangular office. At the other end from his desk was a big mirror that covered the entire wall. He looked in the mirror and groomed himself all day long. He was probably the vainest man I ever knew. I don't mean to belittle him; he was very nice to me.

Mr. Davis asked, "So you want to be an announcer?" I said, "Yes, sir, I'd really like to be." He said, "Let me get Tony Bessan in here.

He's the program director." So Tony came in. He had to be one of the dearest, nicest human beings I ever met. Mr. Davis asked me, "What's your name?" And I timidly told him, "Edmund Barker." I still went by Edmund in those days.

Tony came in and said, "What did you say your name was? Eddie Barker?"

And I said, "Yes, sir, Eddie Barker." That was the end of "Edmund." Tony knew right away it was much too formal for radio.

So Tony Bessan said, "Okay, let's see what you sound like." He gave me a commercial to read. It was as if all of my boyish nervousness just disappeared. Lord knows, I had been practicing for years. I'd read ads out loud. Lockheed used to have an ad in *Time* magazine or something, and the slogan was, "For protection today, and progress tomorrow—look to Lockheed for leadership." And I would put my hand up to my ear, as the announcers used to do, and just read the copy in the ad.

Of course, radio seemed very glamorous to a boy growing up in modest circumstances. My dad, Edmund Asa Barker Sr., grew up in the Hill Country between Blanco and Johnson City. The old family home still stands on Miller Creek. Dad was one of seven children. My mother, the former Nannie Mae Meek, was born into a family of ten children in Kentucky. She came to San Antonio for a visit with a sister who was there for a short time, reason unknown. She met my father and, after a brief courtship, they married in 1922; I was born at home, 102 Kirkwood Street, in the Harlandale section of San Antonio five years later, on August 18, 1927. I was their only child.

My mother and father were not starry-eyed kids. My father was fifty-three years old when I was born, my mother was in her forties (I never knew her true age). As you might guess, my parents were older than the parents of the kids I grew up with, and my aunts, uncles, and cousins were also older. Neither of my parents went beyond high school. My father was the last of seven to marry, and his mother, Leah, lived with him before and after he married.

Dad had been a farmer and started doing carpentry work. It was a struggle for him to find work, and we always lived on the edge financially. In the dark days of the Depression, my mother kept us going by taking in laundry.

As hard as the times were, my dear mother always found a dollar to pay for my "expression" lessons, as we called them. She knew I wanted to do something with my voice. There was a teacher, Maude Reeder Lyons, who taught expression, or "elocution." So when I was in the fourth or fifth grade, I would take a lesson a week from Mrs. Lyons. She would teach me how to put the emphasis on the right word—a very important thing for announcers to know.

I guess it was in the fifth grade when I was chosen to go up on the stage at an assembly and introduce the school superintendent. By this time, my teachers had noticed my above-average speaking ability. Well, in San Antonio the weather was warm most of the time, and so in my poor neighborhood it was not uncommon for children to go to school barefoot. I happened to be barefoot on this occasion. I walked up on the stage, which they had just painted, and my little feet got stuck in the paint. One of life's embarrassing moments.

Until I went to KMAC, I had no idea what I was going to do with the knowledge I had gained from Mrs. Lyons's expression lessons. But when Tony Bessan gave me the copy to read, it did not at all intimidate me. I knew how to read aloud, and I knew how to interpret the commercial that he gave me. Tony apparently liked my reading. Then he gave me a piece of news copy from the old wire machine. I had listened to all the great ones read the news, Kaltenborn and the rest, and so I read it, and the names in the story didn't bother me because I'd heard them so many times.

When I got through, he said, "You're pretty good. I think we can find a place for you." I went back into Mr. Davis's office, and Tony said, "I think he'll work out." Here I was, sixteen years old. A few minutes earlier, I had been fearful of even walking in the door, and now I was about to achieve my fondest dream. My head was spinning. We came to a quick agreement on how much money I'd make — fifteen dollars a week.

But first, I had to quit at the drugstore. The delivery job had been a wonderful experience for me. Like a lot of drugstores in those days, Sommers' had a soda fountain that ran the length of the store. Sometimes I'd stay late at night, get behind the soda fountain, and have a blast. I made some wicked malts. I even learned the soda-jerk lingo from the soda-fountain manager, a guy named Chester. A "Palm Beach on toast" was a pimento cheese sandwich. A "Waco" was a Dr Pepper. "Eighty-one" meant they were out of something.

The old gentleman who ran the store, George Parma, had been quite kind to me. He was very somber, very proper. The other pharmacist was a man named Howard Treadway, who was about to ship out with the navy. During World War II, the druggists worked every day, seven days a week. I remember Howard telling me one day, "Whatever you do, don't be a druggist."

During the war, there weren't many people available to work. They had been desperate for a delivery boy. It was the same for the radio station. It had a hard time finding announcers, which surely is one reason they hired a high school kid. I went back to the drugstore, and it took me about an hour to work up the nerve to tell Mr. Parma I was going to quit. But he was very gracious about it, of course, and wished me well.

I worked hard all the way through high school, and then kept right on working. It used to really bother me that I did not go to college. I was embarrassed for anybody to know that I hadn't gone. Now, it was not at all unusual for young men of my era in South Texas not to go to college. My own family was poor, which is why I worked so much in high school, but so were many other families, and none of the programs we have today existed to help kids of modest means. But my career brought me in contact with people who certainly were well educated, and I was self-conscious about my lack of education beyond high school.

I started at KMAC. In those days, announcers worked split shifts, from 6:00 to 9:00 in the morning, and then again from 3:00 to 6:00 in the afternoon. Because I was in high school, I could work those kinds of hours only on the weekend, so I worked at night. I'd get out of school and take the bus down to the radio station. On Sunday mornings, I remember opening the station. We were on the air 6:00 a.m. to midnight, so I had to get up early on Sundays.

Back then, radio stations didn't have "formats"—rock music, country music, talk, and so on. At certain times, we had country-and-western programs, or "hillbilly," as we called it then. One of the things we had on every night was the Mexican Commercial Hour. I had to spin the records for the program. Everything was in Spanish. I can hear them today, saying, "Una Perla, por favor!" (A Pearl, please!) Pearl beer, which was brewed in San Antonio, was a big sponsor. On a typical shift, I would do everything: play the records, announce the news, read the commercials. A great training ground.

The first time I went on the air, the only thing I had to do was the station break. I opened the microphone and intoned, "KMAC,

San Antonio." My mother and my father knew I was going to do this. I think they told everybody they knew that I was going to be on the radio. And so I rehearsed and cleared my throat, and rehearsed and cleared my throat. "KMAC, San Antonio." Over and over. When it came time to do my bit, I was a nervous wreck, but, somehow, I got it out.

I remember the first big story I reported on the air. A lot of people have forgotten this, but September 11 was not the first time an airplane crashed into a building in New York City. I was in the big record room, and the newsroom with the teletype was right next to it. All of sudden, that thing went wild. I went in and looked at the teletype and saw that a U.S. Army Air Corps bomber had crashed into the Empire State Building. I had a big bulletin to read on the air.

KMAC was the first radio station I ever saw, and I think it was typical. Not all of the station was air-conditioned, only the two studios and the front offices. The control room, where the announcer "ran the board" (the controls) and announced the commercials and the news, the record room, and Tony Bessan's office were not air-conditioned. With the window open, a lot of street noise rose from ten stories below and was heard over KMAC. There was a good bit of live programming in those days, especially guitar pickers. They worked out of a studio. One of the studios had a piano, and that's where all of the church groups set up shop. Since I had never seen anything else, I figured we had a pretty good setup, except for that portion of the station that wasn't air-conditioned.

The first fall I was at the station, we decided to broadcast high-school football from Alamo Stadium. It was the first year the stadium was open. It's still home to lots of San Antonio high school teams. Little did I know that this would be a key moment in my broadcasting career. (More later on my sportscasting days.)

Broadcasting the high school games on KMAC soon led to my announcing Southwest Conference games on the old Humble Network. There, I met Ves Box, the chief announcer at KRLD in Dallas, who also broadcast for Humble. In November 1949, Ves and I were working a Southwest Conference game somewhere. He told me,

"You know, we're getting ready to put television on in Dallas. How would you like to come to work for us?" I said, "Lord, Ves, I don't know anything about television." He shot back, "None of us do. Come on."

I was still at KMAC full time. The station had been good to me. I had never applied for a job anyplace else, but had I stayed in San Antonio, I'd have wanted to go to WOAI eventually. So this new opportunity was too exciting to pass up. KRLD, which in those days was owned by the *Dallas Times Herald*, was offering the whopping sum of $75 a week, a whole lot more than I was making at KMAC. So it wasn't a hard decision at all to leave KMAC.

My first day at KRLD-TV, Channel 4, was Saturday, December 3, 1949, the day that the station signed on. We went on the air at 12:25 p.m. with a brief opening ceremony led by the president of the *Times Herald* and the chairman of the board of KRLD, Tom Gooch. Later that afternoon, KRLD-TV and the two other fledgling television stations in Dallas–Fort Worth, WBAP-TV and KBTV (which became WFAA-TV), jointly telecast one of the greatest college football games ever played, mighty Notre Dame barely surviving a scare from SMU, 27–20, in a jam-packed Cotton Bowl. I hosted a live pregame show from the stadium on KRLD-TV during which I interviewed two of the great figures of the Southwest Conference, University of Texas coach Blair Cherry and TCU coach Dutch Meyer, and then I did a wrap-up after the game.

I wonder how many people saw that game on KRLD? An estimated 17,500 television sets existed in Dallas–Fort Worth at the time, more than half of the estimated 30,000 in the entire state of Texas. Lots of football fans saw the Mustangs and the Irish in church recreation halls or movie-theater lobbies, where dealers showed off the newfangled televisions. Newspaper ads for these demonstrations promised a "50–yard line seat." I'm sure a lot of people in Dallas saw TV for the first time that day.

The next day, a story on the Channel 4 football broadcast in the *Times Herald* said it "came off without a hitch," and viewers described the KRLD signal as "exceptionally good . . . clear and well-defined."

Remember, this was before cable or satellite TV. Reception depended on your "rabbit ears" or roof-top aerial. We were claiming a range of ninety miles, which might have been true if you had an exceptionally tall antenna in Tyler or Stephenville.

Television was taking off like a rocket. The Federal Communications Commission (FCC) estimated that about 2.7 million sets were in use at the time KRLD-TV signed on, but manufacturers were planning to crank out 3 million new sets in 1950. The sets cost more than you might think, but it's always that way with new technology. At Sanger Brothers' or Harris and Co. in Dallas (this was before Sanger-Harris and eons before Best Buy), you could get a little seven-inch General Electric tabletop set for as little as $122, but a combination Motorola TV/radio/hi-fi in a handsomely crafted French provincial cabinet (or whatever style the wife favored) might set you back $850. Pretty steep in 1949.

Looking back at some of the newspaper stories about the start of KRLD-TV, the optimism and the innocence that was so prevalent then is striking. One story observed that it wouldn't be a problem getting a baby-sitter anymore: the kids would be so riveted to the TV, the job would be easy. Of course, children did quickly become mesmerized by television, but there was no sense at all in the story that it might not be such a good thing. Another article actually predicted that TV might somehow lead to a decline in juvenile delinquency. I don't believe that came true.

When KRLD-TV started, we were not on the air full time at all. Remember the old Indian chief test pattern? It had an Indian chief's head at the top and geometric designs and numbers that helped engineers or technically savvy viewers adjust the picture. That's what you'd see most of the time on Channel 4 in the daytime.

We started out broadcasting thirty-four hours a week. We signed on at 5:30 p.m. with *The Cradle Club*, a kid's show that had been retrofitted for television from KRLD radio. Hugh Fowler and the KRLD Orchestra, again coming to TV from radio, did a supper-hour variety show, and we had an assortment of locally produced shows in the early evening hours.

Channel 4 was doing a lot of junky stuff in the early evening hours. We had an organist, Charles Evans, who had a show with a girl singer, Kay Burns. They figured out a way, using the limited technology of the time, to make her a midget and sit her on top of the organ—one of the great early camera shots. Later, we had *Officer Friendly*, another kid's show. But I always thought, "You know, we're making a big mistake here, not having a five o'clock newscast." And now everybody does a five o'clock newscast, and they all make a lot of money on it.

We saved our CBS shows, recorded as "kinescopes" and sent by mail from New York, for later in the evening. These included some of the great names and shows of early TV — Arthur Godfrey, Ed Wynn, *Studio One*, and *Candid Camera*.

When I came to KRLD-TV, they hired me only as an announcer. Of course, Ves Box was the chief announcer. KRLD-TV did not have a news director as such in the beginning. If KRLD radio had one, it would have been a guy whose on-the-air name was "Paul Ross," but whose real name was Charles Simmons. After I had been at KRLD a while, Paul left to open a music store, and I took over as news director for KRLD radio. Some time later, I became the television news director. You might think I'd remember the date of such a career milestone, but I don't. I held both the radio and television news director jobs for umpteen years. This was unusual because I was the "air talent" as well as the news director. Of course, today that's unheard of in television.

The TV news department, such as it was, was involved with a lot of romantic hanky-panky. Once, the news anchor (who also served unofficially as the TV news director) branded a young lady with his initials on her behind. While she may have enjoyed the moment, she later had second thoughts about it. She called the cops, and it was a bit embarrassing for everyone. So the amorous anchor faded away, and I took over.

In those days, radio was not merely an appendage to television. KRLD radio, after all, had been around almost thirty years before Channel 4 ever hit the airwaves. We had a big radio audience. Our 10:00 p.m. newscast used to be a big one. We also did newscasts at noon, 5:30 in the afternoon, and, of course, our morning news on the radio. I was on morning radio for a long time and still did some news on television. We knew a heck of a lot more about what we were doing on radio than we did on TV and were more comfortable with it in the beginning.

When I first came to Dallas, I thought I would be doing only television because the two facilities were separate—the television station, where I worked, was going into a new building across from the *Times Herald* (by the way, Channel 4 is still in the same building, at 400 North Griffin, although the entry has been moved from 1101 Patterson and it's been extensively renovated), and the radio station was in the Adolphus Hotel. They brought the radio station over to the new building within about a year. But in the beginning I did nothing at all on KRLD radio.

Our brand-new studios weren't quite finished when we went on the air, but no matter. Our studio was the upstairs of an old warehouse a half-block down the street from the new building. All of our live programming came from there. The camera cables were strung back to the control room at the main site. We built a small announcer's booth in the main building for station breaks.

I can't say that I was a visionary and saw that television would so quickly overtake radio's position with the public. But I did realize it was going to happen eventually; it was the next step for broadcasting, and for me. Many people predicted that television would be the end of radio, but if you thought about it seriously, you had to know it wouldn't put an end to radio, because you couldn't watch television in the car.

As I said, I was hired as an announcer, not a "news announcer"—just an announcer. So, like everyone else, I did a lot of odd jobs. Besides anchoring the evening newscasts, I hosted a quiz show, *Ring the Bell for Charity*, sponsored by Bell Cleaners. A truly terrible show.

I hosted another quiz show. I don't remember the name of the show now, but I do remember meeting a bright young real estate woman who was a panelist on the show. Her name was Ebby Halliday. One day, I talked to her about going into the real estate business. Who knew if this TV thing was going to last? She didn't give me a lot of encouragement, so I dropped it. Probably just as well.

I'll tell you a great story. Ves Box and I were hosting some show together. It was thought then that you really had to wear a lot of pancake makeup. We had a gal named Peggy Taylor doing our makeup (she's still around as a very successful talent agent). We usually took the makeup off as soon as the show was over, but one night, for some reason, we were both very hungry, so we decided to go get something to eat, and we forgot to take our makeup off.

We went to the old B&B Café, which was then on Akard Street right next to the Adolphus Hotel. There was a long counter where everyone sat. Ves and I sat down, and this waiter came up and gave us a weird look. And then he went back to the kitchen and told the other guys, and they came out to have a look. Ves kind of muttered to me, "What's going on?" I looked at him and said, "Ves, we didn't take our makeup off." Now, this was the early '50s. You still don't see many men with full makeup on, but I'm sure back then they thought for sure we'd just come out of the closet.

It wasn't long, perhaps a year or so, before we quit doing the local game shows. They were a cheap way to fill time in the early days, but soon we were getting more kinescopes from CBS and, gradually, the network began to fill more and more time.

Even though I hosted the quiz shows and announced some sports events, there was never any question in my mind that I was first and foremost a newsman.

KRLD-TV aired newscasts right from the beginning. I hosted a fifteen-minute news program called *The World Today* from 6:30 to 6:45 p.m. Monday through Saturday. Later, the starting time moved to 6:15 p.m.

By today's standards, this was a pretty crude affair. I look back on it and say, "How did we get by doing it that way?" I would write my stories from the wire services or steal something from the latest edition of the *Times Herald*. We didn't have reporters out on the street. For a while, I announced the sports. I even forecast the weather. I stood up in front of the map like I knew what I was doing.

Slowly, the local news programming began to take on the form that we're familiar with today. By 1958, we were doing thirty minutes of news, weather, and sports at 10:00 p.m. We were doing fifteen minutes at 6:00 p.m., followed by fifteen minutes of news from Douglas Edwards and CBS at 6:15. In 1962, Walter Cronkite took over from Edwards, and in 1963, he started his thirty-minute evening news program at 5:30, followed by thirty minutes of local news at 6:00 and 10:00.

We were all learning the business of television news, and we had little to guide us except what had been done in radio news. Back in 1949, Edwards—one of the real TV news trailblazers but mostly forgotten today—wrote a piece on the primitive state of television news that appeared in the *Times Herald*. He had a pretty good perspective on how far television news still had to go: "We know the present-day news product on TV is not the final product, any more than AM radio produced a polished form in its early days. We are progressing every day, trying new techniques, constantly latching on to better ways of making the news interesting and informative for the TV audience. It is a challenge and it is not easy. But it can be attained as long we realize one vital factor. That is: News is our commodity."[5]

Videotape did not yet exist, and we had pretty limited resources for shooting film on the scene of local news events, so, believe it or not, we would often use wire-service still photos mounted on poster board to provide a visual element. Program director Roy George wrote in a special section of the *Times Herald* published on Sunday, December 4, 1949 to celebrate the kickoff of KRLD-TV, "It is impossible to present a late-news broadcast by motion picture, due to the time required to take the pictures, bring the film to the studio and process it. Thus, our emphasis will be on oral news illustrated with still pictures."[6] But, despite this crude state of affairs, our radio experience had served us well. "Since television's principal ingredient is immediacy, news should be up-to-the-minute. People accustomed to the radio expect to get it that way," Roy said.[7]

In the beginning, we had a fifteen-minute newsreel-style program from 6:45 to 7:00 p.m., which we received by mail from something called the Telenews Service, a national outfit. Obviously, it didn't feature any breaking news. At 10:00 p.m., I did a five-minute newscast, and then we signed off for the night.

As a news department, we got better and better. The *Times Herald* wanted to put a good product on the air. Remember, in those days, the television stations (and their radio "sister" stations) were extensions of the newspapers. The *Fort Worth Star-Telegram* had a year's head start on us with WBAP-TV, Channel 5. In December 1949, Belo, the parent company of the *Dallas Morning News*, was already poised to buy KBTV, Channel 8, and would change the call letters to WFAA-TV in March 1950. So it was a highly competitive situation from the start. In 1955, KFJZ radio in Fort Worth put Channel 11 on the air as KFJZ TV, an independent station not affiliated with any network. It became KTVT in 1960, but wasn't much of a player in local news until 1995, when it became the CBS affiliate and Channel 4 hooked up with Fox.

The primary reason I was able to do what I did at KRLD-TV over the years was Clyde Rembert, the managing director. Second, the people across the street running the *Times Herald* — Jim Chambers, Johnny Runyon, and Felix McKnight—appreciated what we were trying to do. I knew I had the backing of the ownership behind me. That meant a lot.

We had a $65,000 "portable television transmitter truck," which we could dispatch to broadcast live events. The early publicity for the station suggested that the truck would be used to cover live news, but that didn't happen much. The greatest use of the big mobile unit was the broadcast of the eleven o'clock services of the Highland Park Presbyterian Church and the Highland Park Methodist Church on alternating Sundays. As NFL football became more and more popular, the truck went around the country covering games for CBS. We never got much use out of it for covering local news. I couldn't say, "Hey, we need the truck to cover a news conference." It was looked on strictly as a money-maker, and it was.

We had a few sixteen-millimeter sound-recording black-and-white cameras. In the beginning, we really didn't have anyone whose main job it was to go out and shoot news film. In rereading the stories about KRLD-TV that appeared in the *Times Herald*, I saw a quote from Hal Hunt, our chief cinematographer (there's a term you don't see in television anymore). It seems quaint. One of the jobs of the cameramen, Hal said, was to "acquire photos and film from amateurs and professional photographers who arrived on the scene earlier," which doesn't show a lot of confidence in our ability to cover breaking news. But then, it's not at all unusual today for TV news departments to buy amateur video and use it on the air (remember Rodney King?), so I guess things haven't changed that much after all.

As the years went by, we started hiring photographers specifically to go out and film the news around town. We had to do this to compete with Channel 5, which was so successful with the *Texas News*, originally a newsreel-style program with dramatic background music and no anchor. So Hal Hunt served as a news cameraman. Another one of our early cameramen was George "Sandy" Sanderson, a newsreel cameraman who had worked in the days of the hand-cranked cameras. He was getting on in years when he went to work for us.

I guess one of the first big stories that we covered using all the tricks of the trade—film and sound as well as scripted stories—was the monstrous tornado of April 2, 1957, which cut a sixteen-mile path right through Dallas, killed ten people, put hundreds of people out of their homes, and caused $4 million in damage. It appeared at about 4:00 p.m. and followed a south-to-north path on the west side of town, starting near Red Bird Airport. It tore up Oak Cliff and ended up at Bachman Lake, barely missing Love Field. We shot lots of dramatic film of the tornado and the havoc it caused. But we also made our mark in radio that day. *Time* magazine in an article entitled, "Closeup of a Twister," quoted the vivid up close-and-personal account of our man Bob Whitten on KRLD: "It's coming our way . . . boiling along, churning rather slowly. It ought to be here in just one minute. Now, we're going to have to step out of the way here to let the tornado go past. There it goes!"[8] Bob described how the tornado tossed a big trailer rig fifty feet into the air. The listeners could hear the sounds of debris crashing into and around Bob's car. Radio can be almost as "visual" as television.

Another one of our early cameramen was a guy named Claude Cox. He ended up working for the Southern Baptist Radio and Television Commission after he left us. Claude was the cameraman who went with me to cover a Braniff Airlines crash in Central Texas. And a good thing he did.

Around 1960, a Braniff Electra (a turboprop commuter plane) going from Houston to Dallas went down close to Fairfield. In those days, I hired a lot of off-duty police officers to be our traffic reporters on radio. One of them was Jim Bowles, who later became the Dallas County sheriff. We had very good relations with the police. One night about midnight, my phone rang. It was a police dispatcher, and he said, "Hey, Braniff has just had a plane crash between here and Houston. I thought you'd want to know about it." I had a list of Channel 4 people and their home phone numbers, so I called Claude Cox and told him, "We've got a plane crash and we need to go cover it."

I went by the station to pick him up. Claude threw a big battery-operated light in the station wagon, and we took off down Interstate 45 for Fairfield. We didn't really know where the crash was. I happened to see a Highway Patrol car parked on the side of the road. "Is this where the plane crash is?" I asked him. He said, "Yeah, but you can't go in." For some bizarre reason, Claude picked up the big light and shined it in the trooper's face. Well, I figured we were about to spend the night in the county jail, but the trooper exclaimed, "You've got a light? My God, they need one. Go on down." We were the only reporters to get in there. It was a horrific scene, but we had great film.

Claude was a real strange one. One Saturday night, a call came in dispatching an ambulance to a railroad crossing fatality on Harry Hines. Claude went to cover it and found that a man had been hit by a train and decapitated. His head had rolled several feet down an embankment, but no one would pick it up. Finally, one brave soul went down and picked up the head by the ears. He brought it back and deposited the head between the poor man's legs on the gurney, like something from *The Addams Family.* You've heard that news-people, who cover all manner of killings and accidents, develop a morbid sense of humor. Cox filmed every foot of it. It never made it on the air, of course, but it gained a prominent place in our infamous reel of the macabre.

Traffic reports on radio are heard more often than the news itself on some stations today. The Texas Department of Transportation has gone into the "television" business by installing cameras all over town, and they're available to every station. But it wasn't always that way.

As I mentioned, our KRLD radio traffic reporters were off-duty Dallas police officers like Jim Bowles; Jim Farr, who played a mean guitar; Murray Jackson, who was the partner of J. D. Tippit, the officer gunned down by Lee Harvey Oswald; Art Hammet, who served as public-information officer for the department; and Jerry Hill. Jerry had been a reporter for the *Times Herald*, where he was known as "Cop" Hill because he dreamed of being one (a very rare ambition for newspaper reporters, I might add). He indeed became a policeman and rose to the rank of lieutenant.

The off-duty officers staffed our police radio monitors and also kept us on top of a lot of things other than the traffic. We always had a close relationship with the police, and having them in the newsroom all the time didn't hurt that relationship at all.

I don't believe I ever said to anyone, "You're a cameraman, and nothing else." Steve Pieringer, our Fort Worth cameraman, was a great example. He became a reporter as well as a photographer. Steve used to set up his sound camera and then run around and pick up the mike and do his report. He was one of the most memorable guys who ever worked for Channel 4.

Steve came to see me one day while he was still in high school. He couldn't have been more than sixteen years old. Channel 5 dominated Channel 4 in Fort Worth for a long time. We didn't have any coverage at all in Fort Worth, but Channel 5 had a bureau in Dallas, so they ate our lunch. Steve, young as he was, saw this and told me, "I'd sure like to be your cameraman in Fort Worth." To paraphrase John Wayne in *True Grit*, I thought, "He reminds me of me." So I told him, "Maybe we can work something out." He said, "Well, just let me have a camera and some film and let me show you what I can do." I think he had a thirty-minute lesson on that camera, and that's all he needed. He was a sharp guy.

Steve got so involved in covering stories in Fort Worth that he was getting tips you wouldn't believe from the police. In those days, we didn't have a film processor in Fort Worth. Everything had to be done in Dallas. So we used to meet him out on the Dallas–Fort Worth

Turnpike, what is now called the Tom Landry Freeway, and pick up his film. The turnpike was then a toll road. He was always running out of money. He'd call up and say, "I'm bringing some film over, but I really need some money." He would hock his watch to the toll taker in Fort Worth and tell him he'd be back. We'd give him some money when he came over, and he'd get his watch back. I don't remember what we paid Steve, but it was not a six-figure salary, as you might imagine.

Steve ended up a legend in his own time. Everybody knew Steve Pieringer, but he came to a sad end. He was the first television reporter in Dallas–Fort Worth to die in the line of duty. He was covering a fire at Mansfield, south of Fort Worth, and there was an explosion. It was late on a Saturday afternoon in 1968, and Doyle Vincent from Channel 5 called me at home and said, "Hey, Steve is in bad shape and they've taken him to John Peter Smith Hospital." I went tearing over there, and the doctor told me, "He needs to be in the burn unit at Parkland Hospital." I rode in the ambulance with him over there, but he died the next day. He was just twenty-eight years old when he died. The Texas Association of Broadcasters still has the Steve Pieringer Award for excellence in reporting.

It took a while for local television news to acquire a certain measure of decorum. We used to do the local commercials live. In the beginning, I would do them myself. I did commercials for Holsum bread and Jax beer. Then as we got a little more sophisticated, we had an announcer whose job it was to present the commercials.

Once, we had a new announcer who was going to do a live commercial on my ten o'clock Sunday night newscast. I got to the commercial break: "I'll be back in a moment, but first this word." And so I threw it to this new announcer. He was just a bundle of nerves. He got a couple of words out . . . and he fainted dead away. The poor guy fell face first. I had never seen anybody fall like he fell. Lights out. Our dear floor director, Benny Molina, started crawling across the floor, the camera still on, and I thought he was going to do something to help the guy. But Benny just took his mike off and crawled back, leaving the fellow lying there. They came back to me and we just skipped the commercial. We got flooded with calls. Everybody wanted to know what happened to the poor guy.

Well, the next Sunday, the guy was back. He had the assignment to do the commercial again. So I read the news and got to the commercial break, and said, "I'll be back in minute." We go to the guy, and I'll be darned if he didn't faint again. But this time he got up, left the studio, cleaned out his locker, left the building, and we never saw him again. He was from San Angelo. His father-in-law had a big sheep ranch out there, and the last I heard, he was riding the range. TV's not for the "faint" of heart.

I always thought I knew what was going on in my newsroom. I didn't micromanage, but I darn well knew who was getting the job done and who was goofing off. But one time, I really did get surprised.

We had a woman working there who wanted to be in the newsroom, although she didn't have a background in journalism. She was very tall and lovely and seemed very prim and proper. This young woman worked the night shift and she mimeographed the scripts and ran the TelePrompTer. She did a very good job.

Years later, after I'd left KRLD, I learned that the maddest affair that ever went on in the newsroom was between this girl and one of our anchors. I had no idea. I had seen her as the purest of the pure. I thought she could walk down the aisle in a white dress and it would really mean something. And here she was banging this very-married anchorman. I wonder what else happened that I never knew.

One thing we did at KRLD radio that I'm really proud of was *Comment*, an interview and call-in show that was a forerunner of today's news-talk format. All of our reporters worked on both television and radio, and we all hosted *Comment*. I did it, Wes Wise did it, Frank Gleiber, Bill Mercer, Jim Underwood, Bill Ceverha (more on these guys later). That way, nobody was tied down to it. We had three hours every afternoon. Our critics said, "Well, we can see you'll get through the first day, but what will you do the second day?" So we had guests who became regulars.

One person we had on quite a few times was Dr. Edward Teller, the Hungarian-born physicist who was instrumental in developing the atomic bomb during World War II. He had friends in Dallas, which brought him into town frequently, and every time he came in, they'd call and ask, "Would you like to have Dr. Teller on again?" Well, sure! He had this deep, Germanic voice, sort of like Henry Kissinger's. Teller is remembered for this bit of wisdom, among others: "No endeavor that is worthwhile is simple in prospect; if it is right, it will be simple in retrospect."

Of course, it was a challenge interviewing someone of his intellectual depth, but between KRLD stalwarts Underwood, Mercer, Gleiber, Ceverha, and whoever we had doing the show that day, we'd carry on a reasonable conversation. Once we had as a guest Dr. Linus Pauling, who won two Nobel Prizes, one for Chemistry and one for Peace. So *Comment* did all right.

Another big interview I did in those early days was with Sen. Joe McCarthy, the anti-Communist crusader. He was then at the peak of his power. McCarthy was exactly what you'd expect, always looking under the couch for a Communist. I didn't enjoy talking to Tailgunner Joe. It was one of these one-sided interviews: he was very wary from the time he came in until the time he left. What could I talk with him about? I couldn't question him too closely, or he'd call me before his committee. I was not a fan of his at all.

A lot of people put Richard Nixon in the same box with McCarthy. I interviewed Nixon several times over the years, but I didn't get the sense of him that I got of McCarthy at all. To me, Nixon was a very good interview. I think that Nixon, and maybe many of the national political figures, regarded local reporters differently from the national types. Nixon, I think, felt much more at ease with the local media— very cordial, none of the defensive stuff you saw during Watergate.

I decided one day that it would be nice to have a contest every day on KRLD radio, using a news story as the question and awarding $100 or thereabouts for the correct answer. I approached Bill Roberts, the radio vice-president, with the idea. "Great idea, but we can't give away $100 a day, " he said. I asked, "Well, Bill, what can we afford ?" He thought a minute and came up with what I thought at the time was an embarrassment. "We can go $10 a day."

I thought about that for a minute and, like a bolt of lightning, an idea hit me that turned out to be a winner. "Bill," I replied, "could you add 80 cents to that ten spot?" Remember, KRLD's frequency is 1080 on the AM band. He grudgingly agreed, and the "1080 News Fax of the Day" was born.

Here's how it worked. At 7:45 every morning, we rang a bell and said, "Time for the '1080 News Fax of the Day.'" We asked a news-oriented question, and the first caller with the right answer walked away with a hefty check—$10.80.

It was amazing how many people stayed by the phone every morning. Winning the "1080 News Fax of the Day" was worn as a badge of high achievement. Some pretty big names around town carried that badge with pride. One I remember was Mike McKool, a top lawyer in Dallas, who listened every morning. One morning he won. You'd have thought he walked away with the answer to the $64,000 question.

Does the name Bob Wooden ring a bell? Probably not, but I understand if it doesn't because it's been a few years.

One afternoon back in 1960, a fellow came into the newsroom and introduced himself: "I'm Bob Wooden, and I'm a stock broker with Merrill Lynch." I tried to brush him off: "Well, thanks for coming by, but I'm in no position to buy any stocks." But that's not what he wanted. "No, no, I don't want to sell you any stocks," he answered. "I want to go on the air every day with a market report."

To my knowledge, no other radio stations were then broadcasting stock market wrap-ups, certainly not in Dallas, so I said, "Why not? We'll give it a try." We did, and every afternoon after the market closed, Bob Wooden came down to the station and did a market wrap. Sort of a pioneer David Johnson, who does the business reports these days on radio and TV in Dallas. Bob moved to Denton after a couple of years, but the market reports were popular and became a regular part of the mix.

We had to be more versatile in those days. Jay Hogan was strictly radio, and a wonderful radio reporter, until we came up with the idea around 1960 to do a light television news program called *People and Places*. Claude Cox shot a lot of it and edited it, and then Hogan would come over and voice it. Hogan became quite a TV personality, although he had no idea what to do with or in front of a camera.

The program was offbeat. For instance, there was a dancer who came to Jack Ruby's Carousel Club. She was a limbo dancer who could bend like a pipe cleaner. Ruby called the station and told Claude he had this great dancer. Not a stripper, he hastened to add. The limbo dancer was Jack's idea of "class." So Cox came in and said, "I got a call from Jack Ruby, and he has this limbo dancer at his club. What do you think about doing a feature on her?" And I cautiously said, "Now, we don't want to do the strippers, but sure, go ahead." And we ran the thing on *People and Places*.

Well, Jack Ruby never forgot it. The first time I ever saw him was in the courtroom after he shot Lee Oswald. And he leaned over and said, "Hi, Eddie." His sister Eva Grant told me one day, "You know, it means so much to Jack that you come down here to the trial every day, because he's always considered you to be one of his best friends."

Jack Ruby, of course, was a little bit unhinged. But one of the things television did was create a sense of familiarity in the viewers. As TV began to take hold, people who saw you on their living room TV set night after night came to feel that they really knew you. For whatever reason, this seemed especially true for me.

In those days, there were very few people on local television. In the beginning, Channel 8 was not a very big factor at all. Channel 5, with its *Texas News* newsreel show, really didn't have a recognizable face, except for the weatherman, Harold Taft, and the sports guy, Bud Sherman, and they were better known in Fort Worth. But in Dallas, there really weren't that many of us.

Today, there are probably twenty to twenty-five people on television in Dallas–Fort Worth who are recognizable. It's kind of hard to zero in on one or two, so it's difficult today to enjoy the level of recognition that I (and the other KRLD-TV announcers) had in the '50s and '60s. And it was that factor of being recognized everywhere in Dallas that helped me get a lot of my best stories.

One of those stories stands out. It was one of the strangest events I ever reported—the suspected bombing of an airliner in November 1959. It was quite a story at the time, but my role in it made news of its own. "How Barker got his story was almost as interesting as the story itself," *Time* magazine reported in a February 1, 1960 article.[9]

An alleged Dallas abortionist named Robert Vernon Spears was the key player. He always referred to himself as "Dr." Spears; his specialty, he said, was "naturopathy," the use of herbs and such to cure an assortment of maladies. He was in his mid-sixties and married to a woman, Frances, who was about half his age. They had two small children, a boy and a girl. Spears had gone to Florida for some reason never fully explained and met with an old ex-con friend, William Allen Taylor. Spears had a long criminal record, and he was about to go on trial in Los Angeles for performing then-illegal abortions. One former associate, quoted in a *Life* magazine story, referred to Spears as "a con man . . . a smooth article."[10]

Spears had taken out a $100,000 insurance policy on a National Airlines flight from Tampa to Dallas with a stop in New Orleans. In those days, National flew the leg to New Orleans, Delta flew it to Dallas, and American continued to Los Angeles. In some manner, Spears allegedly talked Taylor into taking the flight instead of him. He apparently told Taylor he had to finish up some business in Tampa and would be along shortly. Supposedly, he gave Taylor a package and asked him to deliver it to Frances. But unbeknownst to Taylor, so it was speculated, the package he carried contained a bomb timed to go off when the plane was over the Gulf of Mexico. Spears would be shown on the list of passengers, and his wife (and he) would presumably collect the $100,000, so the theory went.

Spears might have avoided suspicion had Taylor not stopped at an insurance machine right before he got on the plane and bought a

$37,500 policy made out to his estranged wife. He put his wife's address on the envelope and dropped it in a mailbox. It was not uncommon for airline travelers to buy insurance that way in those days. Then he, along with forty-one passengers and crew, boarded the flight that would spell their doom.

The plane never reached New Orleans, and the hunt for it got under way. Little was found—only a few bodies were recovered — and no reasonable explanation was forthcoming because investigators had little to go on. One of the passengers aboard the flight was Bob Bumpas, husband of a Dallas actress, Martha Bumpas. I knew Martha, and after I became involved in the case, she called me repeatedly and I gave her the details of what happened as I learned them. In the forty-plus years that followed, every time I saw Martha, she brought up the story and wanted to go over the details again.

Spears had left Florida and gone to Arizona, keeping a low profile. The plot might have worked had Taylor not bought that insurance policy. When news of the crash reached his estranged wife, she knew Taylor was on the plane, although his name was not on the flight manifest issued by the airline. Mrs. Taylor went to the FBI with the policy. Then things started to happen, and very shortly my involvement began.

One of the first people the FBI visited was Frances Spears at the Spears home on Gaston Avenue. Did she know her husband was not on the plane? Had she heard from him? Did she know about the insurance? To all questions Frances Spears answered no. She contacted well-known criminal defense attorney Charles Tessmer, who had defended Spears in many of his early run-ins with the law.

In January 1960, all the media were reporting the story. Several unexplained airline explosions had happened in recent years, and a few weeks after the Spears story broke, another National flight blew up over North Carolina. Suspicion grew that a young lawyer named Julian Frank committed suicide by taking a bomb aboard the flight. Reports then appeared that Frank was Spears's attorney. The plot most definitely thickened, and it became front-page news day after day as the stories became entwined.

Tessmer responded to questions for Frances, but no one was talking to Frances directly. I wondered if it wouldn't be worth a try to contact Tessmer, whom I had known for years, and persuade him to ask her if she would talk with me. He called her, she told him she watched me on television and would like to meet me. We set up a time for me to go to the Spears home.

I met Frances, her two small children, and the live-in maid and nanny. We talked about a lot of things before we got around to why I was there and what I wanted to talk about. She told me basically what she had told the FBI — nothing. "If he were alive, he would be here with me and the babies," she said.

But it had been a pleasant first meeting and, by not being pushy, I think I gained Frances's trust. I told her I would call (now that I had her unlisted phone number) and we'd meet again. But before I could call her, she called me, just to talk. I said I would drop by that afternoon. And that's when I *really* became involved.

To my good fortune, I was at Frances's house when the phone rang. It was Joe Dave Scott, my assistant news director. He told me the FBI had just arrested Spears in Arizona. I hung up the phone and told Frances the news. She blurted out, "I told him it would never work. Eddie, don't you dare tell anyone about this. Don't you dare," she begged me. But I knew I had a story. The first thing I did was close all the blinds in the house and lock both the front and back doors, because I knew the press would be engulfing the house in a matter of minutes, and I wasn't about to share Frances with anyone else.

And sure enough, the press came en masse. I had the screen door hooked and told the press that Frances was distraught and wouldn't be talking to anyone. That's when the picture of me standing in the door of the Spears home that appeared in *Time* was taken. I was on the receiving end of a lot of rather harsh comments (besides *Time's* heartless reference to me as "chubby"). But I held my ground. *Time* reported: "When the other reporters tried to question Mrs. Spears, Barker shooed them away, ushered her back into the house, explaining: 'Her kids have to have a bath.' Growled one newsman contemptuously: 'Are you going to give it to them?'"[11] Oh, those tart-tongued scribes.

I put the other reporters off by telling them that, while I had interviewed Frances, I had not taken any notes and my tape recorder was empty (remember, I was news director for KRLD radio, too). I guess they thought I was stupid, and they let down their guard long enough for us to have the story to ourselves.

Then the FBI came, and, of course, I let them in. They wanted to talk to Frances, and I told them I had the story I was after. They asked me to hold the story until they could get all the pieces put together. I said I would hold up on the story, but I got their promise not to talk to other reporters until my story had aired, and they agreed. And so began a long and rewarding friendship with the FBI that extended into the Kennedy assassination story.

Frances told me she had visited her husband at a hotel in Dallas almost two months after the air crash. She told me she had received a note from an associate of Spears, telling her that he was in Dallas at the Lakewood Hotel:

> BARKER: How did you act when you saw Bob Spears at the Lakewood Hotel? What did he say when you first saw him?
> SPEARS: I don't remember the first words. It was an extremely emotional meeting, of course . . . thinking your husband was dead and seeing him. . . .
> BARKER: Was your reaction that of a wife who loved her husband, who wanted to offer him some sort of protection?
> SPEARS: That was all I could do. He had protected me all my life. I loved him. I still love him. It was the only thing I could do under the circumstances. I just simply couldn't turn him in. . . .
> BARKER: Did you try to get him to turn himself in?
> SPEARS: Yes, desperately.

Frances said Spears told her that he let Taylor take his seat because Taylor had been suffering severe neck pain and wanted to fly to Dallas to have surgery at Baylor Hospital. Spears then drove Taylor's car from Tampa to Dallas. When he heard of the crash, so his story went, he saw an opportunity to give his family some financial security by letting it be thought that he died with the others. I broke the story on the ten o'clock newscast two nights after Frances told me the story, and it immediately flashed around the world.

It was a big story for a long time. This was the crash that caused the FBI to become involved in any and all airline crashes. The FBI said it discovered materials for making a homemade bomb, including blasting caps, in Spears's possession, but it never was able to hang the crash on him. He never went to trial for causing the crash, but they did send him to federal prison for five years on the charge of stealing Taylor's car and taking it across state lines to Arizona.[12]

I felt pretty good about the story and was getting pats on the back from friends and foes alike. Then the phone rang and it was Allen Merriam, the editor emeritus of the *Times Herald*. Usually, the *Times Herald* people were very supportive, but not this time. I awaited his accolades, but instead he said, "I can't believe you would break that story on the *Dallas News*'s time," meaning that by breaking the story in the evening, we gave the *Morning News* a jump on publishing the story. The *Times Herald* didn't hit the streets until the afternoon. Of course, our big newscasts were in the evening, as they are today, and we sure weren't going to wait until morning to broadcast the story, but in Allen's view, baby brother had gotten too big for his britches. Still, it showed local television news was growing up fast.

References:

[1] Ed Bliss, *Now the News: The Story of Broadcast Journalism* (New York: Columbia University Press, 1991), 337-38; another excellent description of Eddie's report appears in: Thomas Doherty, "Assassination and Funeral of John F. Kennedy." In *Encyclopedia of Television*, Volume 2, G-P, Ed. Les Brown (Detroit: Gale Research, 1992), 880-83. Walter Cronkite's account of the reporting of President Kennedy's death appears in: Walter Cronkite, *A Reporter's Life* (New York: Alfred A. Knoph, 1996).

[2] Richard K. Van der Karr, "How Dallas TV Stations Covered Kennedy Shooting," *Journalism Quarterly* 42 (Winter 1965): 647-48.

[3] "A World Listened and Watched," *Broadcasting* (December 2, 1963): 40.

[4] Barbie Zelizer, *Covering the Body: The Kennedy Assassination, the Media and the Shaping of Collective Memory* (Chicago: University of Chicago Press, 1992), 42.

[5] Douglas Edwards, "News Coverage Keeping Pace with Industry," *Dallas Times Herald* (December 4, 1949), Section 10, p. 1.

[6] Frank Chappell, "KRLD-TV Program to Combine Best Radio, Theater Technique," *Dallas Times Herald* (December 4, 1949): Section 8, p. 1.

[7] "Timely, Fresh News Coverage Set on KRLD-TV," *Dallas Times Herald* (December 4, 1949): Section 8, p. 9.

[8] "Closeup of a Twister," *Time* 69 (April 15, 1957): 76.

[9] "News Beat In Dallas," *Time* 75 (February 1, 1960): 58.

[10] "A Far Out, Far Up Mystery," *Life* 48 (February 1, 1960): 13-17.

[11] "News Beat in Dallas."

[12] Hugh Aynesworth, "The Strangest Story I Ever Covered." *D Magazine* 10 (August 1983): 86-89, 137-43.

2

"Your Grandfather Once Stood Side by Side with Edward R. Murrow"

Gradually, as the Bob Whittens and Steve Pieringers came on board, KRLD began to build a really strong news staff. The greatest number of people I ever had for TV and radio was forty-four. Today, Channel 8 has about two hundred people. Everyone had multiple responsibilities in the beginning, and that, I think, built strong reporters and great professionals.

KRLD radio really benefited from television, because we'd have reporters out covering stories for television and then they'd do a report for radio, too. So, by radio standards, we had a good-sized staff. Many of their names are still very familiar in Dallas.

I guess the first person I hired mainly as a reporter, not a cameraman, was Bill Ceverha, who went on to become my assistant news director. He didn't know how to use a camera, but he quickly learned. I never was impressed with people who had college degrees in radio-television. I figured we could teach a person how to run a recorder or how to turn a microphone on and off. I really wanted people who had a broader background than that.

Ceverha had been a captain in the army, stationed in Germany. He had a degree from the University of Missouri journalism school, one of the best in the country, then and now. He was going across the country talking to people, trying to get a job. He was "George" Ceverha then. He just "hit" me right, and I had very few qualms about hiring him. I knew he would do well, and he did. I was very fortunate in the people I hired. We had a couple of sour apples along the way, but not many.

Dick Wheeler, another of the KRLD mainstays, had worked at Channel 8, WFAA, before he came over to us. When Wheeler was at Channel 8 he always wore a boutonniere. Very dapper. He left WFAA and went to Tulsa, but he wanted to come back to Dallas. Channel 8 didn't have a place for him, and so I hired him. He was well known in the market, a proven product. You didn't have to teach him which camera to look at.

Warren Fulks didn't have the television background, but I think he had done some radio. He was a good-looking guy and wanted to learn. I was just impressed with him. Unlike a lot of news anchors, he didn't necessarily want to be a "star" on the air. But he immediately picked up how to speak to the camera, and he was out on the street covering stories. I put Dick and Warren together as a dual-anchor team on the 10:00 p.m. news and they worked as a team until Warren left to go into public relations with Lone Star Gas.

I wanted anyone who worked in that newsroom to have done every dirty job there was to do for a long time before they ever went on camera. That applied to all of them. But Wheeler was a little different because he had a lot of experience. Wes Wise also had a lot of experience, but Wes had never really been anything except a sports reporter. He also came over from WFAA. I told him, "Wes, here we do everything."

When Wes worked for Channel 8, he and the Cowboys' general manager, Tex Schramm, developed a dislike for each other. The Cowboys could be mean. They were cold-blooded in a lot of ways. They went to Mike Shapiro, the general manager of WFAA, who hosted the *Let Me Speak to the Manager* show for so many years, and Mike fired Wes. Poor ol' Wes was out on the street. I got word to him: "Come over and talk to me." He did and I hired him, bam, just like that. I did it as much to gig Channel 8 as anything.

Wes and the Cowboys continued to skirmish off and on. I got a call one day from a court reporter. There was a big stink at the time involving Ralph Neely, who became a great offensive tackle for the Cowboys, his reputation for holding penalties notwithstanding. This was when the battle between the National Football League and the American Football League was still going on. Coming out of the University of Oklahoma, Neely had signed contracts with both the Cowboys and the Houston Oilers of the AFL. The court reporter told me: "I took all the depositions with the Cowboys and Ralph Neely. There's some pretty interesting stuff in there. Would you be interested in it?" (I look back and I'm amazed at some of the people who called and told me things.) I said, "Yeah, I'm interested, but I'd like for Wes Wise to do the story." We made a big story of it, and it just infuriated Tex Schramm. So Wes got a chance to get back at the Cowboys a little bit.

As I said, in those days, we did everything. For example, the night that U.N. ambassador and former Democratic presidential nominee Adlai Stevenson got hit over the head with a picket sign while he was in town to deliver a speech, not long before the Kennedy assassination, Wes Wise was covering it. There's a famous photo of an angry young anti-Communist woman with her tongue sticking out, bopping the scholarly Stevenson on the head with this cardboard placard. Wes learned how to use a camera and became a darn good news reporter.

As I've said, I had some great guys on my staff at KRLD radio and TV over the years (alas, no women until Judy Jordan came along in 1966). Needless to say, they all contributed mightily to whatever I was able to accomplish at Channel 4 and KRLD radio. My friend and coauthor John Mark Dempsey talked to a few KRLD veterans about our adventures together:

It's remarkable how similar are the memories of Eddie's KRLD compadres. On two things they all agree without prompting: (1) Eddie's skills as a "people person" were and are remarkable; and (2) Eddie had a temper that would erupt like a North Texas thunderstorm on a late afternoon in July and disappear just as quickly. The latter is surprising, because in the seven years I've known Eddie, I've never once seen the legendary Barker temper.

"Every now and then, somebody would incur his wrath, and he would just boil over," Bill Ceverha, reporter and assistant KRLD news director, says. "His face would turn beet-red. He just had a real volatile temper. And then it would just pass as soon as it came up."

Dick Wheeler, who, like several others, came to KRLD after working at WFAA-TV and radio, remembers the most celebrated way Eddie defused his anger. "He used to kick wastebaskets from time to time," Wheeler recalls. "He'd get mad at me, but I don't think he ever kicked a wastebasket over something I did. I usually ran about half-scared that I was going to do something wrong and get yelled at. He didn't hold grudges. He was fair, but he really let you know if you did something wrong."

Eddie's penchant for booting defenseless trash cans became so renowned that a member of the KRLD news team once went out of his way to teach the boss a lesson. "It wasn't a conspiracy among us, but we all laughed and applauded it after it was done," news and sports announcer Bill Mercer recalls. "Eddie had a volcanic temper at times. I think it was Claude Cox who came up with the idea of putting a concrete block in the bottom of a trash can nearest to Eddie's door. Every day, Claude would cover it up with old Associated Press newsprint. And every night when he'd leave, he'd throw out the newsprint and put the concrete block under his desk. Eddie didn't blow up every day, but when he did it was really spectacular.

"So one day, Claude has the concrete block in the can, and the paper on top, and Eddie just comes roaring out of his office, yelling some obscenity, probably, and kicked that can and darn neared killed himself. He went limping back into his office. I don't recall what he said. We were all falling out of our chairs. Claude felt he had done a great service to the news department."

Mercer, now semiretired as a professor of radio-television-film at the University of North Texas, says KRLD was a fun place to work. "We had a tremendous time on both sides of that radio-TV station. It's a wonder we all didn't get fired," he remembers ruefully. "Everybody had a great time, and we kidded each other and did pranks. Everybody tried to break up Jim Underwood on the air, and it wasn't hard. When Jim would go into the radio news booth, one of us, Frank Gleiber or I, would slowly start putting his head up in the window and stare at him. Jim just couldn't take it, it just blew him away. Gleiber was really good at it. We'd set people's copy on fire.

"Underwood would break *himself* up. He was just a great human being and a wonderful gentleman. One day, Eddie, Frank and I were doing *Comment*, and Jim walked in and said, 'I just read that a sheik somewhere has died of a heart attack, and at his bedside were his seven wives.' Now that's kind of sad, but Jim thought it was darn funny. He tried to talk and then started laughing. That got everybody else started. By the time it was over, he was pounding the control panel. It was infectious. Some lady called in. She was laughing her head off, and said, "I don't know what we're laughing about, but I'd like to know, because I'm dying [from the hilarity]."

But Mercer says antics like these should not be seen as evidence that Eddie's KRLD news team was unprofessional. "We were very dedicated, with Eddie as leader, to doing the best factual, in-depth, honest job we could," Mercer says. "There was never any thought of bending the news or taking it to one side or the other. If you screwed it up, Eddie would get angry. It was a down-to-earth, hard-working, journalistic news department.

"You know, the folks at Channel 4 when they did their fiftieth-anniversary program in 1999, were surprised that all of us were doing so many different things. They said, 'But you were a sports announcer.' And I said, 'Yeah, but we all worked in the news department.' We all shot film, we all knew the police in town, and the political people.

"When I was doing sports on TV, I kept bugging the photographers to shoot film for me. So one day, they walked in and gave me a sixteen-millimeter Bell and Howell camera with a one-inch lens on it and said, 'Here, go shoot your own darn film.' And I'd never shot film. But that's what we did. I took it out and shot a few rolls of film and figured out how to get the right viewfinder setting."

Wheeler says Eddie set the bar quite high for his staff. "He ran a really tight ship. He was a little more demanding, a little more exacting in the quality of the work you did for him, in your writing. He insisted upon accuracy, which is the name of the game in the news business," Wheeler says.

Mercer came to KRLD in 1953 as a staff announcer, working on both radio and television. He later served as the play-by-play announcer for high school football and minor-league baseball games on KRLD radio, which later led to his work as the radio announcer for both the Dallas Cowboys and the Texas Rangers.

When Mercer arrived, the television newscasts were largely of the "rip-and-read" variety. "We had newscasts on TV, but they were slapped-together affairs. I remember seeing Eddie running down the hall with news copy flying behind him because we were working all different kind of jobs. The TV news department really didn't develop until Eddie brought it into being sometime between '55 and '57. It was due to Eddie's hard work in putting it together.

"When we first started shooting film, we had to take it to a processing place, and then we got a processing machine. It was really a stairstep event, putting the thing together and building it. He deserves the credit for that."

Mercer served as the representative for the American Federation of Television and Radio Artists (AFTRA), the employees' union. "He and I would have these clashes about procedural things that go on," Mercer recalls. "That was part of our togetherness, and at times it would be tense, and others times it was funny."

Ceverha appreciated Eddie's natural talents as a journalist. "The amazing thing is he really didn't have the formal education in it at all," he observed. "It was sort of instinct, seat-of-the-pants judgments and common sense. The news at that time was basically police-blotter news, not only for us but for everybody else. Accidents, floods, hurricanes, murders, bank robberies, that kind of thing. Very little in-depth stuff. And then we started doing some documentaries or special things. I'd say, 'Why don't we do such-and-such?' And he'd say, 'Fine, do it.' So I'd have to go out, shoot the film, edit the film, write the script, and then air it.

"I learned from Eddie to not settle for anything halfway, to make sure everything was done right. For example, if you had an interview, something with a sound track, and then you cut in what's called 'b-roll' [supporting video], he insisted that the picture matched the words. He was a stickler for that. And I learned just to pursue things and make sure you got it right."

The KRLD alumni all marvel at Eddie's ability to develop valuable news sources. "He enjoyed meeting people. He was, and is, outgoing to people," Wheeler says. "He got information that other people didn't have because of that quality."

Ceverha recalls: "He would establish really good contacts. He had great friends within the FBI, the police department, the sheriff's department, the district attorney's office. Because of that, he could sometimes pick up the phone and get some information nobody else could get."

KRLD news and sports reporter, and, later, mayor of Dallas, Wes Wise: "I have said many times over the years that he is the best I have ever seen at taking contacts both in deep friendships and average friendships, and using those contacts in gathering news stories. This could be all the way from a 'scoop,' to the details of a story that's already happening, such as the assassination of President Kennedy.

"It was just uncanny that something would be going on and he would come to me and say, 'Hey, get in touch with so-and-so. I think he might have a story for you.' You'd call the person on the phone, but Eddie had already made the inroads for you. It was your job then to make the most of it. There were many times when we would develop a very good story, but Eddie would really deserve the credit for it because, if it hadn't been for his contacts, we wouldn't have been able to do it."

Eddie's old pals also are unanimous in their affection for the daily *Comment* program on KRLD radio. Mercer calls it "one of the best things that he [Eddie] did. It was the first interview and call-in show in Texas, certainly in North Texas. He and I and Wes Wise and Frank Gleiber and Jim Underwood, we would interview one person. Now, it's kind of unusual to have four or five people interviewing one person, but it got a lot of ideas involved in the program and a lot of different perspectives," Mercer said.

"It really was one of the most enjoyable things I did, other than sports, because I love play-by-play. It was just outstanding. People would stop at pay phones along the highway, because you didn't have cell phones in those days, and call in and ask questions."

Wheeler reflects: "It was something new to me, in 1963 [when he joined KRLD]. I enjoyed it, the informality and the give-and-take. But it took some getting used to. You didn't sit there and read scripted words."

Wise remarks: "Bob Brock [the former *Dallas Times-Herald* broadcasting columnist] used to say the fact that we had people of importance—and people of no importance—on the *Comment* radio program, and then would follow up with a story on television, sometimes the same day, sometimes days later, added prestige to *Comment* and it definitely brought viewers to Channel 4 news.

"I've had listeners back then say to me, 'If you had [piano virtuoso] Van Cliburn on the radio in the afternoon we knew we could tune in Channel 4 that evening and see an interview with Van Cliburn.' So they complemented each other tremendously."

Mercer remembers interviewing George Bush (the elder), Billy Graham, and segregationist Alabama governor George Wallace on *Comment*. Other guests often included local political figures. "We were very careful that we didn't allow people with an agenda to push without facts and figures and actually told some people that they'd have to leave unless they could produce their facts," Mercer recalls. But he especially enjoyed meeting and interviewing the many show-business luminaries who visited Dallas and stopped by to talk.

"I remember Robert Goulet was in town to sing," Mercer says. "And he said, 'I sure would like to play some golf.' Well, we had courtesy memberships at one of the golf clubs. I set him up, and he wrote me a nice little letter after that. It was a great way of meeting people.

"We have a picture of all of us together with Ginger Rogers. She was great. She had such a great personality. She just loved people and she was goofy with us, having a ball and laughing and not being uptight. She invited us all out to see her perform and we all got free tickets. She was just wonderful."

But not all of the guests made such a great impression. Wheeler remembers: "I interviewed Sonny and Cher. The only reason I remember it is that Sonny was so nice, a real nice guy, and Cher was a real a—hole, pardon my French. She was just awful. Just nasty and snide, you'd ask her a question and she'd pooh-pooh it: 'That's a dumb question.'"

Mercer remembers a "big blonde" actress who was a guest once on *Comment*. He can't remember her name. "She was a really 'nothing' actress and she was in this 'B' movie, and she came in to promote the movie," Mercer says. "She was sitting there with her boobs hanging out all over the table. And Eddie asked in a very nice way, 'How did you get into movies?' And she says, 'You've got to be kidding!' Her 'talent' was pretty obvious. And that was another time people wanted to know what we were laughing about."

Ceverha is an example of how Eddie played hunches like a horse-track gambler in hiring reporters. Ceverha took advantage of some free time before his army hitch was up and caught some free hops on military planes to air bases around the country. "I flew around and interviewed. I flew to Chicago, my hometown; Seattle; San Francisco; Phoenix; Dallas; St. Louis; and back to Chicago. Eddie offered me the job in Dallas. That was my first [broadcasting] job. It was kind of a coup for me, starting in a major market like that."

Eddie trusted his intuition, Ceverha says. "He just liked me, I guess. And he only paid me a $100 a week, so I guess he could afford to be wrong. He had an amazing ability to connect with people. He'd just shoot from the hip with hunches. For example, hiring Judy Jordan, the first female television reporter in Dallas, and Norm Hitzges, who had this high little voice, but became a local legend."

Likewise, the relatively experienced Warren Fulks proved Eddie's knack for spotting talent. "Warren Fulks, our ten o'clock newscaster, was just as good as they got," former Channel 4 reporter Bob Huffaker recalls. "He had a natural drama about his delivery that was not the least bit forced or fake. That's just the way he was. He was a dramatic and deeply feeling person, and it came out on the air."

Wise remembers that coming to Channel 4 and KRLD radio turned what seemed like a personal catastrophe into a blessing. He had been the Dallas Cowboys' first television play-by-play announcer in 1960, but the games were broadcast on CBS affiliate Channel 4, which created friction with Wise's regular employer, WFAA, Channel 8. "It caused a constant conflict between Mike Shapiro, Tex Schramm, and the CBS people," Wise says. "And it probably didn't sit too well with the KRLD people, because I broadcast the Cowboys' games on their station while I was the sports director of Channel 8. I was, in effect, fired. They claimed that I was offered another job after being taken off the sports, but that was not so. There was no such offer made. I didn't make a big thing of it in the newspaper, but a lot of [Channel 8 and Cowboys] fans did."

As Eddie has already written, he moved decisively to bring Wes Wise to KRLD, but there is more to the story: "Jim Underwood was the assistant news director. Eddie sent him over to see me after it got out that I was going to be leaving Channel 8 to ask me if I'd be interested in going to Channel 4. And I said, 'Doing what?' And Jim said, 'Doing the same thing you do at Channel 8, doing the sports on the news, weather and sports at 6:20 p.m. and 10:20 p.m.' And I said, 'Heck, yes!' And Jim asked, 'Don't you want to know what it pays?' And I said, 'I don't give a damn what it pays' [laughing]. And he shook his head and said, 'Well, this is a new one on me.' I told him, 'Eddie will be fair.' I did go over there for a cut, not a horrible cut. Barker told me, 'Don't worry, you'll get talent fees that'll bring it up eventually.' And it wasn't even eventually, it was almost immediately. He was extremely fair to me."

Shapiro, remembered for answering viewer mail as the acerbic host of his own weekly program, was irate about KRLD's hiring Wise. "I don't know what happened in the background and at the time I didn't want to know," Wise laughs. "But I think the idea was that, in the past, one station in the market didn't hire a person from another station in the market. When that complaint was presented to Barker and [KRLD manager] Clyde Rembert, they said, 'Hey, this wasn't as if he came over to us and asked for a job, or we went out to get him. You fired him. Then he became available, and we hired a man who was out there in the open.' Worked out great for me. It was probably the best thing that ever happened to me in my journalism career.

"I left Channel 8 on a Friday and on Monday, I started the sports on Channel 4," Wise marvels. "Later on, it was said in the newspaper that Dale Hansen had been the first to do that [although in reverse, going from Channel 4 to Channel 8]. I didn't bother to call and correct them, but I was before Hansen."

Huffaker came to KRLD-TV from the small station in Bryan in late 1961. Right away, he saw that he'd arrived in the big leagues. "Eddie had a good instinct for 'class,'" Huffaker says. "While the other stations had fleets of Fords and Chevys, we had our fleet of Pontiac Catalina wagons, with gold-leaf lettering, 'KRLD News,' on them. I mean real gold leaf. That was all Eddie's doing. He wanted that to be the classiest operation there was, and undeniably back then, KRLD was just one of the best radio-television news operations in the country."

Eddie always says that KRLD had no "stars," but Huffaker respectfully begs to differ: "There was one star, and that was Eddie."

I loved covering the local news, and working with all of my KRLD buddies, but certainly, my association with the great broadcasters of CBS News was a tremendously rewarding part of my career.

The first time I did anything for CBS was in 1950. It was for an hourly radio newscast. A stringer cameraman for CBS named Fred Lawrence was always coming around the station, and I got to know him. Fred was always after me to call the desk in New York and offer a piece on something that could be interesting to the whole country. An earthquake that had rocked Mexico wasn't getting much coverage, so I called the news desk and offered a story.

The first editor I remember talking to was Ed Bliss, who later became Walter Cronkite's editor on the *CBS Evening News* and went on to become a much-honored journalism educator at American University in Washington, D.C. He took my story and said to call anytime I had something newsworthy.

In later years, I was able to repay Ed, at least a little. He came to a Radio Television News Directors convention when I was president of that group. I saw him and asked how long he was staying. "Well, Eddie, I just wanted to look around for a little while. To tell you the truth, I really can't afford to stay for the whole convention," Ed told me. (They really don't pay professors too well, do they?) I took him to the registration desk and told the clerk, "This is my guest. I want him to have a visitor's pass for the whole convention." We became fast friends after that.

You don't see many news directors eating there—they can't afford it. Their news readers, ah . . . anchors, can more easily manage it when the check comes. And where might this be, you ask? The Old Warsaw on Maple Avenue, the epitome of class in Dallas restaurants.

If you have eaten there in past years, you may remember seeing a picture hanging in the front of the restaurant of Mike Wallace, my wife, Jane, and me. Forty or so years ago the phone rang and it was Mike. "I'm in town for the night and would like to meet you and take you and your wife to dinner. Pick a good spot you don't visit often; CBS is picking up the tab."

I immediately thought of the Old Warsaw and its owner, Stan Slavik, whom I had come to know. When I told him whom I was bringing, Stan said, "You'll have the best table in the house." The dinner was great and so was getting to know Mike. We started to leave and Stan pulled out his camera. That picture may still be hanging on the wall. Someone who has been there since I was last there thirty years ago can tell me. But I'm quite sure neither Jane nor Mike has changed at all. Me? Let's move on.

I guess I invited Mike's longtime *60 Minutes* partner, Harry Reasoner, to Dallas to speak to some civic group at least a half dozen times. Harry almost always made these appearances gratis. Only once did he receive a stipend, $2,500, and that was only because the people who invited him offered the fee, and I didn't discourage them from paying it.

It seemed Harry just liked to visit Dallas, and I think I know one reason why: an old flame from his days at the University of Minnesota lived in the area. He asked if I had ever heard her name, and I had. She was involved in some civic project that had put her name in the paper. To my knowledge, he never tried to contact her or see her; he just asked about her.

Harry was doing the Sunday night news on the network at that time and came down on Friday to get the lay of the land for a later story on the Kennedy assassination. Friday night at dinner, Jane mentioned that one of our daughters, Susan, had a horse. "I love horses. Could we go horseback riding on Saturday?" Harry asked. I said, "You bet," and horseback riding we went, but a couple of events developed that we hadn't counted on.

First, we forgot to bring any beer along. It was a hot day and we were thirsty. The pasture bordered on a highway and a liquor store was across the road. Jane said she would stay with the horses, and Harry and I went across to get a six-pack. The place was pretty crowded, and Harry wasn't traveling incognito. Who thought they'd see Harry Reasoner buying a six-pack on Greenville Avenue?

But then something that wasn't funny happened, and it ended up costing Harry about ten days away from the newsroom. He went to mount the horse and something snapped in his back. The pain was killing him, so we called a doctor friend, Bob Stewart, who gave him something to ease the pain. He made it through the night, and we put him on an early flight to New York. I'll be darned if he didn't do the Sunday night news. But it was a couple of weeks before he was "back in the saddle" every day.

The first time I met Eric Sevareid, the distinguished *CBS Evening News* essayist and commentator, was in the CBS Washington bureau. I got him to autograph his book *Not So Wild A Dream*. Frankly, I don't remember whether I bought the book and just happened to run into him, or whether I bought the book and went looking for him to sign it. In either case, it was a short but friendly meeting, and I went on my way.

It took an assassination for our paths to cross again, at Jack Ruby's trial. Eric was in town for a week and did his nightly essays from KRLD. I took him to lunch the first day at El Fenix, when it was on the other side of McKinney. Enchiladas and a Carta Blanca. Tasted so good we made El Fenix for lunch every day he was in town. Since the first lunch was so good, why change? And we didn't.

Eric Sevareid was about as introverted as anyone I ever ran across, but what a mind, and what a way with words. I think he was comfortable with me. I certainly was with him, and we had no trouble keeping a conversation going.

The think pieces he did from the Ruby trial were vintage Sevareid. I'll give you the chance to see what I mean in a later chapter.

CBS News had some rather strange brass manning the helm in the late '70s and early '80s. They certainly blew it when Eric was forced out to pasture.

I've known Dan Rather since the early '60s. We got to know each other quite well during the tumultuous days following November 22, 1963. More on that later. Dan and I have had our differences over the years. I remember, when he wrote his first book, *The Camera Never Blinks*[1], he called to tell me an autographed copy was on the way. But he added, "I should tell you, we don't always remember things the same way." And we don't. But the friendship remains.

When Dan was to be inducted into the Texas Radio Hall of Fame (he started his career at KSAM in Huntsville, and later worked for

KTRH in Houston), I was honored that he asked me to do the induction. And what I said that night pretty well describes my feelings toward Dan:

Where do you start? He's done it all, and done it well. Has it really been over forty years since his dramatic description of that hurricane on a Houston television station caught the eye and ear of CBS News, and he set out on a career that became a journey? And it has taken him far from the Sam Houston State campus to places we only read about. From presidents to paupers, Dan's masterful touch has turned the stories he's covered into our understanding of a complex world.

I said Dan had done it all, but that's not quite right. He was hoping to be here tonight when he was called to do a special assignment for *Sixty Minutes II*. So he hasn't done it all; there's still another story, still an unknown spot on the map that may someday become important to us, and Dan wants to go see for himself.

Dan's no [spring] chicken; he's not as old as I am, but somewhere along the line, will he hang 'em up? I doubt it. I know Dan too well for that; the same burr is still under his saddle that started him off long before many in this room had seen the light of day. So wherever his travels have taken him tonight, it's another notch in the stock of countless notches that make him a worthy member of the Texas Radio Hall of Fame. My friend, Dan Rather.

I first met Walter Cronkite when he was doing the *CBS Morning News* and he came to Dallas for some reason. That was a long time ago, and Walter had yet to hit his stride. *The CBS Evening News*, where Walter really made his name, was a few years away.

When he took over the *Evening News* from Douglas Edwards, it was still a fifteen-minute program. I remember hearing the story of how it expanded to thirty minutes. I'm told that a graphic illustration is what got the change approved. Don Hewitt, who went on to gain fame as the brains behind *60 Minutes*, produced the *Evening News* in those days. Hewitt took the front page of the *New York Times* and blacked out the number of words that would be contained in the fifteen-minute version of the *Evening News*. It was only a tiny fraction of what was on the front page of the *Times*, let alone the rest of the paper. A persuasive demonstration.

With the thirty-minute newscast there was a lot more opportunity for me, as a stringer, to sell a story. We had some good ones through the years. In those days, Walter participated a lot in the makeup of the news, and he was always a part of the decision making. That's not to say he bought everything I submitted. I remember specifically he turned down the Dallas school integration story in the early '60s because the process went too smoothly, so it "wasn't a story."

I heard my old friend Bob Schieffer talking about Walter on the Don Imus show not long ago. Schieffer said, "This is what makes Cronkite so great. If he's on his way to dinner in a limousine, and he sees a police car's lights flashing at the scene of a wreck, Walter will say, 'Stop. I've got to see what's going on.'" He's so inquisitive.

Several years after the John F. Kennedy assassination, CBS made a documentary on the assassination. I was privileged to be part of the program, along with Walter and Dan Rather. (I talk about some of the behind-the-scenes stories of making the documentary in another chapter.) Part of the editing had to be done in New York and would take several days. Walter called and generously invited me and my family for a social visit. "Why don't you bring Jane and Susan and Leslie, too, compliments of CBS?" Daughter Jeanne and sons Allan and Ben didn't get to make the trip.

The weekend was going to be free of work obligations, and Walter invited us to meet him and wife, Betsy, at his boat, the *Wyntje*, in Indian Harbor, Connecticut, on a Sunday afternoon. We would sail out and watch the America's Cup trials. None of the Barkers had ever been on a sailboat, and what a sail it turned out to be.

We were soon under sail: Walter, Betsy, their son, Chip, television director Vinnie Walters, and the Barker crew. Nice sailing for the first half hour and then, whammo! We ran into a storm, and a big one! Walter said, "Women and children below," and to me he said, "Take down the jib."

"What's the jib?" I yelled above the wind, and he shouted back, "That little sail up front." Somehow I managed to get it down, and Vinnie took care of the mainsail. All the while, Walter was at the helm keeping the *Wyntje* pointed into the wind. I stayed on deck and watched a master seaman outwit the elements and see us through the ordeal. On the way back, the harbor was littered with overturned boats of all sizes. But not the *Wyntje*. The first thing I did when we got home was to buy a sailboat, which I hasten to add did not match the size of the *Wyntje*.

One more sailboat story. We were in Miami for a Radio Television News Directors convention, and Walter had the *Wyntje* sailed down to Miami. He called me in the hotel one morning and asked if we would like to go for a noon sail. And we did. Betsy brought pita bread sandwiches, something new for us Texans. A great sail, as we moved alongside a submarine on its way to somewhere. Soon the sub sped off and plunged into the depths. No storms this time.

The most amazing thing about Walter Cronkite is that he's the same now as when I first met him. He never has seemed to catch on that he is held in such high esteem. A good example of Walter's modesty: on the trip to Miami, we went to Joe's Stone Crabs. We didn't have a reservation and the line was around the block. The man at the door saw it was Walter and immediately came up and said, "Right this way, Mr. Cronkite," and started to take us to the head of the line. Walter insisted we could wait: "Please, no favoritism." But Joe's man was about to create a scene, so, reluctantly, Walter accepted the hospitality. Much to the delight of others in line, I should add. Classic Walter.

To this day, he has accepted the accolades, the honors, the attention in stride. I would really put him in the shy category when it comes to accepting the accolades. His hat size remains the same.

When Jane and I married in 1954, we held the ceremony in her old church in Brooklyn. While we were in New York, I went down to CBS News on the seventeenth floor of 485 Madison Avenue to meet some of the folks I had been dealing with on the phone.

Remember back in the opening pages I posed some questions a reader might like to have answered? One of them was, had I ever met Edward R. Murrow? I waffled a bit on the answer and here's why.

Before I went into the CBS newsroom I made a pit stop. I walked up to an available facility and was doing my thing when I noticed someone at the next urinal on the other side of the divider. I glanced up to see who it was and—my God!—it was Edward R. Murrow! The man whose daring reports from the rooftops of London during the blitz had influenced me to become a broadcaster. And what could I do? Not a damn thing. Certainly not offer to shake hands. With his signature cigarette still dangling from his mouth, the great Murrow washed his hands and made his exit. I never saw him again.

So, I'll let you be the judge. Did I meet him, or will I have to tell the grandkids, "Your grandfather once stood side by side with Edward R. Murrow." I just won't tell them where.

Even after achieving some measure of success at KRLD and breaking bread with the likes of Sevareid and Cronkite, I never forgot the folks who were so important to me growing up in San Antonio.

At Harlandale High, I had to attend a music class taught by Miss Ellen Frances Frizzell, whose beauty and talent for wearing Angora sweaters crosses my memory even as I write. One day, we were singing a song that didn't sound right to Miss Frizzell. She halted the singing and, pointing to me, said, "Edmund, I would like to hear you alone." Wow, I thought, she thinks I may be another Bing Crosby or maybe even Ernest Tubb!

Well, she sounded a note on the piano, pointed to me, and I belted it out. I got through a couple of lines before she stopped me. "I've heard enough," she said. And what she said then sent a dagger through my boyish heart: "Edmund, I'm sorry to tell you this, but you are tone deaf." Fearing the worst, I asked, "What does that mean, Miss Frizzell?"

"It means," she said, "that you can't carry a tune and there is no reason for you to continue in the class, but you can stay on if you just don't sing when the others do." It was tough to take.

I thought Miss Frizzell would always remain a lovely memory, the everlasting image of those Angora sweaters erasing the bomb she dropped on me. The years went by, the world turned around many times, and I found myself news director of KRLD-TV and radio. Then one day in 1960 it happened: the first hijacking to Cuba of a U.S.

commercial jet, a Pan Am 707. Jay Hogan saw that the captain of the jet lived in Houston and called the captain's home for his wife's reaction. Just as he was ready to hang up, the captain's wife said, "Do you happen to know Eddie Barker?"

Jay replied, "Yes, I do. He's my boss."

"Well," the captain's wife said, "please tell him Miss Frizzell said hello."

References:

[1] Dan Rather, *The Camera Never Blinks* (New York: Ballantine, 1977).

3

"The Toy Department"

As I've mentioned, one of my boyhood heroes was the sportscaster Bill Stern. Stern had been a stage director and manager, and he brought that theatrical flair to sports broadcasting. He broadcast the Friday night boxing match of the week for years on NBC radio. But he was best known for the *Colgate Sports Newsreel* and, later, *Bill Stern Sports* from the late '30s into the '50s. This was a fifteen-minute show in which Bill told legendary sports tales. Paul Harvey's *The Rest of the Story* probably owes a lot to Stern. I owe a lot to him, too. As much as anyone, he sparked my interest in radio, and sports broadcasting, in particular.

My family had a radio, but we didn't have a phone. One time, Stern had some question on his show about Knute Rockne, the immortal Notre Dame football coach. I knew all about Knute Rockne, so I went tearing next door to the neighbor's and breathlessly asked, "Can I use your phone?" I guess they thought our house was on fire or something and they said okay. There were no 800 numbers in those days, so it must have been a long-distance call. I got through, but I didn't win.

Stern was a master of the motivational, uplifting story. He was so good that if you had only one leg, he made you want to be a placekicker. Did you ever see Woody Allen's movie *Radio Days*? He satirizes Stern brilliantly with an "inspirational" story about a baseball player who played without an arm . . . and then a leg . . . and then another arm. . . . It was probably no coincidence that Bill himself had just one leg.

I loved sports as a kid, all sports. I got very interested in golf. I was about twelve, and when the Texas Open came to San Antonio, I got on the bus and rode out to the Breckenridge Park course. I followed these big-time golfers around the course and stayed out there all day. The one I liked the best was Lawson Little, because he was so nice to me. He chatted with me as we walked the course. The first Cadillac I ever saw was the one Ben Hogan was driving. I saw a lot of the greats that year—Byron Nelson, Cary Middlecoff, Jimmy Demaret, "Slammin' Sammy" Snead. Not all of the pros were so pleasant to kids. "Slammin' Sammy" was pretty crusty. A top golfer named Vic Ghezzi was always breaking his clubs and throwing things. I played a little golf after I grew up, but, you know, rearing five children is a very expensive thing, and I really didn't have the money, the time, or the attention span to get very good at it.

I think of myself first as a broadcast newsman, but sports broadcasting was an important part of my career for a long time and something I truly loved doing. Of course, I never played football. I was always working, either at the drugstore or, later, at KMAC. In today's sports-broadcasting marketplace, it seems everyone has to have been a jock, and so I wouldn't stand a chance of doing what I was able to do back then.

The first interview I ever did at KMAC was with Dizzy Dean, the flamboyant St. Louis Cardinals and Chicago Cubs pitcher, who, by that time, had become an even bigger folk hero as a very improbable baseball announcer. He'd sing the old hillbilly song "The Wabash Cannonball" on the air during games and drive English teachers everywhere to distraction with his imaginative use of the English language: "He slud into third!" When the grammarians howled, Diz explained with great aplomb, "Slud is something more than slid. It means sliding with great effort."

What a great fellow. I was a kid announcer, and for whatever reason, he was in San Antonio, probably something to do with the San Antonio Missions Texas League club. They brought him around to the station and said, "Here's Dizzy Dean. Interview him." My gosh, he was a big guy. I've always had a soft spot for Dizzy Dean, because he was so kind to me. Here I was, this punk kid interviewing this baseball great. I thought, "What a terrific way to start!" It's really something when famous people you admire turn about to be just as you'd hoped they'd be. It's not always like that.

One of my early assignments at KMAC was broadcasting the "midget-car" races on Sunday afternoons. We would go out to a place on Broadway called Playland. They had a Ferris wheel and a merry-go-round and those kinds of things, but they also had a midget-car track. The midget cars looked like miniature versions of the Indianapolis-style race cars. They all used engines made by Offenhauser, the company that supplied the engines for many of the Indy cars. A. J. Foyt got his start racing the midget cars, although that was after I left San Antonio.

To me it was the most boring thing in the world. I had very little interest in these little cars. Not only that, they literally stank. They used something in the fuel that really smelled bad. (It was kind of like chicken. As a kid, I had to kill them, pluck them, and boil them, and the smell turned me off so much I couldn't eat chicken.) Plus, I didn't know how to keep up with the races. After they ran four or five laps, I had no idea who was ahead. Finally, somebody would get the checkered flag, and I would declare, "The winner!" Now, I kind of enjoy watching auto racing. But not eating chicken.

Football—now that was another story. I truly loved broadcasting football games. And, again, I got my start at KMAC. But it was announcing Southwest Conference football for sixteen years on the old Humble Oil Company radio network that is my proudest achievement in sports broadcasting.

As I've mentioned, I started broadcasting football games on KMAC in San Antonio when I was still in high school. The athletic director of the San Antonio schools, Claude Kellum, was excited to have the games broadcast on radio. His brother Jess Kellum was the general manager of Lyndon and Lady Bird Johnson's radio station in

Austin, KTBC (now KLBJ), and I'm sure that had something to do with Claude's enthusiasm for radio. I was just a kid, but he was so good to me. He figured I knew what I was doing, which was about half true.

We hired a couple of guys who were in the army and stationed in San Antonio to do the play-by-play. I was going to do the "color." One of the guys was Bill Whitmore, the other one was Wilbur Evans. In later years, I ended up doing business with both of them. Bill was the sports information director (SID) at Rice University for many years, during the Owls' heyday under head coach Jess Neely. Wilbur, a dear man, went to the University of Texas and was the SID there in the '50s and into the great Darrell Royal era. We kept up our friendship all through the years. About mid-season, Whitmore and Evans got shipped out. So there we were with nobody to do the play-by-play— except me. So I started doing play-by-play the rest of that year and the next year. I guess I did fine.

Of course, I listened religiously to Kern Tips, the wonderfully colorful Humble Network Southwest Conference play-by-play announcer, and tried to learn from him. Kern was born in Houston and went to Texas A&M and Rice. He started as a sports reporter at the *Houston Chronicle* in 1924, and later became sports editor of the *Chronicle*. He got into radio as a sportscaster in 1926, while remaining with the newspaper, but he became general manager of KPRC radio in Houston 1935. He stayed there until he joined the Wilkinson-Schiwetz advertising agency in 1947, which then became Wilkinson, Schiwetz and Tips. It merged with McCann-Erickson in 1954, and Kern became a vice-president. So you can see he was a very accomplished man.

Kern had little idiosyncrasies. He was a Christian Scientist, and they supposedly reject tobacco and alcohol, but he always carried a little flask of Four Roses whiskey and, as soon as the ball game was over, he'd take a little nip. He always stacked chairs to sit on during the game. Most places had these old folding metal chairs, and he'd stack about four together so he'd be sitting at an angle tilting forward as he looked at the field. He'd always undo his pants just before the game, I guess for comfort's sake.

One of the other big-time sportscasters of that era was noted for having a lot of scripted one-liners within easy reach. I've heard that gambit ascribed to Kern, but I don't remember seeing such a checklist the times I was in the booth with him. I'm sure he thought about lines he might use in advance, but it all just seemed to roll off his tongue. I think a lot of fans in those days would rather listen to Kern describe a game on the radio than see the game in person. He was that good.

In doing the research for this book, we came across a 1965 University of Texas master's thesis on Kern Tips's football play-by-play style. Billy Oxley notes that Kern averaged speaking 232 words per minute in the 1964 Texas-SMU game and has a chapter on Kern's distinctive use of language in describing a college football game. Oxley's thesis reminds me of Kern's masterly use of the language. These are some of Kern's descriptions of punts or place-kicks: "tumbles one"; "lays leather to the ball"; "tries to hang one up in the lights." For running plays: "gouge out a little daylight"; "a sunrise-to-sunset leap"; "a high tunafish leap"; "rumbles for a little moonlight" (in a night game). For passing plays: "pulls the trigger on the long ball"; "giving it a long winger"; "goes to the airlanes"; "scooped it up off the daisies"; "the passing game, which had suddenly caught fire, comes to grief in the clutching claws of [the interceptor]." For tackles: "overwhelmed by the mob"; "a billy-goat tackle"; "dropped him for a seat on the 50"; "run over by the heavy trucks."

Oxley notes that in his play-by-play Kern followed this time-honored advice given to writers—use precise nouns, bold adjectives, and forceful verbs: "It was obvious that while Kern Tips had, and used, a number of standard words and phrases to describe the actions on the field, he also had developed a series of very colorful and descriptive phrases which he used from time to time to give variety to his sportscast. The effect of his insertion of these colorful phrases into his descriptions led the listener to believe that his speech was really more colorful than it was."[1]

Like all great artists, Kern knew just where and how to apply the accent strokes to bring his radio portrait to life. Unlike some sports broadcasters, he knew how annoying it becomes if the announcer tries to be clever all the time, and he would use his distinctive phrases only once each per game. In the immortal words of Brylcreem: "A little dab'll do ya."

One of the big songs of the '50s was Bobby Darin's "Mack the Knife," and Kern played off the lyrics of that song and others in his descriptions. He was contemporary in his commentary, very much "with it." His broadcasts flowed. A time-out, a measurement, an injury: there were no long pauses and certainly no second-guessing of anything on the field, which would have been considered very bad form. And remember, Humble play-by-play announcers covered everything that happened between the whistles. They called on the color commentator for a scripted opening (which had to receive the okay of a representative of McCann-Erickson, which produced the games), end-of-quarter commercials, half-time commentary, and a scripted good-bye. That's all.

It's hard to appreciate today the impact of the Humble Network. The Humble Southwest Conference broadcasts had much the same popularity in Texas that the Sunday NFL telecasts have nationwide today. In those days, even after the Cowboys came to town, college football was far and away the most popular sport in Texas. You can see it in the *Dallas Morning News* and the *Dallas Times Herald* sports pages from the '40s and '50s and well into the '60s. The papers gave by far the greatest amount of coverage to the Southwest Conference; everything else was an afterthought. Relatively few games were on television, even in the '60s, and the Humble Network blanketed Texas, on the state's best and most-powerful radio stations—KRLD, WBAP in Fort Worth, WOAI in San Antonio, KPRC in Houston—and lots of smaller stations. It was virtually impossible to be out of the range of the Humble broadcast of any Southwest Conference game on an autumn Saturday in Texas.

Well, I knew that Kern was in charge of the Humble Network. I found out where to write him and sent him a letter. By this time, I was out of high school and working full time for KMAC. Kern wrote me back: "I appreciate your interest. Send me a transcription." We didn't have tapes then. Electrical transcriptions were these oversized records that radio stations played. I sent him a transcription, and, I'll be darned if he didn't write me back: "We can use you, and I'll get back to you with some assignments." Another dream fulfilled.

Humble announcers came from a variety of backgrounds, but none of us made our livelihoods full time from sports, as is the case with many sports broadcasters today. Kern was an advertising executive; Bill Michaels was general manager of KABC in San Antonio;

Charlie Jordan ran KFJZ and the Texas State Network in Fort Worth; Ves Box was the chief announcer at KRLD in Dallas; Dave Russell was with a radio station in Beaumont; I worked at KMAC in the beginning, and then went to KRLD as a staff announcer.

I started broadcasting Southwest Conference football games on the Humble Network in 1947 while still working full time for KMAC. My first game was Texas A&M versus Oklahoma at Norman. The crew I had to work with included some of the best. The play-by-play man was Charlie Jordan, the ad agency rep was Dave Williams, and the engineer was the legendary Truett Kimzey—who demonstrated the first working television system in Texas a good ten years before WBAP-TV officially became the state's first TV station and who, as a part-time announcer at KFJZ in Fort Worth, became first to declare, "The Light Crust Doughboys are on the air!" I handled the color commentary.

We stayed at the Skirvin Towers Hotel in Oklahoma City. Game day for that Sooners-Aggies game in Norman dawned clear and hot with a capital *H*. Our booth on the east side of the stadium had a corrugated tin roof. We were right above the OU student section, with no men's room, no water, and no soft-drink stand anywhere nearby. But we were up to the task as Coach Bud Wilkinson's Sooners battled Coach Homer Norton's Aggies. If it matters, OU won that day, 26–14. That game was where I had my baptism into the way Humble did things on its broadcasts.

The games were entirely sponsored by the Humble Oil Company (now Exxon/Mobil). The commercials were all for Humble Oil, and we read them live from the game site. The company's great slogan was "Let Humble take you to the games, or bring the games to you!" We always broadcast the school songs of both schools and never talked over the music. Humble permitted no mention of injuries to particular players for fear of alarming moms and dads listening at home. We never criticized a referee's call. No dwelling on coaches' bad decisions or players' mistakes. Humble announcers would report that a team was penalized but not identify the player who committed the penalty, so as not to humiliate the tender young athlete. It was a gentler, more chivalrous time.

If a disaster of any kind occurred during a broadcast, we were not to mention it. For example, Kern was broadcasting a game during which a section of the stands collapsed. Though the sirens wailed, he said not a word about it. He and Humble were very proud that he didn't yield to the temptation and do a live report. In the Humble playbook, we reported only what was happening in the game on the field. And Kern had his own way of saying things. One thing he would never say was *"the* Cotton Bowl"; it was always just "Cotton Bowl." Don't ask me why.

We never anticipated the outcome of the game. If a team was leading 48–0 in the fourth quarter, we'd never say, "This is a runaway," or "There's no doubt A&M has this one sewn up," or anything like that. We'd never say, "Well, this is the third defeat in a row for Coach Jones, and he's really got his tail in a crack." Humble wanted listening to the Southwest Conference games to be a very pleasant experience, with no controversy or anything of an unsettling nature intruding at all.

The Humble Network's strict format for the Southwest Conference games wasn't always easy to follow. In 1950, I was the color commentator for the Presidential Cup bowl game between Texas A&M and Georgia in College Park, Maryland. Charlie Jordan and I were the only announcers to say in their vitas that they ever did a Presidential Cup game; there never was a second one. The start of the game was delayed because it was being televised on the old DuMont Television Network, and the TV crew was having some sort of technical problem, which was not at all uncommon in those days.

As I mentioned earlier, the color announcer and the play-by-play announcer each had rigidly defined roles. The play-by-play man did nothing but the play-by-play, and I mean *nothing* but. It was the color commentator's job to do everything else. No banter between the play-by-play man and the color man at all. The color man would usually keep statistics, and on rare occasions the play-by-play announcer might turn to him and ask, "How many first downs does SMU have?" But no more than that.

Well, Charlie Jordan was the play-by-play announcer for the game and, under our rules, he couldn't help me at all. Maybe that's where I learned what to do if you don't get a call on a radio talk show. So I had to keep talking . . . and talking . . . and talking while we waited. When they finally got ready to start the game, a plane was going to fly over the field and drop the game ball in a parachute. The plane came over and the darn wind just took the ball right out of the stadium. And rather than start the game with another ball, they waited until they brought that fool ball in from the parking lot. And old Charlie was just looking at me and laughing the whole time.

Coincidentally, I met my boyhood hero Bill Stern at that game. He was announcing the game on television. The thing I remember about him is that he was broadcasting the game from high in the stands and eating an apple between plays. When he finished the apple, he tossed the core over his shoulder and out of the stands. Funny what you remember about people.

One of the great things about sports broadcasting is the people you meet. Some are celebrated; some will become so. Ves Box and I started broadcasting high school playoff games in Texas and Oklahoma for the Magnolia Oil Company after the regular-season Southwest Conference season was over. Magnolia—the forerunner of Mobil, best known for its famed symbol of Pegasus, the flying red horse, which dominated the Dallas skyline for years—operated a high school football radio network. We did one season of the Magnolia games and had started a second season.

One day I got a call from Kern: "Well, I've had some complaints from Humble. One of their hot shots heard you doing a Magnolia game and they don't like it. If you want to keep working for Humble, I suggest you give it up." Humble and Magnolia, of course, were bitter competitors. So I said that's fine, and we quit announcing the high school games. But the Magnolia people asked Ves and me if we could go and supervise the broadcasts for them. Sure, we said, we can do that.

One day I was supervising a high school playoff game in Oklahoma, and the play-by-play announcer was a young fellow named Curt Gowdy. Of course, he was just starting out at that time. I have no recollection of the game or Curt's performance at all. He was just a pleasant guy. It must have been '48, because by 1949, Curt was doing the New York Yankees games with Mel Allen. He went on to become the voice of the Boston Red Sox, but, of course, he really made his name as the lead announcer for NBC's Major League Baseball Game of the Week and AFL and NFL games, including the Super Bowl. When I first heard him on a national broadcast, I said, "Hey, that's Curt Gowdy from Oklahoma!" I hadn't really thought about him since, but I think it was his unique name that I remembered more than anything else.

I remember most of the Southwest Conference coaches of the '40s and '50s well, not from the personal relationships I had with them but from seeing them in action and following them in print. Newspaper reporters, then as now, were closer to coaches than were other media people. They spent time with them on a daily basis, and good newspaper coverage was highly valued by the coaches and the schools. On the Humble broadcasts, we didn't even carry interviews with the coaches on the pregame shows, and we certainly didn't have a long sit-down with them the way the network TV announcers do today. I did get to know the SMU coaches well from doing shows with them on KRLD and living in Dallas.

Matty Bell, who coached the Mustangs to the national championship in 1935 and remained on the Hilltop until 1949, could have managed a big-time business instead of coaching a college football team. He was a charming guy, a very articulate man. You could see him as the maître d' of a swanky restaurant or as a chairman of the board of a major company. He was always an easy interview. You didn't have to feed him much more than a word or two and he would take it from there. Matty had a tremendous amount of confidence in himself.

It hurt me to see Rusty Russell come along as head coach in 1950, the year after Doak Walker left. Matty knew when to get out, and he did. He retired to become the athletic director. Rusty had come to SMU with Doak from Highland Park High as an assistant coach. It was like when a popular preacher leaves a church; whoever follows him has a tough act to follow. They just didn't have much of a ball club at SMU after Doak left.

SMU's head basketball coach, Doc Hayes, was just great. I loved him. He was such an easy guy to work with, a genuinely nice guy, not to mention a pretty good roundball coach. He won eight Southwest Conference championships and carried the Mustangs to the Final

Four in 1956. I was very saddened when he and his wife both died in a car accident.

Jess Neely of Rice, Dutch Meyer of TCU, Blair Cherry at Texas, Bob Woodard and George Sauer at Baylor, and Bear Bryant at A&M were memorable personalities. Even though I broadcast a lot of A&M games, I really can't say I got to know the Bear well. Because of *The Junction Boys* by Jim Dent and the movie that ESPN made of the story, people ask me what I remember about Bryant's brutal 1954 preseason camp in the Southwest Texas desert. It was not a secret at the time. It was the big talk of the summer leading up to that season that Bear Bryant was coming in with his iron-handed tactics to mold a champion. There was a lot of publicity about it, but I don't think many people realized at the time how really tough that camp was.

But it was a Baylor assistant whom I remember most, Frank Broyles. It was his job to be in the coaches' booth in the press box and communicate with the bench, and did he communicate! The coaches' booth was next to the broadcast booth, and there was little in the way of insulation to keep sound from traveling, and Frank's voice *traveled*. He got himself worked up into a lather and used language that wouldn't have passed muster with the Baylor deacons had they heard, but he *was* heard on our broadcasts. Humble never, ever wanted to make waves, but it was worked out that the coaches' booth would be moved to the other end of the stadium, where the newspaper types could be Frank's audience.

Frank went on to greater heights as the head coach at the University of Arkansas and, at the time of this writing, is the revered (and rightly so) athletic director at Fayetteville. Ironically, he also spent quite a few years with Keith Jackson as a color commentator on ABC's telecasts of college football games. I don't remember him having any trouble controlling his language.

While I've said we didn't have much close contact with the coaches, there were exceptions. Seven schools were in the Southwest Conference when I started—Arkansas, Baylor, Rice, SMU, TCU, Texas, and Texas A&M. Texas Tech came in as number eight in 1960. There had been rumblings for years that Texas Tech should be in the conference. There were strong feelings on both sides, but Humble executives saw the handwriting on the wall and decided Tech games should be broadcast. I did the first one, and I did the first game in Lubbock when Tech became an official member of the SWC.

The Tech coach was DeWitt Weaver. He decided that the Humble crew should be invited to his little Friday night gatherings for great Chinese food upstairs at the Ming Tree restaurant in Lubbock. Bill Holmes, the longtime Tech sports information director and "evangelist" for the Red Raiders, issued the invitation and, for as long as DeWitt was there, Humble announcers were welcome. We got a pretty good idea of what he intended to do the next day. Now that I think back, when George Sauer came to Baylor, he went out of his way to know who we were, too.

I called Bill Holmes an evangelist, and that he was, in spreading the word about the giants who wore the scarlet and black: E. J. Holub, who went on to play linebacker for the Dallas Texans and the Kansas City Chiefs, for one. Holmes was one of those people you couldn't help but like, and you always wanted to go the extra mile for him. His budget didn't rival those of other state-supported schools (you know whom I mean, orange bloods).

Gosh, I almost forgot another one of my favorites, Herman Morgan at SMU. Everybody called him "Sleepy." Sleepy scouted a lot of upcoming games for the Ponies, and he would often ride home with me after a game that I had broadcast. He loved SMU, and he loved "Varsity," the SMU school song. He said it always brought tears to his eyes when he heard it, and I'm living proof that it did. We were driving back from a Baylor game while SMU was playing Texas in Austin. The Humble broadcast came on the radio, and the announcer said, "And now the SMU alma mater." Sleepy grabbed my arm and said, "Please pull over and stop." I did, and as the strains of "Varsity" came over the radio static, Sleepy's tears rained down.

When I went into television at KRLD, local sports events were an obvious source of programming. Someone got the bright idea to televise some of the minor-league hockey games from the Fair Park Coliseum, and, of course, I was supposed to be the announcer. I had no more idea of what was going on than the man in the moon. We decided probably the best place for me to be was up in the rafters. So I said to a guy from the hockey club, "Look, I need help. Why don't you get up there with me and guide me." I remember he said,

"There's one thing that's really important, you've got to remember." What's that? I asked. "Icing the puck," he told me. Well, I still don't know what icing the puck is, but it still sounds just as funny as it did then.

We did a lot of things spontaneously, on the spur of the moment. Once Kern Tips came up to Dallas for some reason and was curious to see a football game on television. This was at the very beginning of the 1950 high school football season. Ves Box said, "Kern wants to watch some football on television. So we're going to broadcast the game, and I want you to go out and do it." Just like that, at the last minute. We trundled our $65,000 mobile unit out to P .C. Cobb Stadium, originally DalHi Stadium—for decades the Mecca for high school football in Dallas. I didn't have any knowledge of the teams; I hadn't talked to the coaches. The only roster I had was the program they were selling, and it was half wrong. Just so Kern Tips could see how football looked on television.

How far have we come in football broadcasting? In the late '40s, Doak Walker was the hero of Dallas. He played first at Highland Park High and then became an All-American halfback at Southern Methodist University. And then he signed with the Detroit Lions of the NFL. Bobby Layne, a charismatic guy who played at Highland Park with Doak and then went on to the University of Texas, was the Lions' quarterback. So in the early '50s, Channel 4 made a deal with the Lions to send us their game film each week.

A week late, on Sunday afternoon, I would go down and re-create the ball game live, working from the printed play-by-play rundown. It was a little like the re-creations of baseball games they used to do on the radio. This was the coaches' game film, taken from a high angle—black and white, no close-ups, no replays. By today's standards, it would be a tough thing to watch. I don't know whether we had a great audience or not, but we probably did. It was the only game in town.

I announced the first televised Texas-OU game, a regionally televised affair. I had assumed Kern was going to do the game, but I learned the week of the game that I was going to do it. It seemed funny to see Kern in the radio booth right next to us.

We had a ton of mail on that game. It was the darnedest thing. The pros and the cons added up to the same number. We got twenty-some-odd letters saying they liked it, and twenty-some-odd who said it was awful. The fans of whichever team lost thought the telecast was terrible; those who won thought it was great. Even today, many fans think the announcers hate their team, when, most of the time, they couldn't care less who wins or loses. Fans are incredibly passionate about their teams, as I would later learn to my regret.

If I'm known for anything in my broadcasting career, I guess it is my role in covering the JFK assassination. Ironically, I probably would have had little to do with the story had I still been broadcasting Southwest Conference football.

For sixteen years prior to 1963, I had been an announcer for the SWC games. The broadcast setup was certainly unusual compared to broadcasts today. Humble, the sole sponsor of the games, was supersensitive to any reaction from any member school or important alumnus. The Texas Aggies were not having the best of seasons in 1962. Under coach Hank Foldberg, they lost 6–3 to the University of Houston, which the Aggies have always derisively referred to as "Cougar High." They lost at home to TCU, 20–14, and the Horned Frogs were no one's idea of a football factory in those days. A&M ended up 3–7 in '62, the Aggies' fifth straight losing season after Bear Bryant left College Station behind for Alabama. It fell my lot to get a heavy number of Aggie games.

Remember what I said about getting fired once? Well, you know the old saying about "shooting the messenger." One day in midseason, Ves Box walked into my office, closed the door, and said, "I don't know how to tell you this, but Kern called and told me to tell you that you won't be doing any more Humble games." I was floored. I managed to ask, "Ves, what did I do?" And he said, "I don't know. Kern just asked me do it." I think Ves would have been honest with me if he'd known, because we were very close.

This was so strange. There seemed to be no complaints about my work. To my knowledge, no other Humble announcer was ever fired right in the middle of a season. I hadn't robbed a bank or violated any moral clauses. Every year, I was getting better games, and when we got down to only three games remaining in the season, it was Kern, Ves, and me doing them.

I tried to get Kern to tell me why I was fired. He wouldn't take my phone calls. He wouldn't answer my letters. It really disappointed me. For whatever reason, he couldn't bring himself to tell me why he had fired me.

Usually, there's a way to find an answer to almost any question if you go looking hard enough. The reason that Humble dumped me was that I was the announcer of too many Aggie gridiron defeats. The diehard Aggies, many in powerful positions, complained. The A&M alumni (or "former students," as they're called), athletic department, and university administration were very particular about what was said about A&M and how it was said, and I'm sure that's still true. Humble was not about to let a relationship like theirs with the Aggies be endangered by an all-too-easily-replaced play-by-play announcer.

Even though he lacked the courage to tell me himself why I was fired, I still admired Kern. He was the best at what he did. But I often wonder if anyone ever really knew the man. He died in 1967 at the age of sixty-two, a legend then and to this day.

The abrupt firing haunted me for many years. It crushed me. It was a humiliating experience. It was tough to explain to my wife and co-workers why I was so unceremoniously dumped after sixteen years. It wasn't the loss of the income that bothered me—I think I was making $125 a game—although when you're bringing up five kids, every little bit helps. It was the prestige of broadcasting Southwest Conference football that I loved most. But, besides the respect that came with being a Humble Network broadcaster, I enjoyed the games, I enjoyed the people, I enjoyed being a part of it all. I enjoyed the opportunity to express myself in the extemporaneous, free-flowing medium of play-by-play announcing. But I survived. And late on the afternoon of November 22, 1963, standing outside the emergency entrance to Parkland Hospital, it hit me. Had I not been fired from the football job, I would be spending this afternoon far away preparing for Saturday's game. Funny how that old saw about one door closing and another opening really works at times.

The end of my Southwest Conference broadcasting career was not the end of my involvement in sports broadcasting. I had some broadcasting opportunities with the Dallas Cowboys as the team gradually grew into a national phenomenon.

In the '60s, CBS involved the local affiliate stations in the regional telecasts of the NFL games. Frank Gleiber, our sportscaster, became the play-by-play man for many CBS telecasts of Cowboys games. At the end of the ball game, CBS wanted an interview with the winning coach, and on a few occasions, I served as a postgame interviewer for the broadcasts.

One of the games was Dallas–Green Bay at Milwaukee in 1965. I did an interview with the Packers' legendary coach, Vince Lombardi. Probably the hardest interview I ever did. I just asked the normal, routine questions after a 13–3 Green Bay win. But he looked at me like, "Who in the hell are you? Why am I standing here talking to this nobody?" Lombardi was exceedingly gruff. He was ready to get out of there. In his biography of Lombardi, *When Pride Still Mattered*, David Maraniss writes how he had no use for reporters, except the New York writers he met while he was an assistant coach at West Point and with the New York Giants in the '50s. I believe it.

Frank and I weren't the only Channel 4 folks involved in CBS' NFL telecasts. Floor manager extraordinaire Benny Molina worked on the games, too. I'm sure there is a more sophisticated way of doing it now, but in the early days of the telecasts, the referee needed to be told when to call a time-out for a commercial and when to resume play. The job of providing this vital information fell to Benny, the man with the white glove. Benny stood on the sidelines, and the referee had to be on the lookout for the white glove. Sure enough, when Benny placed the hand with the white glove over his heart, all activity on the field came to a halt. When Benny lowered his hand from over his heart, the referee could sound the whistle to resume play.

I came home from the Green Bay game and other road games on the Cowboys' team plane. I'll always remember Bob Lilly, the Hall of Fame defensive tackle, sitting in the back of the plane chewing gum and reading a stack of comic books. Now, Bob has become a distinguished gentleman, a fine photographer, but he was still just a kid in those days. I didn't know too many of the Cowboys from that era. I did get to know Lee Roy Jordan, the undersized but gritty middle linebacker, a little after he retired. He got into the redwood lumber business. He always seemed a really genuine guy to me.

The rise of the Cowboys in the late '60s was much more than a big sports story; it was a key to the boom that Dallas enjoyed at about the same time. It would have been hard to imagine such a thing when the Cowboys started out as an exceptionally humble expansion team in 1960. The Dallas Texans of the upstart American Football League, owned by young Lamar Hunt, also rolled onto the scene in 1960. Both teams played in the Cotton Bowl. The Texans moved to Kansas City in 1963, right after winning the 1962 AFL title, and became the Chiefs.

Someone from each of the teams would come down to KRLD every week and give me a package of two dozen tickets to give away. They were trying to put some faces in the stands to avoid the embarrassment of acres of empty seats. The Cowboys announced the attendance one rainy Sunday in 1960 as a generously padded ten thousand. One sportswriter cracked, "Five thousand fans came disguised as empty seats." Most of the fans moved under the overhang of the upper deck on each side of the Cotton Bowl, and so, from the press box, the stadium appeared nearly deserted. The Cowboys' droll quarterback, Don Meredith, once suggested that, rather than the customary pregame player introductions, the Cowboys should go into the stands and introduce themselves personally to each fan.

The Southwest Conference was king in those days. One of the guys with Wilkinson, Schiwetz and Tips, Dave Williams, had a real love for Baylor, even though he never went to school there. One time we were talking about pro football, and Dave said, "Well, pro ball is not going to go over down here." I said, "Why not?" He said, "Pro ball is the game for all of the hard-hats and the working class, people who don't have a college. They go to the pro games. But down here, everybody's got Baylor, or Texas, or A&M." In the beginning, I think there may have been some truth to that. But then when all of the names they knew from college ball came into the Cotton Bowl on the pro teams—Texas' Bobby Layne with the Steelers by the time the Cowboys came along, SMU's Kyle Rote with the Giants, A&M's John David Crow with the Cardinals—interest started picking up. When the Cowboys started winning big in '66, they started filling up the Cotton Bowl every Sunday.

After the Kennedy assassination, people around the country hated Dallas. But I have always said that what brought Dallas back was the Cowboys. All of sudden, we went from the most-hated city in the world to the home of "America's Team." Of course, Dallas was ready to grow anyway, especially when Dallas–Fort Worth International Airport came in and we got away from the rivalry with Fort Worth. But the Cowboys—with their shiny silver-blue helmets—certainly helped Dallas create its glittering image, no two ways about that.

On a few occasions, Cowboys players got into trouble with the law, and that would often mean a call from Bob Strauss. Strauss was a big-time Dallas attorney who, as the chairman of the national Democratic Party, later became known as "Mr. Democrat." He also served for a time as ambassador to Russia in the first Bush administration. But in the '60s and early '70s, he was on retainer as the Cowboys' lawyer. I always loved Bob Strauss; he was a great character.

Lance Rentzel was a star receiver for the Cowboys, tall, blond, handsome as the devil, married to the sexpot movie starlet Joey Heatherton. Well, of all things, Rentzel got arrested for exposing himself to a little girl. He lived not far from where we lived in University Park. I got a call from Strauss. He said, "Say, you know, one of the Cowboys has a little problem." I said, "Are you talking about Lance?" I'd already heard about it. He said, "Yeah, I'd appreciate it if y'all didn't use that story." Well, of course, we could hardly call ourselves a news department if we looked the other way when a Dallas Cowboy star got arrested for exposing himself to a child. I said, "Bob, I love ya, but you know we can't sit on that story." The Cowboys' general manager, Tex Schramm, had told him to try to quash it, but Tex was an old newspaper man and he should have known better. The next season, Lance was playing again, with the L.A. Rams. I wonder if he'd get off so lightly today with our higher sensitivity, and rightly so, to sexual offenses against children.

After I left KRLD in 1972 and started the Eddie Barker Associates public relations firm, we produced the syndicated *Tom Landry Show*, which aired in Dallas and around the Southwest. Channel 4 had been producing the show and the preseason games, most of which were not televised by CBS. The producer of the Landry show and the games, Nevin Lyerly, came to me and said, "If you hire me, I think we can get the Landry show and the preseason games." I thought, "What the hell am I doing hiring Nevin? I'm not making enough yet to pay myself." But I was always a gambler, so I hired him. I went to Tex Schramm and said, "We'd like to produce your preseason games. I can't guarantee they'll be on Channel 4." Well, he said, "Great, let's do it." We also got the Landry show, and we produced the preseason games and Tom's show for quite a few years.

Poor Tom could never pronounce "Toyota." In his Texas drawl it always came out, "Ty-yota." But he was a dear man. He called me one day and wanted to send one of his daughters, Lisa, to talk to me about a career in broadcasting, or whatever she wanted to do. Sadly, she died of liver cancer as a young woman.

Tom was absolutely top rate. I'm sure he had some flaws, as we all do. The very eccentric and talented running back Duane Thomas famously called him "a plastic man." But many years later, after his football career was over, Duane got his life on track and talked about how much he had come to admire Tom Landry. What you saw—the quiet, strong demeanor of a man who flew thirty combat missions in World War II, the Christian faith, the unassuming manner—that's really how he was. I never questioned him. He was one of those people whom you just accept as a first-rate guy, because it's apparent that's what he is.

I also admired Schramm a great deal. We had a good relationship with Tex while producing the Cowboys preseason games all those years, until the networks started to televise so many of them that it no longer was practical for us to do them. I was always fond of Tex, but also I was a fan, because his mind was so darn fast. The Cowboys were already wildly successful, but Schramm came along and created the Dallas Cowboy cheerleaders, with the low-cut tops, and added a little sex to the mix. They became as big as the Cowboys themselves. That was Tex. A genius.

Some of my best friends over the years have been sportswriters and newspaper people in general. One of them is Blackie Sherrod, the great *Dallas Times Herald* sports editor and columnist, who later moved on to the *Dallas Morning News*. I got to know Blackie when we were doing the *Comment* program every afternoon on KRLD radio. We'd have guests who appeared again and again, and Blackie, always nearby in the *Times Herald* office and being the witty, interesting guy he is, was a favorite. He was just so natural.

I've never known a sportswriter quite like Blackie. He's so well read that he's equally comfortable quoting Homer or Damon Runyon. One of Blackie's many illustrious protégés, Dan Jenkins, the author of *Semi-Tough, Dead Solid Perfect,* and many other raunchy but hilarious sports novels, puts it very well: "A myth exists in Texas newspaper circles that working for, or alongside, Blackie Sherrod at some early station in your life was the equivalent to a journalism degree. I wish to correct this myth. It was better than a doctorate." I've always felt very close to Blackie, even today. Not long before he retired from the *Morning News,* he wrote a column about me. In his delightfully off-center style, he wrote, "Eddie Barker is now ensconced in an East Texas cave, from which he occasionally emerges to lay in supplies and issue righteous growls at civilization. Or to mail enlightening messages to old pals."[2]

In one of his columns, Blackie had quoted a half-remembered bit of doggerel about the rookie baseball players who shine in the spring but fade in the harsh glare of the regular season. I happened to remember the poem and its author, New York sportswriter John Kieran. One of the verses goes as follows:

The morning glories blossom just as springtime hits the trail,
But when April melts in Maytime, they begin to fade and fail.
And the lad who "looked like Heilmann"
meets the guy who "hit like Cobb,"
On the way to Niles, Ohio, and his former plumbing job.

Another name Dallas sports fans will know is Norm Hitzges. Norm has made his career opining on sports over the Dallas airwaves—on the old WFAA radio, KERA-FM, KLIF, and, most recently, KTCK, "The Ticket." I think he's the best-informed sports authority to be found, here, there, or yonder. Norm showed up one day in my newsroom saying he was working on his master's degree at the University of Texas. His thesis was on the old Humble football network, and he wanted to interview me. The more we talked, the more I became aware of the fact that this guy with the big nose, high squeaky voice, and grating laugh—later to become his trademarks— was a walking sports encyclopedia.

At the time, CBS News every Saturday evening had an out-of-the- mold "think piece" produced by a theatrical fellow named Heywood Hale Broun. Heywood had been a stage actor in New York before CBS hired him as a decidedly different sports broadcaster. He wore loud, splashy sports coats, sported a large mustache, and did some off-the- wall pieces about sports that I found fascinating. He wrote things like this, on outfielder Carl Yastrzemski's Triple Crown 1967 season and the heretofore lowly Boston Red Sox' unlikely American League pennant: "He was not just hitting home runs but was, in fact, accom- plishing the ninth labor of Hercules, bringing a championship to Boston, a city whose previous baseball idol, Ted Williams, resembled that other Greek, Achilles, who fought a great fight but spent a lot of time sulking in his tent."[3]

The more I looked at and talked to Norm, the more I pictured him as my local Heywood Hale Broun. The conversation went on and, in the end, I offered Norm a job, a decision that could have cost me *my* job. He learned the fundamentals and I put him on the air. As soon as his maiden broadcast was over, my phone was ringing. The big boss wanted to know who this guy was, where did he come from, and did I have any idea what I was doing putting him on the air. I had to do a lot of fancy footwork in getting my boss to have the same vision I had for Norm, that of being our own Hale Broun. But it worked, and Norm, with that not-for-broadcast voice, was on his way. He's still the best of the best in sports broadcasting, and I'm privileged to have been in on the launching.

My partner John Mark Dempsey recently talked to Norm:

I asked Norm if he agreed that, if not for Eddie, he might very well not be working in broadcasting today. "Oh! Big nose, thinning hair, funny voice? The world was just discovering hair spray at that time. There weren't any jobs for people like me in broadcasting."

Hitzges said Eddie gave him tremendous freedom in creating unusual sports pieces for Channel 4. "Eddie turned me loose to do a lot of weird, wild stuff for the time. I'm sure he thought, 'Oh, you've got to be kidding,' when I did a three-minute piece on the roller derby queen,

Joanie Weston, and I set it to Joni Mitchell's song 'The Circle Game.'"

Norm remembers learning a valuable lesson from Eddie. Norm had been running around frantically trying to get a piece completed at the last minute, yelling and shouting. "Eddie called me over after the newscast and said, 'See you a minute?' Then he asked, 'What was that all about?' I told him I was up against a deadline. He told me, 'I'll tell you something. Either you get it done on time, or you don't get it done on time. Either way, we're going on the air.' There's no need for the yelling.

"I love Eddie Barker. I learned more from Eddie Barker and my college basketball coach than from any other two men in my life. I didn't always love him [Eddie]. But as the days and months went on and I got better and better, and I later worked with people not close to his level, I realized we didn't have any idea how good he really was."

As you're reading this chapter, you might wonder why I've called it "The Toy Department." I'm sure you remember the late Howard Cosell of *Monday Night Football* fame. He gets the credit. Howard used to say sports are "the toy department of human life," so I borrowed the phrase from him.

I put sports in more or less the same category as show business. Working in television and radio also has brought me in contact with a string of celebrities—musicians, movie stars, television stars. One of the first interviews I did when I started at KMAC in San Antonio was with clarinetist and big-band leader Woody Herman, probably best known for "At the Woodchopper's Ball." He was playing over at the Anacacho Ballroom in the St. Anthony Hotel, both of which are still going strong. It was "the" place to go in those days. I don't know what possessed me to do this, but I went over to the hotel and told them I was from KMAC and would like to interview Woody Herman. I was still in high school. And, sure enough, they took me to meet him. I said, "I'd really like to interview you." And he asked me, "Where's your recorder?" I said sheepishly, "Well, I don't have one.

It's over at the station." He said, "Well, tell me where the station is and, on a break, I'll come over there." And he did! And we had this great interview. He was a great guy, just like Dizzy Dean.

And then you get farther into your career and you meet people like Lucille Ball and Desi Arnaz. They were in Dallas promoting *I Love Lucy*, and KRLD was a CBS affiliate, so they came to the station. I did an interview with them. I know millions of people still "love Lucy," and I don't want to disillusion anyone, but I have to say I just didn't like them at all. Very difficult to interview. They were terribly demanding about this or that camera angle. They really played the "stars." I thought she was pretty funny on TV up until then, but that killed it for me.

Another couple that was "on" all the time was Allen Ludden and Betty White. Ludden was the host of the game show *Password* on CBS and White was his actress wife, who often appeared on the show. Of course, she later had great success with *The Mary Tyler Moore Show* and *The Golden Girls*. They came to KRLD on a promotional tour. But they were just so phony, very "show biz" in their behavior. Ever since that interview, I've had the image of them getting ready for bed at night, just the two of them, still putting on the Hollywood act. They got the "gong" from me.

One of my favorite guests on *Comment* was World War II hero and movie star Audie Murphy, who grew up in the country east of Dallas, near Greenville. Here was this little kid from the sticks—he stood just five feet, five inches tall and weighed 110 pounds—who went off to war and won the Medal of Honor and literally every other medal for bravery on the battlefield in Europe to become the most decorated American combat soldier of the war. But the last thing in the world I thought Audie Murphy would be fit for was a movie actor.

We had Audie on *Comment* several times over the years, and he was so low-key, such an unassuming person. I was always concerned that he was not doing what he ought to be doing. Now, he was a terrifically handsome guy and had lots of success as an actor in some very good movies, including *The Red Badge of Courage* (in which, iron-ically, he played the role of the Youth, a Civil War solider who lost his nerve under fire) and the movie version of his book *To Hell and Back*. But I just felt he was out of his element in Hollywood. If he had an ego, I never saw it. He was almost humble.

Audie had a troubled life after he left the army, and I wonder if the life of a movie star was good for him. He had nightmares about his experiences on the battlefield. Today, we would probably say that he suffered from post-traumatic stress disorder. He died in a plane crash in 1971 at the age of forty-six. But what a life he had. A statue of Audie in combat uniform now stands outside the American Cotton Museum in Greenville on Interstate 30, and every time I go by there, I have a good feeling about him.

I once interviewed an even more legendary movie actor, Humphrey Bogart. We did that interview at the old Dallas Athletic Club downtown. In those days, that was quite a place for visiting celebrities. I don't remember why Bogart was there, but the interview must have been arranged by a fellow named Skipper Cherry, a very good public-relations man, who was with Interstate Theaters. I don't remember anything extraordinary Bogie had to say about *Casablanca* or *The Maltese Falcon* or any of his other great movies. I just remember that Bogart was a great guy, very relaxed. He'd talk about anything you liked.

My all-time favorite musical is *Guys and Dolls* (an affection I share with my friend Blackie Sherrod). I once met and interviewed Frank Loesser, who wrote the lyrics and music for *Guys and Dolls*, which is a jolly romp inspired by a Damon Runyon story. Loesser was an incredibly versatile man. On the totally opposite end of the spectrum, as a young enlisted man he wrote a hit song during World War II, "The Ballad of Roger Young." Roger Young was a young fellow who won the Medal of Honor in the Pacific war, and the song includes the following lyrics: "Oh, they've got no time for glory in the infantry/Oh, they've got no time for praises loudly sung/But in every soldier's heart in all the infantry/shines the name of Private

Roger Young." It's a beautiful thing.

We had Loesser on *Comment* one day at Fair Park during the State Fair. I commented to him, "It really amazes me that you can turn from doing a *Guys and Dolls*, and then do something as moving as 'Roger Young.'" Like most talented people, he was quite matter-of-fact about it. He just kind of shook his head and said, "Well, you write what comes to you."

Rudy Vallee was the first pop-music star, even before Bing Crosby. He had a long career in radio, TV, and movies, and always maintained his jaunty, preppy image. We had him on *Comment* once, also out at Fair Park. He was a genuinely charming guy. Jim Underwood, our KRLD news- and weatherman, had just found out he was diabetic. Jim was doing the show with me that day. We were just getting ready to go on and Vallee was there. We made small talk, and I said to Rudy, "Jim just found out he's diabetic." Vallee looked at him aghast, and said, in that tight-jawed, cultured Eastern dialect, "My God, I'd rather have cancer."

When you write a book, you hope a misspelled word or factual error doesn't show up in the final product. And I certainly hope none show up on any of these pages. I've got my fingers crossed. But let me tell you about one author who recalled his life's experiences and wasn't so lucky. There was a big goof in the book. And how did he find out about it? Well, if you must know, I was the messenger.

The Statler Hilton Hotel on Commerce Street in Dallas had a grand opening, and all of us freeloaders were invited. Conrad Hilton himself was there. Earlier that year of 1957, Mr. Hilton had written *Be My Guest*, a fascinating book about his life. And he had quite a life, including a marriage to Zsa Zsa Gabor in the early '40s. I had stayed in a Hilton hotel about a month before and read *Be My Guest*; it was in every Hilton hotel room everywhere. But what I'm about to tell you caused a major book burning and total reprint.

In the book, Mr. Hilton tells a lengthy story about his friendship with Texas governor Beauford Jester, but in the first printing, the name wasn't Beauford, it was "Beaumont" Jester. I introduced myself to Mr. Hilton at the party and complimented him not only on the fine new hotel but also on his book. And then I said, "I guess you know Jester's name is misspelled." This mighty titan of business went as pale white as anyone I've ever seen. "What . . . what are you saying?" he managed. And I told him. His color turned to a crimson red. He went to one of his underlings, standing nearby, uttered some angry words, and the two of them departed the scene. I hated to tell him, but it had to be done. Incidentally, Conrad Hilton is buried in Calvary Cemetery, the "official" cemetery of the Dallas Catholic diocese, out on Lombardi.

But the topper of my encounters with fame and glamour has to be the time I interviewed Jayne Mansfield. I don't know how many people remember Jayne today. She died in a terrible car crash in 1967 at the age of thirty-four, but in the '50s and '60s she was second only to Marilyn Monroe as a blonde bombshell. She had a Betty Boop–like, girly-girl voice. She had some big hit movies, like *The Girl Can't Help It* and *Will Success Spoil Rock Hunter?* As cartoonish as Marilyn seemed, before she became a "serious" actress, Jayne was even more so. Taller, blonder, bigger—in every way.

Jayne grew up in University Park. In January 1958, she married a former Mr. Universe, Mickey Hargitay, in Los Angeles, and they took an overnight flight to Love Field in Dallas to see Jayne's mother, Vera, and stepfather, Harry "Tex" Peers. Well, I thought, I'll go out to Love Field and interview them. The Peers knew me from Channel 4, which was always helpful, and they introduced themselves and told me, "We watch you all the time."

Jayne and Mickey got off the plane. Jayne was wearing the wedding gown she had worn the night before, a pink number, as I remember. And of course, it displayed her voluminous breasts—unbelievable. Everybody was oohing and aahing. We did the interview, which was uneventful, but Jayne and Mickey couldn't have been more pleasant. And Vera said, "Well, Harry, I guess we'd better get a cab so we can go home." I don't know why they didn't have a car there. Well, I saw my opportunity for a unique experience. "I'll be glad to take you," I told Mrs. Peers. "Well, we have our luggage," she said uncertainly. "It's all right, I'm in a station wagon," I replied.

So we go around and put the luggage in the back. Mr. and Mrs. Peers and their granddaughter—Jayne's daughter by a previous marriage—got in the backseat. I was in the driver's seat, and muscleman Mickey sat in the passenger seat, with the voluptuous Jayne in his lap. And so off we headed for their house right off Hillcrest in University Park. On the way, Mrs. Peers said, "Oh, Harry we don't have any milk." I said, "Well, that's no problem, there's a 7-Eleven up here. We'll stop and get some milk."

It was the break of dawn and the store was just opening. All of these construction workers and plumbers were coming in to get their coffee and a doughnut. And they all looked over at my station wagon, and there was bosomy Jayne Mansfield sitting atop muscle-bound Mickey Hargitay. I can just imagine one of them saying, "There's something you don't see everyday, Bob." I had a little sign made for that seat: "Jayne Mansfield Sat Here."

Meeting and reporting on the show-biz celebrities of the day was a blast. But nothing in my career compared with covering the story that exploded one gorgeous fall day when the ultimate "celebrity"— John F. Kennedy—met his shocking fate on the streets of downtown Dallas.

References:

[1] Bill Oxley, "A Descriptive Analysis of the Radio Sportscasting Techniques of Kern Tips" (Master's thesis. University of Texas, August 1965).

[2] Blackie Sherrod, "Erudition Erupts Where Some Least Expect It." *Dallas Morning News* (April 5, 2001): 21-A.

[3] Stan Isaacs, "Once Around the Bases of the National Pastime." http://thecolumnists.com/isaacs/isaacs166.html, accessed July 20, 2005.

4

"I Think Lee Shoot Kennedy"

I've already described how I reported President Kennedy's shocking death: the whispered tip from a doctor acquaintance; the snap decision to trust the source; the unexpected attention that came from breaking the bitter news on CBS. Of course, the story didn't end at the Trade Mart or Parkland Hospital. We just kept going, hour after hour, all weekend long and—in fact—for years to come.

I interviewed everyone—from the police officer who saw Lee Harvey Oswald in the Texas School Book Depository after the assassination but let him go when the building manager vouched that he was an employee to the bus driver and cab driver whose vehicles Oswald rode in to get back to his rented room in Oak Cliff. (Incidentally, Oswald tipped the cabbie a nickel. A young man in a big hurry . . . or just cheap?)

I interviewed the witnesses to the shooting of Dallas police officer J. D. Tippit and the officer who finally wrestled the gun from Oswald's hand in the Texas Theatre. I interviewed Dallas police detective Jack Revill. He told me they had gone over the parade route with the Secret Service. "We've got an awful lot of windows," Jack fretted. The agent replied, "With all the windows, we can't cover them all."

Bob Huffaker, then a young Channel 4 reporter, considered my assistant news director Jim Underwood to be his mentor at KRLD. Bob had served in the army and admired Underwood's experience as a marine on Guadalcanal in World War II. He remembers that Jim was certain the shots came from the windows of the Texas School Book Depository. Underwood rode in the third press car, eight cars behind the president's limousine, with *Dallas Times Herald* photographer Bob Jackson, who would find his lasting place in history less than forty-eight hours later. "The car that Bob and Jim were in had just turned onto Houston Street off of Main when the shots were fired," Huffaker says.

> Bob Jackson looked up and saw the rifle. Jim heard the three shots and jumped out of that car and ran toward what at first seemed the greatest danger, where people were throwing themselves on the ground. He then ran pell-mell through the rail yard behind the School Book Depository until they thought they had the shooter inside the building.
>
> Jim gave one of the first reports from the scene after he ran into the building and breathlessly made the first report, which began by saying, essentially, "I heard three loud shots from right above my head." He had a combat marine's sense for the direction of sniper fire. So his initial report is one of the most valuable and accurate that we have.

Near midnight on the night of the assassination, the police staged a bizarre press conference in which they marched Lee Oswald out into the glaring lights to answer the shouted questions of the world press. Bill Mercer was our man at police headquarters that night. Bill remembers: "I was emotional that afternoon, trying to talk to people, like in Boston, around the country calling in. But that night, it was more like survival trying to be sure I grabbed everybody I could. I thought about it later, as years passed, now forty years, and I thought, 'I wonder what the heck I did,' because I can't remember all that. There were so many things going on that you didn't have time to think about what this all meant."

Wes Wise, another of our versatile guys who doubled in news and sports, also played a big role in covering the assassination. "Without any question, it was the greatest journalistic experience of my life," Wes says.

It was a horrible story to have to cover. But since it happened, I was really privileged to be able to cover it as I did. You don't realize what a privilege it was until it's all over and years have passed. Barker was very adept at assigning the right people to the right tasks on that story.

On Saturday, Eddie assigned me to go back and cover Oswald's tracks as close as we could from the School Book Depository building to where he got off the bus and took the cab in downtown Dallas, took the Houston Street viaduct, was let off by the cab a block or two beyond his rooming house, went back to his rooming house, went over to Tenth Street and shot and murdered J. D. Tippit, and on over to the Texas Theatre. My assignment was to take a camera and retrace his steps as well as we could, and we traced them pretty close to what it turned out to be. After doing all that, I had to go back and do the 6:20 sports.

I saw some of the evocative film Wes shot that day again in the fortieth-anniversary TV specials on the assassination.

On Saturday, it was difficult to keep the story going. There was very little to update. It was perhaps the first experience television had with the twenty-four-hour news cycle we hear so much of today. It looked like it was a closed case at the time. I interviewed Sarah T. Hughes, the federal judge who had been appointed by President Kennedy and who swore in Lyndon Johnson as president on *Air Force One*. She was a tough old gal. She was all business and I liked her. Judge Hughes had been a police officer when she was a young woman going to law school in Washington, D.C. Couldn't have been too many female cops in those days. I think lawyers who went into her court knew they had been in a courtroom. Judge Hughes was not soft at all. I think part of her not being soft was that she was trying to prove that, as a woman, she could not be intimidated.

I don't remember a lot about the interview, but I remember while I was waiting, her husband, George, a nice man, was flitting around their home. "Oh, the judge will be with you in a few minutes. Can I get you some coffee?" Sarah T. was definitely the "alpha" personality of that pair.

I worked that weekend from professional instinct. I did what I was supposed to do. I was a reporter. People ask me, "What was your reaction to the president being assassinated in Dallas?" Really, I didn't have a personal reaction. I was too busy reporting the story. The full weight of what happened didn't hit me until Saturday night, when I finally had a chance to sit back and take a breather.

A few weeks earlier, we had had the infamous incident when Adlai Stevenson, the Kennedy administration's ambassador to the United Nations and the twice-nominated Democratic candidate for president, visited Dallas for a speech. Dallas really did have a very militant, far right element in those days, and they came out in force to jeer Stevenson for supposedly being soft on communism. The incident ended up with a young woman whacking poor Stevenson on the head with a big cardboard placard. It did a lot of harm to Dallas's reputation and, of course, it was reprinted many times after the assassination.

Anyway, the station covered Stevenson's speech live. When it started getting ugly, the director ordered the cameraman to pan up to the ceiling so we would not show any of the turmoil. I was sitting at home watching and I thought, "What in the world are we doing?" What a dumb thing to do.

On the other hand, our regular news coverage of the Stevenson incident shows what a great staff I had in those days. Wes Wise and Jim Underwood covered it. "To be very frank with you, I think that Eddie assigned us to that story because he knew that Adlai Stevenson was a pretty liberal guy hosted by two liberals, Stanley Marcus and Judge Sarah T. Hughes, on United Nations Day," Wes recalls.

Eddie knew the far right-wing fringe, not just the conservatives, but the radical right wing, was going to be there to
demonstrate. And he had Underwood and me cover it

The natty young radio announcer.

Mallet in hand, Eddie prepares to sound a tone. Announcers at KMAC would strike the xylophone-like instrument between live and recorded commercials.

The first interview that young Eddie Barker conducted at KMAC was with baseball Hall of Famer Dizzy Dean. "He was so nice to me," Eddie remembers.

In the early days of KRLD-TV news, Barker handled everything, including the weather report.

Eddie (in hat) and Dave Williams (far right) with their spotters during a play-by-play broadcast from Alamo Stadium on KMAC.

Eddie at KMAC with his first broadcasting boss, the amiable Tony Bessan.

Eddie broadcasting the Battle of the Flowers parade in San Antonio from atop the Gunter Hotel for KMAC radio.

Eddie interviewing then-University of Kentucky head football coach Bear Bryant at a 1952 Cotton Bowl event.

*Eddie interviews band leader Woody Herman
at KMAC in San Antonio.*

Primitive conditions in the KRLD studio. Jim Underwood must hold the phone to the ear of an unidentified guest in order for her to hear the caller's question. Bill Mercer is standing.

The Democrats' "dream team" at the opening of the Rayburn Library in Bonham in 1957. Left to right, Lady Bird Johnson, U.S Senator Lyndon Johnson, former President Harry Truman and wife Bess, and Speaker of the House Sam Rayburn.

'Facts' Lead Oswald's Widow To Believe He Shot Kennedy

Dallas, Jan. 27 — Marina Oswald said today, in a copyrighted exclusive interview with radio-TV station KRLD, "the facts" tell her that her late husband shot and killed President Kennedy.

"I don't want to believe . . . but I have too much facts and facts tell me that Lee shot Kennedy," the 22-year-old native of Russia told Eddie Barker, KRLD news director.

"A Very Bad Surprise"
Her husband, Lee Harvey Os-

AP photo
MRS. MARINA OSWALD
'I don't want to believe"

HOUSTON CHRONICLE

investigation into the assassination.
the televised interview, Mrs. ... aid said she knew nothing

WIDOW WANTS TO BE U.S. CITIZEN

'Facts Tell Me Lee Shot JFK,' Young Mrs. Oswald Says in Dallas

Dallas (UPI)—Mrs. Lee Harvey Oswald, widow of President Kennedy's accused assassin, ... a nationwide TV audience ...

TIMES-UNION
ALBANY, N.Y.

Mrs. Oswald, then a pharmacist in Minsk, met Oswald after defected to Russia and married him.

"I'm busy with my children day," she said "I try to ... an house, wash diapers, and ... le bit cook and play with ... ldren outside."

Mrs. Oswald Finds Facts Convincing

Dallas, Tex., Jan. 27 — Marina Oswald said today, in a copyrighted exclusive interview with Radio-TV station KRLD, "the facts" tell her that her late husband shot and killed President John F. Kennedy.

"I don't want to believe . . . but I have too much facts, and facts tell me that Lee shot Kennedy," the attractive, 22-year-old native of Russia told Eddie Barker, KRLD news director.

Her husband, Lee Harvey Oswald, was charged with the President's death here Nov. 22. Oswald was shot to death two days later by Jack Ruby, Dallas night club operator. Ruby's trial for murder is set for Feb. 17.

It was announced in Washington that Mrs. Oswald will be the first witness called in the investigation into the assassination.

Mrs. Oswald said she knew nothing about her husband's ... "It was a very bad surprise for me."

She said she loved Oswald and is sorry for him because "he died very young. I visit his ...

Mrs. Marina Oswald

She said that she felt sorry for Lee "because he died very young" and that she visits his grave "one time or two times a week."

"Only Conclusion"
Mrs. Margaret Oswald, Oswald's mother, said Monday night at her home in Fort Worth that her daughter-in-law was disillusioned because she has been held in seclusion by the secret service too long.

"Her 'facts that lead her to believe that Lee killed the President' are only conclusions," Mrs. Oswald charged.

The 56-year-old grandmother said the secret service would not allow her to see Marina when the two accidentally met at Lee's grave Sunday.

They whisked her away,"

THE CINCINNATI ENQUIRER

'I Don't Want to Believe, But--Lee Shot Kennedy'

DALLAS, Jan. 28—(UPI)—Marina Oswald, unsure of her English but calm and determined, last night thanked Americans for their generosity and told them they "have very big hearts."

The attractive Russian-born widow of Lee Harvey Oswald, accused of assassinating President Kennedy, told a national television audience she had roots in Texas and wanted to stay here.

She said she did not want to believe she husband shot the assassinated President ...
and later tell me that Lee shot Kennedy.

AMERICAN CITIZENS

Her appearance, an exclusive copyrighted interview with news director Eddie Barker of station KRLD, was broadcast nationally

Mrs. Marina Oswald during television interview Monday in Dallas. (AP)

Oswald's

Wife Feels Lee Oswald Was Slayer

By Ronnie Dugger
Special to The Washington Post

DALLAS, Jan. 27—"I don't want to believe, but I have too much fact, and fact tell me that Lee shot Kennedy," Marina Oswald said in an exclusive interview on a Dallas television station last night.

"He never tell me this, and this was a very bad surprise for me," Lee Oswald's 22-year-old widow said. "I love Lee, and I sorry for him ... cause he died very young."
... Oswald wanted her

MRS. OSWALD

Oswald Widow on Television

Oswald's Widow: 'Facts Tell Me . . . Lee Shot Kennedy'

NEW YORK (UPI)—Mrs. Lee Harvey Oswald, the widow of the man accused of assassinating President Kennedy, Monday night told a nationwide television audience that the facts tell her that Lee shot Kennedy.

In her first television interview since the November 22 assassination, and the slaying of her husband in a Dallas police station two days later, the Russian-born Mrs. Oswald said she has no desire to return to the Soviet Union.

she visits his grave "one time or two times a week."

Mrs. Oswald, who has received more than $35,000 from persons wishing to express their sympathy, concluded her interview by thanking the American people for their generosity.

accused assassin of President, her youngest daughter, at interview from Dallas Monday. First public appearance ... at in Dallas Nov. 24.

'Thank You; American People . . .'

DALLAS, Jan. 28 (UPI)—Marina Oswald last night thanked Americans for their generosity and told them they "have very big hearts.

The 22-year-old Russian-born widow of Lee Harvey Oswald, accused assassin of President Kennedy, told a TV audience she had roots in Texas and wanted to stay on.

"FACTS TELL ME"

*Eddie's exclusive interview with Marina Oswald
produced headlines around the world.*

Judge Sarah T. Hughes, who gave the presidential oath of office to Lyndon Johnson aboard Air Force One following the assassination of President Kennedy. She was a guest on KRLD radio's "Comment" program, a forerunner of today's talk-radio format.

DARO23A

B U L L E T I N

(RUBY--DALLAS)

A DALLAS RADIO STATION (K-R-L-D) QUOTES AN "EXCELLENT SOURCE" AS

SAYING JACK RUBY HAS DIED OF CANCER. SO FAR, THESE HAS BEEN NO

OFFICIAL CONFIRMATION. THE RADIO STATION SAYS THE BODY WAS TAKEN TO

THE MORGUE.

BR1043ACS 1/3

Bulletin announcing the death of Jack Ruby.
A tip from Sheriff Bill Decker gave Eddie and KRLD a "beat."

Secret Service re-enactment of the John F. Kennedy assassination,
Dealey Plaza, 1964. Channel 4 cameraman Joe Dave Scott shot this
photo.

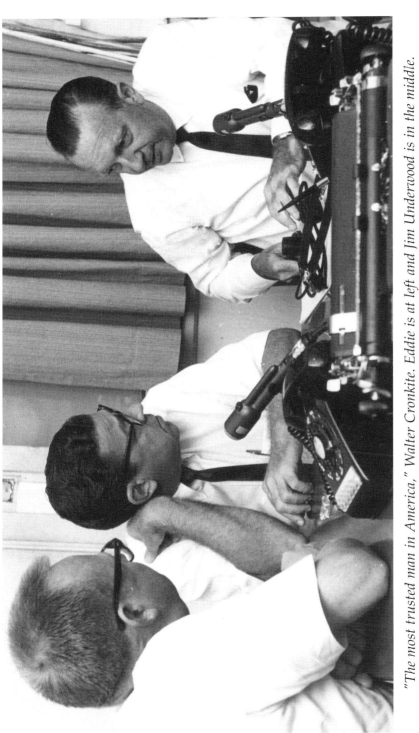

"The most trusted man in America," Walter Cronkite. Eddie is at left and Jim Underwood is in the middle.

Eddie interviewing John Connally, the former governor of Texas, who was severely wounded in the assassination of President Kennedy.

Sixth floor window from which Oswald shot Kennedy.

BOB BROCK

★

Exclusive On
An Exclusive

FOUR WEEKS of touch-and-go manuevering and "pins-and-needles" waiting paid off Monday as KRLD News Director Eddie Barker obtained the first filmed interview with Marina Oswald, Russian-born wife of accused presidential assassin Lee Harvey Oswald.

In fact, it was the first time that Mrs. Oswald had sat for a formal face-to-face interview with any representative of the news media since that fateful Friday, Nov. 22.

Five minutes of the exclusive interview was used as the lead item of Walter Cronkite's CBS Television News at 5:30 p.m. Monday. The interview was run in its entirety on Channel 4 newscasts at 6 and 10 p.m. and 12 midnight.

Tuesday, Barker related how the interview had been brought about after a number of conferences with Mrs. Oswald's lawyer, John Thorne of Grand Prairie, and her business manager, Jim Martin of Dallas. Barker said that the first query concerning an exclusive interview with Mrs. Oswald was made around Jan. 1.

Monday. KRLD newsmen and cameramen Jim Underwood, Joe Scott, Warren Fulks and George Sanderson, in addition to Barker, participated in the interview.

Barker said they were all asked not to divulge the location of the Oswald home.

"Since Marina is a very shy

Dallas Times Herald television columnist Bob Brock's story on Eddie's exclusive interview with Marina Oswald.

November 22, 1963. KRLD-TV news director Eddie Barker and CBS reporter Dan Rather. Barker and Rather would clash over coverage of the assassination a few days later, but remain friends today. (Courtesy of The Sixth Floor Museum at Dealey Plaza, KRLD-TV/KDFW Collection)

because this was an assignment of some responsibility and controversy.

When it got to be about 9:30, Stevenson had been interrupted several times. He made that classic line that got applause from the audience there at the Memorial Auditorium theater: "Sir, do I have to come all the way from Illinois to teach Texans good manners?" And they ushered that guy out. With the deadline for the ten o'clock newscast very near, Underwood and I got together, and he said, "We can't leave this thing." By this time, all the other TV stations had left because it was getting close to their deadlines. He says, "Look, you stay on here. My weather comes before your sports. If I have to, I'll do your sports." So sure enough about 9:40 or so, Stevenson left the place, and I turned on my camera, and this woman attacked him over the head with a placard. It was really a heck of a scoop for us.

I ran it back in and gave it to Henk DeWitt, who was the engineer who developed the film. I took it off and looked at it through a small preview machine. I knew that the woman had done something bad. I didn't know she had actually hit him over the head. Her tongue was sticking out, and the whole thing. So I did an outline for our anchorman, Warren Fulks, and didn't even edit the film. I told him, "Do the best you can with this outline." And Warren delivered the outline like it was a finished script. I give him more credit than I do me. It was fantastic. The next day, Walter Cronkite played it over and over in slow motion. Cronkite said, "Thanks to our alert young cameraman, Wes Wise, we have this film of the incident." I've always thought Barker put him up to saying that.

In the days, weeks, and months that followed the assassination, I like to think I played an important role in CBS' coverage of the events that followed the assassination. I was not employed by CBS but, for a long time, I might as well have been. I was the anchor of the principal television newscasts on KRLD and had a lot of radio exposure as well. In those days, the bosses—and the news director is a boss—did a lot of street reporting. My name, face, and voice were known to a lot of people. And that opened a lot of doors, figuratively and literally, especially while I was covering the events of November 22, 1963.

My knowledge of the market and my ability to open those doors was my ticket to become part of all of the magnificent work that CBS News did following the assassination. I was privileged to work with Walter Cronkite, Dan Rather, and Don Hewitt, among others. Among the "others" was Bernie Birnbaum, the field producer whose tenacity and friendship remain an important part of my life to this day. Anyone who ever had the privilege of working with Bernie will "amen" these lines. And Jane Bartels, the researcher par excellence, tended to detail more efficiently than anyone who has crossed my path before or since.

Don Hewitt was always coming up with ideas. Lee Harvey Oswald had used the name "A. Hidell" when he ordered the Mannlicher-Carcano rifle to shoot JFK. Don called me up one day. "Eddie, I want you to see if you can order a Mannlicher-Carcano under the name of A. Hidell," he told me. And he wanted me to rent the same post-office box that Oswald had rented. So I got a magazine full of ads for mail-order rifles and went to work. I ordered M-Cs using the name A. Hidell. I tried to rent the same post-office box, but it was no longer in use. I used money orders to order the rifles.

Well, it didn't take long for results. A total of eleven M-Cs came in, and I received a note for the twelfth saying that the dealer didn't have it. Of course, a rifle wouldn't fit in the post-office box, so I had to take the paper in the post-office box to the window and retrieve the merchandise. Not once did anyone at the post office bat an eye or look like either the rifle or the name was familiar to them. We, of course, then did a story for CBS showing all the rifles and describing how we got them. "Homeland security" wasn't so good in those days, either.

So what to do with the eleven M-Cs? I had a closet in my office and stored them there. I gave a few away to folks around the station who asked for one. The years went by and I thought little about the rifles until then-President Nixon came to town for an appearance and they used our big studio to stage it. Naturally, the Secret Service came to check out the building. I was with the lead security agent on the first floor of the building. Suddenly, his two-way came to life. An agent in the basement newsroom, in a more-than-urgent voice, said,

"Come to the basement ASAP!" Okay, you're ahead of me: the agent, searching my office, looked in the closet, and I got a stare you wouldn't believe.

The Secret Service agents appreciated the story, but what to do, since the president and his family were going to use my office for a few private minutes after the event? Following the telecast, President and Mrs. Nixon and their two daughters, Julie and Tricia, came downstairs and used my office for about twenty minutes, since they were all going in different directions when they left. The Secret Service told me to lock the closet and they put an official seal on the door. But all the same, I felt there was more than superficial attention paid to that door.

I said in the beginning of this book that I'd tell you the story of when I kicked my friend Dan Rather out of our newsroom. It's become a part of newsroom lore.

Right after the assassination, there were all kinds of stories making the rounds about Dallas's being a "city of hate." Even its kids were said to be seething with hatred. And one of the spreaders of such untruths was a young Methodist minister who was saying that when the news of the president's death was announced on the public-address system of an elementary school in conservative University Park, the students let out cheers of joy, said unkind things about the now-dead president, and streamed out of the school.

"Do you know anything about this?" Dan asked me.

"The school he's talking about is University Park Elementary, and our children all go there," I answered. "I checked with the principal, and he said the kids were cheering because they were told they were getting out of school early."

"Okay," Dan replied. "That's one we can forget about."

In those days immediately after the assassination, Dan and his crew would process all of the film they shot during the day in our lab. And when he was going to screen the film, Dan always invited me in see what he had. But on this day he didn't invite me into the screening room, nor did he invite me to look at what he was feeding up the line for the *CBS Evening News*.

"Dan's doing his feed live tonight," one of my guys said. "Wonder why?"

We didn't have to wonder long. The evening news opened with Walter switching immediately to Dan in Dallas. And the story? You're right: it was the Methodist preacher telling Dan about all of those "right-wing" children who cheered the death of the president.

Well, I lost it. I was noted, of course, for kicking wastebaskets when something went wrong. This time, none missed my boot.

When Dan walked into the newsroom, the first thing he heard me say was, "OUT!" He looked at me and realized I meant it. I laid into him. Certainly he had every right to report anything he wanted to report, but to say he wasn't going to do the story and then do it behind my back—and from my newsroom—was a whole new ball game.

I told him again to get out and take the whole damn bunch with him, the "bunch" being the thirty-odd cameramen, editors, and so on that made up the CBS crew in town.

"He means it, fellows. Get your gear and let's get out," Dan said.

And get out they did.

We quickly got three teachers from University Park Elementary down to the station. Only one, fourth-grade teacher Mrs. Genevieve Cleveland, appeared on air, interviewed by Bill Mercer. She explained what had happened and categorically denied that the kids were cheering the president's assassination.

It didn't take Dan long to call New York, and it didn't take long for New York to call, not me, but my bosses. And what bosses I had. As Jackie Gleason would say, "the greatest." They stood behind me all the way. Of course, the threat from the New York higher-ups was they were going to cancel our affiliation contract, but we knew that would never happen. They needed us. Even Jim Chambers, the *Times Herald* publisher and CEO, came down before the night was over. And I think Jim, a reporter who rose through the ranks, got a chuckle or two out of the fact that I had the *cojones* to stand up to the network.

Remember that old Bob Wills song, "Time Changes Everything"? Well, it did here, too, and it didn't take long. The fences got mended, and Dan and the "bunch" were operating out of my newsroom again the next day.

I can understand why people believe the assassination must have happened differently from the way the Warren Commission described it. There are still doubting Thomases who will never accept that a punk kid—Oswald—could have caused so much damage. So the argument will go on and on. And why not? If we all agreed on what happened, look at all of the authors who would be looking for steady jobs.

Of course, a key link in the conspiracy chain is Jack Ruby. As it happened, the Sunday that Ruby gunned down Oswald, my friend Blackie Sherrod was working a temporary assignment as an editor on the city desk. I think Blackie might have been thinking beyond writing his sports column, and the *Times Herald* management was thinking, "This guy is a genius. What can he do on the news side?"

Jack Beers, a *Dallas Morning News* photographer, took a terrific photo of Ruby just as he stepped forward to shoot Oswald, with his gun hand pointing at Oswald's midsection. It was sensational. The *Times Herald* didn't have anything—or so the editors thought. Felix McKnight, the *Times Herald* editor, called me and said, "We've got to do something on the Oswald shooting. What have you got?" I said, "Well, we've got some film here. It's the greatest you'd ever want to see. He kills him plain as day—bang!" He said, "Blackie and I want to come over and look at it." So he and Blackie came over to Channel 4, and we looked at this film. Our cameraman George Phenix shot it on a sixteen-millimeter camera.

Felix asked, "What can you give me out of that?" I said, "Tell you what we'll do. We'll give you sixteen frames. It's the whole, dramatic thing." And he said, "That's great." So we printed sixteen frames for Felix and Blackie. Off they went. They were going to print the sixteen frames, four rows of four frames, showing the sequence of the officers walking Oswald out into the garage and Ruby stepping out to shoot him. It would have been as good as or better than what Jack Beers shot.

About an hour later, McKnight calls. "Barker," he said in his gravelly voice, "you can take those frames of yours and shove 'em up your #%*! You're not going to believe what we've got." It was the famous

Pulitzer Prize–winning photo taken by Bob Jackson of a doubled-over Oswald, snapped at the moment that Ruby shot him, a fraction of a second after Beers snapped his photo.

The local folks looked with a skeptical eye on the press corps that came into Dallas after the assassination, because very little was being said about the city that wasn't derogatory, and in many stories the city was actually blamed for the president's death. As a result, the people of Dallas were less than anxious to talk to any of these back-East types.

But on the other hand, lots of people in Dallas trusted me and knew I wouldn't do them wrong when it came to reporting the story. The networks, the wire services, and all other media were after the same story. But CBS won out as the network that did the best job at the time and in the months and years to follow. The connections I had developed and my ability to open doors definitely gave us an advantage. As the story unfolds, you'll see what I mean.

An example, not related to the assassination, of how I was able to help CBS out in Dallas: The phone rang one day and the caller from CBS said, "I need a big favor and you're the only person I know who could deliver on this." I replied, "Well, fire away, and tell me what you need." (He's gone on now, but I can't use his name. His co-workers at CBS who don't know this story will just have to guess. My friend knew he could trust me always to keep his name between us.)

His request caught me a bit off guard: "I need a driver's license." Turns out that he had been given a DUI ticket, his license had been suspended for one year, and he needed to drive. I always prided myself on being able to produce when the network called and I didn't want to break my record. "Tell you what," I told my caller, "hang loose today and I'll be back to you tomorrow."

What to do, what to do? And then it hit me: call my old friend "Sergeant John" at the Department of Public Safety and see if he could help. Ol' Sergeant John was like me: he prided himself in helping folks along life's way and he said, "I think I can handle this. Get your friend down here and I'll get on it." He was on the plane the next day, and we went to see Sergeant John. And true to his word, the good sergeant saw my friend safely through the test, and this New York was behind the wheel again, with a license and insurance. The sergeant even suggested an insurance agent over on Lemmon Avenue who could handle it.

CBS asked me for a lot of favors through the years and knew I would deliver, from driver's licenses to Marina Oswald exclusives.

At the start of the book, I told you I'd tell how I managed to become the first person to interview Lee Oswald's widow, Marina. Every reporter in town, in fact, in the country, or the world, if you want to take it that far, wanted to talk to Marina Oswald. But she didn't want to talk to any reporters. Still, like so many others, I persisted, and through a series of lucky breaks in January 1964, got the first interview Marina gave.

A little background. After the assassination and Oswald's arrest, Marina and their two young daughters, Rachel and June, were placed in protective custody. Originally, they, along with Oswald's mother, Marguerite, were taken to the Inn of the Six Flags located near the Six Flags over Texas amusement park in Arlington, but it would never have worked to have the two "M's" under the same roof. The sales manager of the motel was Jim Martin. He lived in East Dallas not far from White Rock Lake. He told the Secret Service that there was room in his home for Marina and her two children, and it would be a more normal life than staying indefinitely in a motel. Oswald's family was moved to the Martin home. No one in the media knew where they had been taken, but a lot of speculation circulated.

The old axiom that you will never know until you ask was certainly proved here. Marina had retained an attorney in Grand Prairie, John Thorne. I did not know John but made a point to call him. When I told him I was interested in meeting Marina and interviewing her, John didn't slam down the phone, tell me to get lost, or ask how much I would pay for an interview. Instead, he said, "She watches you every evening, and I'll be glad to ask her." He did, and she said she would meet me and do the interview. I understand John has passed away, but I still have to say, "Thanks again, John."

So the drama began. Thorne told me where Marina was staying and that she would expect me at eight o'clock that evening, after she had put the two girls to bed. I went to the house in East Dallas. Jim Martin answered the door, invited me in, and introduced me to Marina Oswald. Her English wasn't that great, and my Russian was zilch, but we managed some idle chatter. Then she suggested we go out in the backyard for a get-acquainted talk. Jim stayed with us and was Marina's source of cigarettes. I remember how she patted Jim's pocket for another the second the one she was smoking was finished. I told her I wanted very much to interview her, that we could do it right there in Jim Martin's home, and that I would bring with me some of the other people she watched on the news every evening. She said yes, she would do the interview. We set a time of eleven o'clock in the morning, two days later.

I told the newsroom staff what we were about to do. All were sworn to secrecy on the threat of a pox upon on them if they even whispered what we were up to. To go with me, I chose Jim Underwood, Wes Wise, Warren Fulks, and Joe Dave Scott, a fine cameraman. I had the closest of relationships with Walter Cronkite, Sandy Socolow, Don Hewitt, and all of the great CBS News folks, but I didn't tell them we were about to do the interview because, I guess, someone could be listening in to the telephone conversation.

Our modus operandi would do justice to a real cloak-and-dagger operation. The Martin house was on a street without sidewalks, and you entered the garage from the alley. We went in two unmarked cars. "Move your cars to the street," I instructed Martin. "We'll drive into the garage and close the door behind us." It may be hard to imagine now just how hard everybody was trying to get to Marina. I didn't want some rival reporter to drive down the street and see us there. Or, who knows, maybe a neighbor across the street knew someone at Channel 5 or Channel 8 and would tip them off that we were there.

The interview went well, and Marina uttered those words that made headlines around the world the next day: "I think Lee shoot Kennedy." Of course, she has since changed her story. I was talking to Gary Mack of the Sixth Floor Museum one day about Marina and said, "I wonder if she would repeat now what she told me so many years ago." Gary said he doubted it, based on her recent stance. But I think she just might if the two of us had a chance to sit down and visit again.

Marina knew that Lee was inclined to violence and rash action. In our interview, she remembered her husband coming home after trying to assassinate retired U.S. Army General Edwin A. Walker, a controversial figure with alleged connections to the hard-right John Birch Society: "He came in the house 11:30. He was so pale, nervous in what happened to him. He told, 'I tried to shoot General Walker.' And I asked who is General Walker and he told me he is a fascist. And I asked if he had wife and children and he said, no, he is single. He said but this does not make it wrong or right. And he told me if Hitler was shot before war, this was better for most people."

Marina's reaction to the news that President Kennedy had been shot was much the same as anyone else's, but more poignant because of what she did not know and what was yet to come. And, as happened when she heard of her husband's attempted shooting of General Walker, her thoughts were of family and children: "I think about Jackie [Kennedy] and the children. And at the same time I thought of myself in that position, you know, with children. When this happened, I think about how it would be if this happened with me. . . . You know, mothers, with children, the same as if it were me. . . . Mrs. Paine [Ruth Paine, Marina's landlady] told me that somebody from where Lee worked, the School Book Depository, had shot the president. And, you know, my heart went down, you know, because I wondered if it was Lee. And I go into the garage where the rifle was, and I saw the blanket and I said, 'That's good, it's not Lee.'"

But, of course, Lee Oswald's rifle had been taken from the blanket.

We got back to the station and processed the film. Thank the good Lord the lighting was right, the sound was good, and we had a keeper. Remember, this was before videotape and instant replay. We had to "soup" the film, our term for processing. I then called Cronkite and Hewitt and told them what I had. You can imagine how ecstatic they were, knowing that they'd be giving the shaft to NBC and ABC in a few hours.

"When can we see it?" Hewitt wanted to know. There were no satellites in those days, at least not for our use, so any stories we sent to New York went over lines leased from the telephone company and were usually sent prior to broadcast time. But not this time. I didn't want to run the risk that someone in some control room somewhere might see what we had and, perish the thought, pirate it. So I told CBS we would feed the film live at 5:30, our time. New York agreed. We edited a piece that ran over six minutes. Walter opened the broadcast with the news that America was about to see the first interview with Marina Oswald.

Like all stories our newsroom did that were exclusively ours, I always called the AP and UPI and gave it to them as a copyrighted story. That was to make sure any of the local opposition would have to credit us before they could use it. It was a real winner for us!

A little sidebar: Joe Dave Scott, who was assistant news director at the time, was a good friend of Bert Shipp at Channel 8, a prince of a guy and the father of Brett Shipp, the very fine investigative reporter at Channel 8 today. Joe Dave and Bert had this friendly rivalry about who got the best stories. Joe Dave called Bert about 5:25, just before the *CBS News*, and told him to be sure to watch. Joe Dave said, "Well, we really got [Channel] 8 this time."

That interview began a long and certainly interesting association with Marina Oswald. I had gained her trust, and she felt comfortable talking with me. I saw Marina frequently in the months ahead and had the occasion to ask her about her life in Russia and then with Lee. I remember asking her one time, "Marina, what in the world did you see in Lee that would cause you to marry him?" She didn't hesitate; those icy blue eyes looked straight at me and she said, "A way out of Russia."

She was a cold, calculating woman, even at the tender young age of twenty-two. And I would imagine that life with her at times wasn't very pleasant, especially if you didn't have any money, no job, and no place to live. No doubt in my mind that she was the "Type A" personality in that twosome. Why did Lee Harvey Oswald kill the president? Some political motive? Not on your life. In my book, Oswald killed Kennedy to prove to Marina that he was a man, even though, as she told me, his "manhood" didn't show itself in the bedroom. She taunted him about it, and he reacted by performing the dastardly act that he did.

It was some time later that a Russian basketball team came to Dallas to play an exhibition game. Marina called me and asked, "Eddie, can you find out where they're staying?" They were booked at an old motel on Harry Hines Circle. I got the room number of the person in charge of the group and gave it to Marina. She took a cab to the motel and went to the room. She told me that she knocked, the man opened the door, recognized her, and slammed the door in her face. The former Marina Nikolaevna Prusakova was crushed. "I just wanted to talk to someone from home," she sadly told me.

It may seem out of place, but the Fort Worth barbecue king, Walter Jetton, figures in the story of how we broke the news that Marina had remarried. Jetton was a favorite of President Johnson's. Johnson loved to host old-fashioned, trail drive–style barbecues at the White House and at his ranch on the Pedernales, and Jetton was the man he called on to stage the events. Walter actually published a cookbook of his LBJ barbecue secrets.

One day in 1965, Walter came into the KRLD newsroom. I had met him a number of times, and we always had a very friendly relationship. He said, "I want to do something for you." I warily said, "Walter, what are you going to do for me?" He said, "I want to have a barbecue for you. You've always been so nice to me." I said, "Gosh, Walter, that's kind of a big thing." He said, "No, I want to do it. I'd like to do it here. You can invite anyone you want to invite."

We set a date, and Bob Cook, the fellow who owned the parking lot next to the building, said we could use it for the barbecue. About 5:00 a.m., here came Walter Jetton with all his barbecuing gear. I don't know how many people I ended up inviting, but it was a big crowd. At about one o'clock we were right in the middle of the barbecue, and somebody came out of the newsroom and told me, "You have a phone call." So I go in and I'm greeted with, "Well, how'd you like to know that Marina Oswald's remarrying today?" It was one of my well-cultivated sources. I said, "You're kidding! Well, tell me about it." And he said, "She's marrying a guy named Kenneth Jess Porter. They're going to get married this afternoon."

The source told me that Porter had lived in Richardson and had recently divorced. The source gave me Porter's Richardson address and his Social Security number. So Jim Underwood and I hightailed it out to Richardson to get the former Mrs. Porter's reaction to her ex's marrying the widow of the alleged assassin of the president. We drive up to the modest house in East Richardson and ring the doorbell. The former Mrs. Porter came to the door, and I introduced Jim and myself. "Mrs. Porter," I said, "we would like to get your reaction to your ex-husband marrying Marina Oswald." She lets out this howl: "WHAT DID YOU SAY?!" Before I could repeat it, she had slammed the door. It was the first word the poor woman had of the upcoming marriage.

As the former Mrs. Porter adjusted to the shocking news Jim and I had delivered, Jess and Marina started leading the media on quite a chase, as far north as Lake Texoma. But they shook off the local paparazzi and ended up having a quiet wedding, performed by the local justice of the peace in the little town of Fate, near Rockwall. They still live a few miles from where they were married in 1965.

What an afternoon Walter Jetton's barbecue turned out to be.

CBS called a few years later and wanted me to see if we could do another interview with Marina. I didn't think she would agree to one, but, as usual, I said I would give it the old college try. Marina was working in Foley's at the Town East Shopping Center. Bernie Birnbaum and Jane Bartels flew down from New York to go with me.

We went into the department store, and when Marina saw us, she immediately ran toward a dressing room. I told Bernie and Jane to stay back. I knocked on the dressing room door and said, "Marina, come on out; we just want to talk." So she came out slowly, and Bernie and Jane came over. It was about lunchtime and there was a Luby's cafeteria in the mall, so I said, "Let's go have lunch and we can visit there."

We stood in the cafeteria line and, though it was crowded, not a single soul recognized Marina, but three people recognized me. How quickly a face not seen every day fades from memory.

That was one time I couldn't persuade Marina to talk for the cameras. I didn't push her; she was genuinely trying to get lost in the crowd.

Marina later went to work in the army-navy store on McKinney Avenue. Jane—my Jane—and I were in there one day and Jane said, "Who is that woman over there that keeps looking at you?" I didn't know Marina was working there so I said, "I don't know."

By then the woman was approaching us and asked, "Don't you

remember me?" Of course I did. Time had changed Marina from the frightened twenty-two-year-old whom people remembered from the time of the assassination. In her years at the army-navy store, how many people realized the clerk who spoke with an accent was once the most-talked-about woman in the world? Not many.

I hadn't met her husband, Jess Porter, but did have a long and pleasant conversation with him as the fortieth anniversary of the assassination approached. Marina had a distaste for the *Dallas Morning News* and would have nothing to do with any of its reporters who tried to talk to her. The paper, knowing of my long association with her, asked if I would try to open a door so they could interview her on the anniversary. I said I would try.

I called Marina at home, and Jess answered the phone. I identified myself and asked if I could speak to Marina. "She's not here," Jess replied.

"Will she be back soon?" I asked.

"Not for a couple of months, she's in Russia visiting her family," Jess answered.

Jess said he was sure Marina would talk with me if she were there. We talked about their thirty-eight years together and about Marina's daughters. Jess is retired now. He said that Marina had been back to Russia several times. I got the feeling she made this particular trip just to be unavailable for the hordes of reporters she knew would be looking for her on the fortieth anniversary. I didn't tell Jess that I was running interference for the *News* in wanting to talk to Marina.

I enjoyed our visit and hope that, somewhere along the way, I'll get to visit with Jess again. As for Marina's skipping town when she did, I don't blame her. After all, reporters can be a pain, can't they?

5

"He Seemed to Pause
for a Moment . . ."

Like every other network, CBS wanted to interview certain people associated with the Kennedy assassination. As the story developed, otherwise obscure names (like Howard Brennan, as we shall see) became important parts of the tale. And CBS wanted to get into certain buildings, such as the Texas School Book Depository. Like the other national media representatives, it found it was not trusted, not believed, and didn't receive a lot of cooperation. That's where I came in.

Some incidents that happened then wouldn't take place in today's world of broadcast journalism. But times were different in 1963–64, especially when it came to reporters trusting cops and vice versa. In those days, we'd scratch their backs and they'd scratch ours. The cops I especially liked were the gumshoes, you know, the plainclothes types who moved in more "interesting" circles.

The coziness—I can't think of a better word—that existed in the relationship between reporters and judges or people in high local government offices would make many of today's journalists shudder. Nevertheless, it was my good fortune to enjoy a lot of those kinds of relationships.

CBS broadcast a documentary on September 27, 1964, the Sunday night that the report of the Warren Commission—a blue-ribbon panel appointed by President Johnson to investigate the assassination—was released. I did a number of interviews for the program. One of the interviews I obtained for the Warren Commission report documentary was with Texas governor John Connally, who, as you know, was wounded in the assassination of President Kennedy and nearly died himself. Connally did an interview in the hospital with NBC's Martin Agronsky a few days after being shot, but it didn't last very long, and I did the first major interview with Connally on June 22, 1964, after he returned to office.

Connally vividly remembered the shooting—"My, God, they're going to kill us all," the governor remembered thinking. He shared with me his vivid and strongly held memories of the assassination: "I did not hear the second shot, the one that hit me. I understand there's some question in the minds of the experts about whether or not we [Kennedy and Connally] could both have been hit by the same bullet, and that was the first bullet. I just don't happen to believe that. I won't believe it, never will believe, because, again, I heard the first shot, I recognized it for what it was. I had time to turn to try to see what had happened. I was in the process of turning again before I felt the impact of a bullet."

Prior to the broadcast, I told then-CBS News president Fred Friendly that we had an exclusive interview with the governor. I got a Friendly-sized guffaw in return. "The governor of Texas would not turn down NBC and ABC when they ask for an interview," Fred confidently assured me.

After all the network documentaries had aired, Fred said, rather grudgingly as I recall, "Well, you were right." He came up to me and said, "Come into my office, I have a little something for you for all the hard work you've done for CBS."

"Wow," I thought, "he's going to give me a nice bonus check." We went into his office, he closed the door, sat down at his desk, and motioned me to sit. On pins and needles, I watched as he opened his desk drawer. But instead of the check I hoped was there, he handed me an LP of Ed Murrow's *See It Now* program, autographed by Friendly. I looked for that record when I started making these notes and couldn't find it. It must have been lost in the move from the city to the country, where we live now.

The governor was not the only exclusive that night.

You may have forgotten or never have heard some of the names in our coverage of the JFK assassination, but these people are part of the mosaic. Their stay on center stage did not last long; they said what they had to say and moved on. But their contributions, however minor, helped put the puzzle together.

Unless you are one of those assassination buffs who know chapter and verse the names of every individual who played some role in the story, you may have forgotten Howard Brennan. His testimony was crucial to the Warren Commission. His is a key story, a fascinating one, and how he ended up on the CBS Warren Commission report documentary is, well, a bit unusual.

Brennan was sitting on the low wall across the street from the front door of the Texas School Book Depository as Kennedy's limousine passed by. He saw the assassin in the sixth-floor window and watched him fire his last shot. He gave the police a description of the gunman. But unlike some people who saw some of the happenings that fateful noontime, Howard Brennan had no desire ever to go public with his story. He did only one television interview to my knowledge, and that is the one he did with me. I interviewed him for the CBS News documentary, "November 22nd and the Warren Report"[1]:

BARKER: Among the witnesses here in the plaza, the Commission relied heavily on the testimony of Howard Brennan, who, watching from just about here, said that he actually saw the assassin firing.

BRENNAN: I looked directly across and up, possibly at a 45-degree angle. And this man, same man I had saw prior to the president's arrival, was in the window and taking aim for his last shot. After he fired the last of the three shots, he didn't seem to be in a great rush, hurry. He seemed to pause for a moment to see if for sure he accomplished his purpose, and he brought the gun back to rest in upright position, as though he was satisfied. . . . The president's head just exploded. . . . The Secret Service man asked me for a description. I gave him a description of a man in his early thirties wearing light khaki-colored clothing, height, five-foot nine or ten, weighing 170 pounds.

As eyewitness descriptions go, Howard's impression of Lee Harvey Oswald was pretty close. True, Oswald was twenty-three, but with his thinning hair, he easily could have been mistaken from a distance as a man of thirty or more. The Warren Commission report notes that, while Brennan's was not an exact description, it was similar to the descriptions given of the man who shot policeman J. D. Tippit a short time later, a killing that only a few diehards dispute Oswald committed. As a testament to Howard's eyesight and memory, he also remembered seeing three men in the window below Oswald and later correctly identified two of them, who appeared before the Warren Commission. Not too bad.

Howard Brennan was the man who put Lee Harvey Oswald in the sixth-floor window, the eyewitness who would have been the key witness had Oswald lived and faced trial. But while he had the opportunity to do so, Brennan chose not to pick Oswald out of a lineup. My friend Gary Mack, curator of the Sixth Floor Museum, located in the old Texas School Book Depository, reminded me of this. Additionally, he felt that, since Brennan had seen Oswald on television, that might have influenced his memory. Gary reminded me that Brennan's reluctance to finger Oswald in a lineup has been grist for the mill of the conspiracy buffs.

However, Howard did give detectives reason to believe Oswald was their man. Here's what Chapter 4 of the Warren Commission report says:

During the evening of November 22, Brennan identified Oswald as the person in the lineup who bore the closest resemblance to the man in the window but he said he was unable to make a positive identification. Prior to the lineup, Brennan had seen Oswald's picture on television and he told the Commission that whether this affected his identification "is something I do not know."

In an interview with FBI agents on December 17, 1963, Brennan stated that he was sure that the person firing the rifle was Oswald. In another interview with FBI agents on January

7, 1964, Brennan appeared to revert to his earlier inability to make a positive identification, but, in his testimony before the Commission, Brennan stated that his remarks of January 7 were intended by him merely as an accurate report of what he said on November 22.[2]

Howard was afraid there was a conspiracy of some sort and that, if others in the conspiracy found out that he had fingered Oswald, his own life would be in danger. Here again is the Warren Commission's explanation:

> Brennan told the Commission that he could have made a positive identification in the lineup on November 22 but did not do so because he felt that the assassination was "a Communist activity, and I felt like there hadn't been more than one eyewitness, and if it got to be a known fact that I was an eyewitness, my family or I, either one, might not be safe." When specifically asked before the Commission whether or not he could positively identify the man he saw in the sixth-floor window as the same man he saw in the police station, Brennan stated, "I could at that time, with all sincerity, identify him as being the same man."[3]

The story of the Howard Brennan interview is without parallel. You might not believe what happened, but believe me, it did.

Howard Brennan was a steam fitter working on piping systems for the Republic Bank Building. When he got off the early shift, he went downtown to see the president. Howard lived in the Pleasant Grove section of southeast Dallas, a blue-collar area, and it was there that his wife waited for him to come home and tell her about the visit of the president. What he told her when he got home, of course, was that he saw with his own eyes a man fire at the president. But before he headed home, he sought out a Dallas policeman and asked to be taken to a Secret Service agent. And there he told what he had seen. Howard told me later that the only thing he asked of officials was that his name never be made public, as he didn't ever want to tell in public what he saw.

Howard became the key witness to appear before the Warren Commission. Something that has always baffled me is why no reporter, me included, picked up on his name before the report was released (even though he appeared briefly in some of the news film we shot on November 22). When the report was handed out on Friday afternoon with an embargoed release time of 6:00 p.m., eastern time, Sunday, September 27, 1964, Howard Brennan's name suddenly became a hot property.

The CBS report on the findings of the Warren Commission would be broadcast at the time designated in the embargo, and so would the broadcasts of the other networks. The wire services would supply newspapers with the details they would need for Monday's editions. Because of all of the groundwork I had done for CBS in Dallas, I would be a part of the final preparations and airing in New York. I had reservations on a mid–Friday afternoon flight and went home to pick up my bag. On the way, I stopped off at the cashier's window of the *Dallas Times Herald*, parent company of KRLD, and drew a cash advance. It was lucky I did, as you'll see.

I kissed Jane good-bye and was headed out the door when the phone rang. It was for me. Jane Bartels, who probably knew as much, if not more, about the assassination as anyone I ever knew, was on the phone. "Have you ever heard of Howard Brennan?" Jane asked.

"No, who is he?" I replied, forgetting the brief sound bite we had with Howard on the day of the assassination.

Jane spelled out what was in the advance copy of the *Warren Report* she had. She said it named Brennan as the man who fingered Lee Harvey Oswald as the man who shot JFK. "Do you think you could find Brennan and get an interview with him?" Jane inquired. Of course, I would try.

I made a quick thumb-through of the Dallas phone directory and found Brennan's address and telephone number. I dialed it and Mrs. Brennan answered. I asked for Howard and she said he wasn't home. When I told her who I was, she said, "Oh, they promised Howard he would never have to talk to the press about it." I wanted to keep the conversation going, so we talked about how he felt about what he had seen, and so on. Mrs. Brennan told me that they watched my news broadcast every night and Howard liked me. She said Howard would be home shortly. "Why don't you just drive out and meet him?" she asked. I told Mrs. Brennan I was on my way.

I called the newsroom and told reporter Jim Underwood to be out in front and to have a sound camera and a recorder with him. Jim was also our weatherman, had as much on-television exposure as I had, and was a darn good cameraman. As I've mentioned, we did it all in those days: shoot film; run a tape recorder for radio; "soup" (develop) the film; put the razor blade to the audiotape; write the copy; and air it. Things have changed a bit.

We got to the Brennans' modest home and knocked on the door. Howard answered, looked us over, and invited us in. We passed a few pleasantries, then Howard brought up the reason for the visit. Again he informed me that he had been promised his name would never be released. Well, of course, there it was in the most eagerly anticipated government report in history. I told him there was no way the press (I still call us the "press"; "media" is not my choice) would let him rest in peace. Why didn't he just do the interview with me and he wouldn't have to do it again? How I could say that with a straight face I don't know, because the "mob" would find him sooner or later. And then something happened that made my promise to him a true one.

I was desperately trying to think of some way to convince him to do the interview. Surely, I wasn't the only reporter in town with the good sense to look in the telephone book for a name and address. Or, maybe, no one else had a person as sharp as Jane Bartels reading the fine print in the report and coming up with the name. I tend to believe the latter. Then an idea: How would the Brennans like to go to New York? We would do the interview there.

Mrs. Brennan smiled, looked at Howard, and said, "Howard always promised me we would go to New York some day, but we just couldn't afford it." Eureka!

"Mrs. Brennan, why don't we fly up to New York this evening?" I suggested. "I'll do the interview with Howard and we'll see to it that you have a wonderful weekend and Howard won't have to talk to anyone but me."

Her reply: "But I don't have a thing to wear." That did it! Remember, at the beginning of this book, I wrote that I'd tell you if I ever paid for a story? And how I mentioned getting that cash advance for the trip? Well, I reached in my pocket, pulled out a $100 bill, and said, "Here, go buy something to wear."

She took the hundred, and I knew I had my interview.

I had to tell CBS what I'd done, arrange for some airline tickets, and so on. I knew there was a Braniff Airlines flight to New York that left about six o'clock. I called Jere Cox, the workhorse of a public-relations man for the airline, and told him I needed three first-class tickets and for him to make up the names, any names as long as they didn't spell "Brennan." Jim Underwood would pick up the Brennans and bring them to Love Field for the flight. I then got on the phone to Les Midgley at CBS, who was the producer of the show. He was ecstatic, to say the least, and said there would be a limo at LaGuardia Airport and the rooms would be waiting.

Underwood produced the Brennans on schedule. Howard was wearing a large white cowboy-type hat that later proved to be a great help in making sure no one else got an interview with him. The plane trip was uneventful. Braniff first class in those days was superb, and the Brennans enjoyed every minute of it.

When we arrived at LaGuardia, there was a mob scene. Somehow, the name "Howard Brennan" had surfaced and the word had gotten out that I had him in tow. A CBS rep, whose name I have long since forgotten, told me the limo was ready and to make a beeline for it. Howard was surrounded by the typical screaming, shouting throng of journalists, but he said not a word beyond that he was with me and was going to talk only to me.

We made it to the limo, a first for both Brennans, and a lot of press types followed in hot pursuit. But the driver, skilled in the ways of the world, shook them off, and we arrived at a small hotel on the East Side with nary a reporter in sight. The Brennans were quick to bed with the understanding we would meet in the coffee shop at eight o'clock the next morning and go to CBS to do the interview. Midgley and I retired to the bar and raised one. If it held together, we had a segment of our Sunday show that would leave the competition just looking on.

Eight o'clock the next morning, Saturday, and the Brennans were right on time for breakfast. Midgley joined us and we talked over the day ahead. We'd do the interview, then CBS had arranged for a network employee and his wife to meet the Brennans, and for the next three days they would see everything there was to see in New York and then some.

Just as we were finishing breakfast, Howard remembered he had left his hat in the room. "I have to go back for it," he insisted. He didn't come back for an uncomfortably long time, and I was getting a little worried. Then I heard my name being paged. It was Howard: he told me the hall was full of reporters and cameras looking for "that guy in the white hat." They didn't recognize him without it. What should he do? "Forget the hat, Howard, and get on down here," I told him. He did and we were off to CBS for the interview.

For the September 1964 CBS special on the Warren Commission report I talked to a lot of the witnesses to the Kennedy assassination and subsequent events. Mostly, they were ordinary people unwittingly caught up in an extraordinary event. Even so, their observations on Oswald help create a more complete portrait of the assumed assassin. What follows is a "collage" of sound bites from the CBS program.[4]

Lee Oswald's mother, Marguerite, was always available for an interview after the assassination. Still, she seemed to be a lost soul, never quite able to admit to herself that her son had been a terribly troubled, damaged young man:

> He [Lee] was a happy-go-lucky youngster, actually. He had a dog. He had a bicycle. He belonged to the Y. He used to go to the Y and go swimming. . . . He loved to play Monopoly. He knew any and everything there was to know about animals. He studied animals, was often in the zoo, and, as we know, he was picked up in the Bronx Zoo in New York playing hooky from school. And I consider that normal, also—playing hooky from school—many, many boys do this.
>
> We know, and it's sad, and unfortunate, that Lee was deprived of his father, and he was born two months after his father had expired. But we must understand that Lee had two brothers, so he was not raised just with a woman alone.

I interviewed Ruth Paine, in whose home Marina Oswald and the Oswald children lived when the Oswalds moved to Dallas from New

Orleans in September 1963. Oswald himself took a room in a board-inghouse, but visited Marina and the children at the Paine home. Ruth had some very telling insights into Oswald's personality, including things that show even assassins are human:

> I thought of him [Lee] as a dissenter, a pamphlet passer, a person not contented with society as it was, nor with himself, nor his—the credit he was getting—for being the sort of person he was. I think he felt he wasn't noticed or given suffi-cient credit. His wife complained of him as having an overblown opinion of himself, and I think he did. He was not a particularly capable person. And he certainly had very little training, so that he was not able to get jobs that interested him. He was lucky, indeed, to get any job.
>
> He argued some with his wife. I never saw him violent with her. He was here as a guest, and recognized that fact, polite to me at all times. And I could see that he cared about Marina a great deal. I really felt that she was his only human contact of real value to him. He was by himself a great deal. He didn't try to make friends. But he valued his closeness with Marina and knew that she was a good wife for him.

Ruth's memory of hearing the news of the president's assassina-tion was very much like Marina's: "I lit some candles and Marina asked me if that was a way of praying, and I said that it was. And even then I thought he was mortally wounded. And then we heard that he [the president] was dead. And Marina said to me, 'What a terrible thing this is for Jacqueline Kennedy and for her children. Now they will have to grow up without a father.'"

Mrs. Earlene Roberts rented a room in her Oak Cliff home for eight dollars a week to Oswald, who gave the assumed name of O. H. Lee:

> MRS. ROBERTS: He wanted to see the room that I had for rent, and I showed him the only one that was for rent. And he'd taken it, said he wanted to be closer to his work. But he didn't have the job then at that Texas bookstore. He got it that day and went to work the next morning.
> BARKER: Did he pay his rent on time?

MRS. ROBERTS: Oh, yes, all except but one weekend, and that was on Armistice Day, and he came back in and said, "Well, I had a long weekend"—which was on Tuesday—and paid his rent. He always paid on Monday afternoon when he came in.

BARKER: What did you talk to him about when he paid the rent?

MRS. ROBERTS: Well, I'd just take it, and I'd say thank you, and he'd turn and walk off and never say nothing. I didn't get a good grunt out of him.

I interviewed the man who gave Oswald a ride to work on November 22, Buell Wesley Frazier. Normally, Oswald spent his weekend at the Paine home with Marina and the children and rode to work with Frazier on Monday morning: "Well, he come to me the Thursday, November 21, and asked me could he ride home with me that afternoon. And I said, 'Why, yes,' and I said, 'Why are you going home this afternoon?' And he replied that he wanted to go home and pick up some curtain rods so he could put some curtains up in his apartment. And I said, 'Oh, very well.' And then I said, 'Well, will you be going home with me tomorrow also?' And he said no, said he wouldn't be going home with me on the 22nd."

Of course, the Warren Commission determined that the package containing "curtain rods" Oswald carried with him to work on November 22 actually contained the rifle he used to kill President Kennedy.

Target shooter Garland Slack had a strange encounter with Oswald at a rifle range in the weeks before November 22. He noticed that someone else was shooting holes in his target:

SLACK: So I went to the fellow [the rifle-range attendant] and told him, I'm paying two bits for targets and putting them up and somebody's shooting a hole in them before [I shoot]. So we got to looking at who it was, and it was this fellow that turned out to be Oswald.

BARKER: Well, what did you say to Oswald?

SLACK: Well, I just kidded him like I would anyone else. . . . And, of course, if I had known the kind of guy he was I probably wouldn't have said anything. But I made a remark that he wasn't going to get any prize, he wasn't going to win a turkey by rapid fire and shooting someone else's target.

BARKER: What did he say to you?

SLACK: He never said anything to me. In other words, he didn't say he was sorry for doing what he was doing.

BARKER: Now you say that he was shooting rapid fire. How rapid fire was he shooting?

SLACK: Well, for instance, he was shooting six times, say, in seven or eight or nine seconds.

It took about six seconds, maybe a little longer, for the three shots to be fired that ended John F. Kennedy's life.

Many of the interviews I did for the Warren Commission special helped piece together Oswald's actions on the afternoon of November 22. When the shots were fired, Dallas police officer James Foster was stationed above the triple underpass, in front of the motorcade. Lots of assassination buffs believe that shots might have come from above the underpass:

BARKER: Officer Foster, was there any doubt in your mind about the direction from which those shots came?

FOSTER: No, sir, there wasn't, not after I had moved to the railroad [above the underpass]. There was no doubt that the shots were coming from back of the motorcade toward Elm and Houston.

Motorcycle officer Marion Baker heard the shots. He was certain that they came from the Depository and he dashed into the building: "I heard those shots come off, and they seemed like they was high, and they were directly ahead of me. And as I tried to figure out . . . where they came from and [I realized] the building that I had in mind was directly ahead of me. And that was the Texas Book Depository Building." Baker hustled up the stairs and encountered Oswald in an employee lunchroom on the second floor, calmly sipping a soft drink. Building superintendent Roy Truly accompanied Baker and told him that Oswald worked for the Depository. Satisfied, Baker let Oswald go.

Investigators reenacted Baker's and Oswald's movements and determined that Baker arrived in the second-floor lunchroom about ninety seconds after the shots were fired at Kennedy and Connally. I asked Baker if that was enough time for Oswald to make it from the sixth floor. "He could have done it if he'd have been awful fast, if he'd have preplanned it that way," Baker told me. Indeed, the Warren Commission found that Oswald could have hotfooted it from the sixth-floor window to the second floor in as little as seventy-four seconds.

Cab driver William Whaley picked up Oswald at a bus station in downtown Dallas and carried him to his boardinghouse in Oak Cliff:

BARKER: What did you talk to him about?
WHALEY: Well, I didn't talk very much. I didn't know the president was shot at that time, and with police cars and sirens running all around this end of town, making a lot of noise. So all I said to him was, "I wonder what the hell all the commotion is, in this end of town." And he didn't answer me. So I didn't say any more to him. I figured he was one of these people that didn't want to talk. He had something else on his mind.

For some reason, Oswald told Whaley to let him out about four blocks beyond his boardinghouse at 1026 North Beckley and then hurriedly backtracked to Mrs. Roberts's house:

MRS. ROBERTS: I was watching *As the World Turns*. It comes on from 12:30 'til one o'clock. And this had been on a few minutes and they said a special bulletin [Cronkite's famous announcement: "In Dallas, Texas, three shots were fired at President Kennedy's motorcade in downtown Dallas"]. Well, I was listening—had the television on —listening and trying to find out what'd happened to President Kennedy when he came in. . . . He wasn't running, he was just in a fast walk.
BARKER: Well, when he came in that day . . . did you say anything to him about the president being shot or not?
MRS. ROBERTS: No, sir. I just said, "You sure are in a hurry."

And he didn't answer me. He didn't say anything. When he went out, he went out walking fast the same way.

A waitress at the popular Eatwell Restaurant downtown, Mrs. Helen Markham, witnessed Oswald shooting policeman J. D. Tippit a short time later, near the corner of Tenth and Patton. She told me how Oswald stopped and leaned in through the front-seat passenger-side window of Tippit's patrol car, as if responding to a question from the patrolman: "Well, he [Oswald] got out of the window, put his hands back down to his side and stepped back about two steps. The policeman calmly opened the door, he calmly got out. And me, I didn't pay no attention because I thought they were talking friendly. And the policeman walked . . . to the front wheel on the driver's side and this man shot him in the wink of the eye. Just bang, bang, bang." Although we didn't use it in the CBS program, I vividly remember Mrs. Markham describing how the blood was pumping out of Officer Tippit's temple.

Oswald ducked into Hardy's Shoe Store on West Jefferson, about six blocks from where Tippit had been shot. The twenty-two-year-old clerk, Johnny Brewer, told me he was immediately suspicious of Oswald: "Well, it was right after the president was shot. They broadcast the description on the radio of this man, about five-eight, five-nine, 150 pounds. And this Oswald matched the description, and, oh, just a few minutes before he walked into the lobby on the radio they had a bulletin that an officer had been shot here in Oak Cliff. And he walked in, he matched the description, looked scared. Just the way he stood there."

Brewer followed Oswald after he left the store and saw him go into the Texas Theatre. He described Oswald to the cashier, who had her back to the entrance and didn't see anyone sneak in. On Brewer's suggestion, she called the police, and Brewer entered the theater through the back exit:

BARKER: What happened when the police came?
BREWER: Well, just before the police got there, they turned the houselights on in the theater, and I looked out the curtain and saw Oswald. And he stood up and walked to the aisle there and then turned around and sat back down almost where he had been sitting. Then I heard this noise outside and

opened the door, and the police grabbed me and asked me what I was doing there and I told them. And they asked me if the man was still in the theater. I said yes. And they asked me to point him out, so a couple or three of the policemen and myself walked out and I pointed to him, and Officer McDonald—he was the first one to him—he approached him and Oswald stood up.

Police officer Nick McDonald told me how he escaped death when Oswald tried to shoot him with the pistol he apparently had used to kill Tippit. McDonald used his own gun to show me that Oswald's pistol didn't misfire, as has been reported: "If you'll cock it, I'll show you the position my hand was in whenever it snapped on me. The fleshy part of my hand between the thumb and forefinger was between the hammer and the firing pin, [and the hammer] hit the skin and then struck the primer, which slowed the action down. It sort of pinched the fleshy part of my hand in there."

I asked Dallas Police Chief Jesse Curry if the Dallas police had ever heard of Oswald before the assassination: "No, sir. We did not have any information on this man in our criminal intelligence file, and that's normally where it would have been, in our subversive file, as we refer to it."

After the humiliation of Jack Ruby gunning down Oswald in the basement of City Hall—in full view of a live television camera—I asked Curry what he would have done differently: "I can very definitely say this, that I am afraid that I would be criticized again, but probably it would be from the news media, because I wouldn't let them inside City Hall."

President Johnson hoped that the Warren Commission report would quell the American public's doubts about the assassination. Instead, it created a cottage industry of professional doubters. CBS and I would return to the Warren Commission report in less than three years.

When the time came for Jack Ruby to go on trial, a friendship I had nurtured with State District Judge Joe Brown proved very helpful. When Judge Brown first ran for office, he bought ads on KRLD radio. He got elected and felt those ads were what put him in office, and he never forgot it. That had to be the key to the rapport I developed with him through the years. By the time of the Ruby trial in early '64, the judge and I had been on a first-name basis for a long time.

Ruby, of course, shot and killed Oswald in the basement of City Hall, on live national television, no less. Just about everyone in Dallas had seen it, but then everyone else had seen it, too, either live or on the many playbacks. Anyway, there was tremendous pressure to move the trial out of Dallas, and with good reason besides the television coverage. Emotions ran high over the Kennedy assassination and the screw-up that allowed Ruby to murder Oswald. It was hard to lay a bet that Ruby would walk out of that courtroom a free man. But the Honorable Judge Joe Brown heard his own drummer, and its cadence made his courtroom a place you weren't likely to forget.

The appeals of Ruby's lawyers, the flamboyant San Francisco dandy Melvin Belli and the East Texas country boy Joe Tonahill, were falling mostly on deaf ears. But it was only the ears of the judge that mattered. Would he move the trial out of Dallas or wouldn't he? The judge retired to his chambers to make his momentous decision, and on the way he glanced over and motioned for me to come with him. Just the two of us were there and I asked him, "Well, Judge, what do you think?" I hardly had the question out of my mouth when he shot back, "Eddie, you know darn well I'm going to keep the trial right here in this courtroom, but you can't say that now." And that little exchange set up something I hadn't seen before and am sure I will never see again.

The judge said he would reconvene court at 1:30 p.m. and it would probably take him about twenty-five minutes to actually get to the ruling. By knowing the exact time that he would announce his ruling, I could go on the air with the story that he had decided to turn down the motion to move the trial. The judge and I then synchronized our watches, down to the second. He went into the courtroom, and I waited in his chambers. At the agreed-upon time, 1:58 p.m., I did a feed to CBS from his office for the two o'clock news that the change-of-venue request had been denied. Meanwhile, in the courtroom the judge instructed his bailiffs, "No one is to leave the court-room until I leave the bench," and it took him several minutes to leave. A very unusual way to get a beat on a story, but a beat nonetheless. Thanks, Judge!

It's always gratifying to receive recognition for your hard work, but especially when it comes from someone whose own work you greatly admire.

As a newscaster, Lowell Thomas was ahead of his time. He traveled the globe many times over and played a major role in making Lawrence of Arabia known around the world. He had an afternoon newscast on CBS radio for years, at 5:45 p.m. as I remember, and before that he broadcast many years for NBC. Thomas set the bar high for broadcast news, and he's very deservedly in the Radio Hall of Fame. "So long until tomorrow" was his famous sign-off. I had never met him and never expected to, because there was little likelihood our paths would ever cross. But they did.

The phone rang in the newsroom one afternoon and it was for me.

"Lowell Thomas here," came the oh-so-familiar voice.

"How are you, sir?"

"I'm fine. I'm in Dallas to address the Knife and Fork Club this evening," he said. "The purpose of my call is to tell you how much I admired your work on the Kennedy assassination story and I was hoping to meet you."

Wow!

"Mr. Thomas, it would be my pleasure. Where are you staying, sir, and I'll come over."

He was at the Fairmont, not too far from the station, and I went to meet him in the lobby. No mistaking him with his rose-colored glasses and that distinguished mustache.

We talked for half an hour. I then asked him to come over to the station, and we taped another half hour for playback on KRLD radio.

I took him back to the Fairmont, we shook hands, and as he walked away he waved and called out "so long" as only Lowell Thomas could say it.

As I've said, there are many characters who played key roles in the events surrounding the JFK assassination whose names are not at all well known. Ever hear of Baxton Bryant? Most people haven't. But Bryant, without realizing it, was a minor player with a major role in what happened that strangely sunny day. He was a Methodist minister with as much, if not more, interest in Democratic Party politics as in his pulpit.

To show you what manner of man Baxton Bryant was, here's a little story. On Thanksgiving Day, 1950, Bryant, pastor of the Methodist church in the little North Texas town of Bells, and another man were burning trash or burning off the dry grass around the church, depending on whose story you read. The eighty-year-old church caught fire and burned to the ground. Well, after the church's small insurance settlement came in and the members pledged what they could, the pastor still needed $10,000 to rebuild the church. That was a tidy sum in a little farming town. So the resourceful Reverend Bryant came up with the ingenious idea of a Mile of Dollars—a ribbon of dollar bills a mile long, donated dollar by dollar by the hard-working folks of Bells and the surrounding area. They strung the dollars on a wire along U.S. Highway 69 south of town.

Bryant didn't raise all of the money the church needed from the Mile of Dollars, but he got so much publicity that he soon raised the rest. *Life* magazine gave the story prominent coverage, including a photo of Bryant wrapped up in dollar bills. Donations poured in from all over the country. This was a man who knew how to get things done.

Originally, there was to be no parade when President Kennedy came to Dallas—off the plane at Love Field and straight to the Trade Mart to deliver a speech. The Dallas Citizens Council, among others, sponsored the luncheon, and not many, if any, blue-collar types had membership in the organization or would be at the event. And that's where the Reverend Bryant entered the scene.

By 1963, Bryant had become the pastor of the Elmwood Methodist Church in Oak Cliff. He was well connected in the Democratic Party. For example, he was a friend of "Mr. Sam" Rayburn, the venerable

Speaker of the House from Bonham. When President and Mrs. Kennedy arrived at Love Field, one of the first people to greet them was Baxton Bryant, who brought a large crowd of Kennedy supporters with him. Bryant told the *Dallas Morning News* in 1988, "I talked to Kennedy, and he was amazed at how many people were there. . . . Kennedy said, 'This doesn't look like an anti-Kennedy crowd.'"

But Bryant would not have been satisfied merely by greeting the president with a gaggle of supporters at the airport. The pastor made it known in no uncertain terms that the plan for JFK's visit was lousy. He sent a telegram to the president complaining about the apportionment of tickets at the luncheon. Too many business-community Republicans and conservative Democrats. The common folk would not be able to see their president. The Reverend Bryant's telegram read, "One would think Nixon won and was coming to Dallas to greet his dedicated workers. Better not to have come if the visit is used to reject supporters and reward opposition. Please do something. We can't win the John Birchers, but can fire up our own workers in '64." Baxton succeeded in getting the Trade Mart balconies opened up for rank-and-file Democrats. And I've always wondered if his telegram influenced the president's decision to ride through Dallas in an open car. Here's why.

Governor Connally opposed the motorcade, for reasons that became all too obvious. On November 15 — just a week before the assasination — a headline in the *Morning News* said, "JFK Motorcade Seems Unlikely," because of "a tight schedule and security regulations." But the story reported that "Democratic leaders" had requested a motorcade so "rank and file party workers" could see the president. Also on November 15, the story on Baxton's telegram appeared in the *Times Herald*. On November 16, the plans for the motorcade were announced in a *Times Herald* story.[5]

Well, you know the rest. I later half-jokingly told Bryant, "You might be the man most responsible for what happened to the president." Understandably, I guess, he didn't see a lot of humor in the comment.

References:

[1] "CBS News Extra: November 22nd and the Warren Report." CBS Television Network script, September 27th, 1964. Collection of Eddie Barker.

[2] *Report of the President's Commission on the Assassination of President John F. Kennedy.* United States. Warren Commission. (Garden City, N.Y.: Doubleday, 1964), 135.

[3] *Report of the President's Commission on the Assassination of President John F. Kennedy.* United States. Warren Commission. (Garden City, N.Y.: Doubleday, 1964), 135.

[4] "CBS News Extra."

[5] "Politics and Presidential Protection: The Motorcade," Staff Report of the Select Committee on Assassinations. U.S. House of Representatives. Ninety-fifth Congress, second session, March 1979; "Education Needs JFK Topic Here," *Dallas Times Herald* (November 14, 1963): A-1, A-9; "Demo Ranks Split on JFK Luncheon," *Dallas Times Herald* (November 15, 1963): A-23, A-28; Carl Freund, "JFK Motorcade Seems Unlikely," *Dallas Morning News* (November 15, 1963): Section 4, p. 1; "Increased Seating Readied for Kennedy Luncheon," *Dallas Times Herald* (November 16, 1963): A-1.

6

"Only in Fiction Do We Find All the Loose Ends Neatly Tied . . ."

As the years went by, rather than gradually fading away, the controversy over the assassination of President Kennedy grew ever more intense. Jack Ruby, more than anyone or anything else, saw to that when he murdered Lee Harvey Oswald, thereby preventing a trial from ever taking place. And so CBS revisited the Kennedy assassination in a four-part documentary, "CBS News Inquiry: *The Warren Report*," which aired June 25–28, 1967.[1]

Again, I'm glad to say my hard-earned Dallas contacts played a role in the success of the program. I think the CBS series—which strongly argued against the conspiracy theories that have popped up over the years like yard weeds in March—still stands as one of the best works of journalism on the assassination.

Some might say, "Well, so much more information has come out since 1967." I would counter that, generally, the closer in time to a murder an investigation is conducted, the better the chance of finding out what really happened. If more recent investigations would be convincing to you, my coauthor, John Mark Dempsey, and I refer you to Gerald Posner's excellent *Case Closed* and the 2003 ABC-TV special hosted by Peter Jennings on the assassination, both of which convincingly conclude that Lee Harvey Oswald was the lone assassin.[2]

One more note. A group of journalists who covered the JFK assassination firsthand, including me, gathered for a reunion at SMU in

1993. Laura Hlavach and Darwin Payne document this event in *Reporting the Kennedy Assassination*. In response to a poll of those journalists, seventy-five said Oswald acted alone, six said no.[3]

To this day, the sixth-floor window of the old Texas School Book Depository remains one of the most famous—or is the word *infamous?* — landmarks in the world. And you know why: it was the perch from which Oswald assassinated JFK. But for years it was off limits; no reporters or photographers were allowed, period.

Four years passed and still no reports from that window. CBS wanted to reexamine the assassination in an unprecedented four-hour documentary. The network wanted to film a re-creation of the assassination from Oswald's presumed point of view. And again it was Don Hewitt who called me and said, "We need to get in that window and we know you can get us in. Any questions?" I've got to tell you that Hewitt was, and still is, a genius without equal.

I knew what I had to do and set about doing it. The building superintendent was a dear man named Roy Truly. He was the keeper of the window, and he kept it closed to all comers. So there was no point in going to him.

I learned a long time ago that, if you want to get something done, start at the top. The top in this case was the owner of the building, Colonel D. Harold Byrd. The rank came from his many years and dollars devoted to the Civil Air Patrol. So I called Colonel Byrd and told him of our plan for the documentary and the fact that access to the window was critical. He didn't pause a minute and said, "Why, Eddie, that's no problem. I'll call Roy and tell him to let you do whatever you have to do. You'll like working with Roy." I called Roy Truly, and after briefly quizzing me about what CBS and I planned to do, he could not have been more cooperative.

CBS wanted to do this over a weekend, and figured I could get some streets blocked off as well. I went to Police Chief Charles Batchelor (Jesse Curry having retired the year before) and told him what we wanted to do. The chief never batted an eye. "Just tell me the streets and the hours and I'll do the rest," Batchelor told me.

The questions about what happened in the operating room at Parkland Hospital when the doctors tried to revive President Kennedy have always been central to the debate about what "really happened." Dr. Malcolm Perry was one of the emergency-room surgeons who operated on the president. In a news conference on the afternoon of the assassination, a reporter asked him, "Which way was the bullet coming on the neck wound? At him?" Dr. Perry replied, "It appeared to be coming at him." But Dr. Perry told me that he did not really intend to say that a bullet came from the front of the president. The reporter's leading question could have influenced the doubtless exhausted and emotionally drained Dr. Perry's answer. As Walter Cronkite observed in the program:

> At the hospital, the scene was turbulent and disordered. The press and public were clamoring for news. Dr. Perry was rushed from the emergency room to a news conference, where he was badgered into giving a description of the wounds.
>
> The neck wound, he told the press, looked like an entry wound, and he pointed to the front of his neck. In the transcript of that news conference, there's no doubt that Dr. Perry made it sound as if he had a firm opinion. Well, the reporters flashed the news, and in that moment of confusion and misunderstanding established once and for all in the minds of a great many people a conviction that at least one bullet had been fired from the front to the motorcade.

Here's what Dr. Perry said in the interview we did for the 1967 CBS program:

> PERRY: I noted a wound when I came into the room, which was of the right posterior portion of the head. Of course, I did not examine it. Again, there was no time for cursory examination. And if a patent airway cannot be secured, and the bleeding cannot be controlled — it really made very little difference. Some things must take precedence and priority,

and in this instance the airway and the bleeding must be controlled initially.

BARKER: What about this wound that you observed in the front of the President's neck? Would you tell me about that?

PERRY: Yes, of course. It was a very cursory examination. The emergency proceedings at hand necessitated immediate action. There was not time to do more than an extremely light examination.

BARKER: There's been a lot said and written about was this an exit wound or an entry wound? Would you discuss that with me, sir?

PERRY: Well, this is a difficult problem. The determination of entrance or exit frequently requires the ascertation [sic] of trajectory. And, of course, this I did not do. None of us did at the time. There was no time for such things.

The differentiation between an entrance and exit wound is often made on a disparity in sizes, the exit wound generally being larger, in the case of an expanding bullet. If, however, the bullet does not expand—if it is a full-jacketed bullet, for example, such as used commonly in the military, the caliber of the bullet on entrance and exit will frequently be the same. And without deformation of the bullet, and without tumbling, the wounds would be very similar—and in many instances, even a trained observer could not distinguish between the two.

BARKER: Did it occur to you at the time, or did you think, was this an entry wound, or was this an exit wound?

PERRY: Actually, I didn't really give it much thought. And I realize that perhaps it would have been better had I done so. But I actually applied my energies, and those of us there all did, to the problem at hand, and I didn't really concern myself too much with how it happened, or why. And for that reason, of course, I didn't think about cutting through the wound, which, of course, rendered it invalid as regards further examination and inspection. But it didn't even occur to me. I did what was expedient and what was necessary, and I didn't think much about it.

BARKER: You did not turn the president over?

PERRY: No, there was no reason to. There was not time. . . and there was really no reason to. It made very little difference to me, since my immediate concern was with an attempted resuscitation.

For some reason, Dr. Perry was intent on making the distinction that he performed a tracheostomy on the president, not a tracheotomy. The dictionary definitions of these two words are very similar, so I'm not sure why he was so concerned about it. I suppose it makes a crucial difference to other surgeons.

I interviewed Governor John Connally again for the 1967 documentary. He only slightly moderated his view that the Warren Commission was wrong in saying that one shot hit both him and President Kennedy:

BARKER: Do you believe, Governor Connally, that the first bullet could have missed, the second one hit both of you, and the third one hit President Kennedy?
CONNALLY: That's possible. That's possible. Now, the best witness I know doesn't believe that.
BARKER: Who is the best witness you know?
CONNALLY: Nellie was there, and she saw it. She believes the first bullet hit him, because she saw him after he was hit. She thinks the second bullet hit me, and the third bullet hit him.
NELLIE CONNALLY: The first sound, the first shot, I heard, and turned and looked right into the president's face. He was clutching his throat and just slumped down. He just had a—a look of nothingness on his face. He—he didn't say anything. But that was the first shot.
　　The second shot, that hit John—well, of course, I could see him covered with blood, and his—his reaction to a second shot. The third shot, even though I didn't see the president, I felt the matter all over me, and I could see it all over the car.

So I'll just have to say that I think there were three shots, and that I had a reaction to three shots. And—that's just what I believe.

CONNALLY: Beyond any question, and I'll never change my opinion, the first bullet did not hit me. The second bullet did hit me. The third bullet did not hit me.

Now, so far as I'm concerned, all I can say with any finality is that if there is — if the single-bullet theory is correct, then it had to be the second bullet that hit President Kennedy and me.

While Connally questioned the Warren Commission's finding that a single bullet hit both the president and himself, he did not dispute that the shots came from behind:

CONNALLY: All of the shots came from the same place, from back over my right shoulder. They weren't in front of us or they weren't at the side of us. There were no sounds like that emanating from those directions.

BARKER (to Nellie Connally): Was there any doubt in your mind, the direction that those shots came from?
NELLIE CONNALLY: No. They all came from the same direction.
BARKER: Which was?
NELLIE CONNALLY: It was behind us, over my right shoulder.

Of course, I talked to witnesses who thought they saw and heard things that would cast doubt on Oswald's guilt, or at least would suggest that he didn't act alone. Arnold Rowland and his wife stood in the crowd across from the Depository. Rowland told the Warren Commission that he saw an elderly black man in the window from which Oswald supposedly fired the fatal shot. But he said he also saw a gunman in another window of the Depository, at the far end of the building from Oswald's alleged perch:

ROWLAND: And I was just lookin' around and we noticed a man up in the window and I remarked to my wife, tried to point him out. And remarked that he must be a security guard or a Secret Service agent.

BARKER: So, the window, then, that you're referring to is on the opposite end of the building from where the main entrance to the building is? [The notorious sixth-floor window is directly above the main entrance.]

ROWLAND: Yes, it is on the other side of the building. And he had a rifle. It looked like a high-powered rifle because it had a scope which looked, in relation to the size of the rifle, to be a big scope.

Caroline Walther went further. She said she saw two men with guns in the Depository:

WALTHER: I looked at this building and I saw this man with a gun, and there was another man standing to his right. And I could not see all of this man, and I couldn't see his face. And the other man was holding a short gun. It wasn't as long as a rifle. And he was holding it pointed down, and he was kneeling in the window, or sitting. His arms were on the window. And he was holding the gun in a downward position, and he was looking downward.

BARKER: About what floor would you say these two men were on that you saw in the window?

WALTHER: The first statement that I made, I said the man was on the fourth or fifth floor, and I still feel the same way. He was about—in a window that was just about even with the top of that tree. I saw the man had light hair, or brown, and was wearing a white shirt. That—I explained to the FBI agents that I wasn't sure about that. That was my impression on thinking about it later. . . .

BARKER: Now, what about this other man who was in the window?

WALTHER: This other man was wearing a brown suit. And that was all I could see, was half of this man's body, from his shoulders to his hips.

A railroad worker, S. M. Holland, was standing above the triple underpass just in front of the president's motorcade. We returned to the underpass and the nearby "grassy knoll" for the interview. Holland thought the first two shots came from the direction of the Texas School Book Depository but maintained that he heard a total of four shots. The last two, he said, came from the legendary knoll: "And about that time, there was a third report that wasn't nearly as loud as the two previous reports. It came from that picket fence [on the grassy knoll], and then there was a fourth report. The third and the fourth reports was almost simultaneously. . . . And I glanced over underneath that green tree and you see a—a little puff of smoke. It looked like a puff of steam or cigarette smoke. And the smoke was about eight or ten feet off the ground, and about fifteen feet this side of that tree."

Holland told me he ran from the triple underpass to the place behind the picket fence at the top of the grassy knoll. There, he said, he saw evidence that someone had been standing behind the fence near a station wagon:

HOLLAND: I did find where a man had been standing and walking from one end of the bumper to the other, and I guess if you could have counted the footsteps there'd have been two hundred or more on the muddy spots—footprints. And there were two mud spots on the bumper of the station wagon. . . .
BARKER: Were they fresh footprints?
HOLLAND: They were fresh. It had been raining that morning. There was footprints—mud on these two-by-fours—there was mud on the bumper of the station wagon, and there was only two sets of footprints that I could find that left this station wagon. They went behind a white Chevrolet car that was settin' over there.

What to make of these conflicting reports? Journalists and detectives know that in a large group of people who supposedly have observed the same event, witnesses will tell strikingly different stories. I believe most of these people were sincere in giving their accounts. The Warren Commission, and we who produced the CBS series on the assassination, simply had to weigh the balance of the evidence. Most of the interviews we did, like the one with Howard Brennan in 1964, more or less substantiated the basic facts contained in the Warren Commission report.

Amos Euins, fifteen years old at the time of the assassination, was standing on the corner across the street from the Depository. Nearly four years later, he returned to Dealey Plaza with me. He said he saw what he thought was a pipe sticking out of the sixth-floor window:

EUINS: I happened to look up and I seen a pipe, you know. So I never did pay no attention thinking it might be a pipe, you know, just a pipe sticking out. So it was sticking out about a foot, about that high, you know.
BARKER: Point out for me, Mr. Euins, the window where you saw the pipe.
EUINS: It was about on the sixth floor, right below the banister.

Associated Press photographer James Altgens was standing near the street, in front of the grassy knoll, facing the Book Depository. He snapped a photo that shows the president reacting to the shot that hit him in the neck. He then saw the shot that hit Kennedy's head. Altgens said it was "obvious" to him that the shot came from behind:

ALTGENS: The one thing that did seem to be a little bit strange, immediately after the car proceeded on to Parkland Hospital, men with drawn guns ran up the terrace of this plaza, up into what is considered to be and referred to as the knoll area. And thinking that they had the assassin cornered up in this knoll area—and it seemed rather strange, as I say, because knowing that the shot came from behind, this fellow had to really move in order to get over into the knoll area.
BARKER: You had no thoughts about another assassin behind the fence or on the knoll?
ALTGENS: I've had a lot of people to contact me in that they felt there was another person involved, and trying to get me to verify either photographs they had or to work out some information they felt they had come across to substantiate . . . the fact that there was another assassin. But at no time has any of this evidence proved to me beyond a shadow of a doubt that there was another assassin.

The driver of Vice-President Johnson's car, a short distance behind the president's car, was a Department of Public Safety trooper, Hurchel Jacks:

> JACKS: The car in which I was driving, which occupied the vice-president, . . . had just completed its turn, and I felt a blast which appeared to be a rifle shot come from behind me. I turned and looked up to the School Book Depository.
> BARKER: Well now, what about these people who say shots came from this fence area up here? Would you agree with that at all, or not?
> JACKS: No, sir. I . . . don't think there was. I heard three shots and I could feel the concussion from all three.

And I returned with Abraham Zapruder to the wall at the edge of the grassy knoll, from which he filmed the legendary home-movie footage of the assassination. Shots from behind the picket fence would have whistled by his ear. Zapruder agreed that no shots came from the knoll: "I'm not a ballistics expert, but I believe that if there were shots that came from my right ear, I would hear a different sound. I heard shots coming from—I wouldn't know which direction to say—but they were driven from the Texas Book Depository and they all sounded alike. There was no difference in sound at all."

One of the inconsistencies in the reporting of the assassination that raised suspicions was the initial description of the rifle found on the sixth floor of the Depository as a "German Mauser." A Dallas County deputy constable, Seymour Weitzman, and a deputy sheriff, Eugene Boone, discovered the rifle. Weitzman explained to me that he made a simple mistake:

> WEITZMAN: I'll be very frank with you. I stumbled over it two times, not knowing it was there.
> BARKER: Just went right by it.
> WEITZMAN: Went right by it. And Mr. Boone was climbing on top, and I was down on my knees looking, and I moved a

box, and he moved a carton, and there it was. And he in turn hollered that we had found a rifle.

BARKER: Well, when did you first get a full view of the gun?

WEITZMAN: When the crime lab brought the gun out, after they had gone over it. I could see portions of the gun while they were doing a partial investigation of it here in the building.

BARKER: What kind of gun did you think it was?

WEITZMAN: To my sorrow, I looked at it, and it looked like a Mauser, which I said it was. But I said the wrong one because just at a glance I saw the Mauser action, and—I don't know—it just came out [in the wrong] words, "It's a German Mauser." Which it wasn't. It's an Italian-type gun. But from a glance, it's hard to describe, and that's all I saw it was, at a glance. I was mistaken, and it was proven that my statement was a mistake, but it was an honest mistake.

The bullet that apparently passed through President Kennedy's throat and then tore into Governor Connally's chest and wrist, the bullet that Warren Commission doubters derisively refer to as the "magic bullet," has also been a huge source of controversy over the years. Oliver Stone, who made the movie *JFK*, fancifully portrays Jack Ruby planting the bullet on Governor Connally's stretcher at Parkland Hospital. The casual handling of the crucial evidence no doubt contributed to the conspiracy theories that grew around it.

I interviewed two Parkland Hospital employees, Darrell Tomlinson and O. P. Wright. Tomlinson found the bullet when it fell from the governor's stretcher:

TOMLINSON: There was a doctor that went into the doctor's lounge and he had to pull this stretcher out, the one I'd taken off the elevator, and whenever he came out he failed to push it back up against the wall. So I just stepped over and gave it a little kick to get it back in line, and then I turned to walk away and I heard a rattle, and I turned around and looked. I didn't see anything at that time, but I walked back over to the stretcher and there was this bullet [that] was laying there. So, I picked it up, looked at it, put it in my pocket. . . .

BARKER: Well, now, as you think back, is there any doubt in

your mind today that the stretcher on which you found that bullet was the stretcher that came off of the elevator?
TOMLINSON: Well, I know that. That I know. I just don't know who was on the stretcher.
BARKER: But the stretcher was on the elevator?
TOMLINSON: Right.
BARKER: And this was the elevator that Governor Connally would have taken, or would have been placed on to go to the operating room, is that right?
TOMLINSON: Yes, sir, . . . that's the one he went up on.

Conspiracy theorists claim that the bullet fell off of President Kennedy's stretcher, which, if true, would discredit the "single-bullet" explanation.

Tomlinson then offered the bullet to Wright, the hospital's chief of security. Wright said he instructed Tomlinson to keep the bullet in his pocket while Wright contacted the federal authorities:

WRIGHT: I contacted the FBI and they said they were not interested because it wasn't their responsibility to make investigations [perhaps because, at that time, the murder of the president was considered a local crime, just as any murder would be]. So, I got a hold of a Secret Service man and they didn't seem to be interested in coming and looking at the bullet in the position it was then in. So I went back to the area where Mr. Tomlinson was and picked up the bullet and put it in my pocket, and I carried it some thirty or forty minutes. And I gave it to a Secret Service man that was guarding the main door into the emergency area.
BARKER: Mr. Wright, when you gave this bullet to the Secret Service agent, did he mark it in any way?
WRIGHT: No, sir.
BARKER: What did he do with it?
WRIGHT: Put it in his left-hand coat pocket.
BARKER: Well, now, did he ask your name or who you were or any question at all about the bullet?
WRIGHT: No, sir.
BARKER: How did the conversation go? Do you remember?
WRIGHT: I just told him this was a bullet that was picked up

on a stretcher that had come off the emergency elevator that might be involved in the moving of Governor Connally. And I handed him the bullet, and he took it and looked at it and said, "Okay," and put it in his pocket.

As Cronkite said in the program following this interview, "There is little to praise in such treatment by the FBI and the Secret Service of perhaps the most important single piece of evidence in the assassination case."

Still, the predominance of evidence, then and now, points to Oswald as the lone assassin. One of the first big conspiracy books is Mark Lane's *Rush to Judgment*, in which Lane accuses the Warren Commission of botching the investigation.[4] But Lane himself plays fast and loose with some of the details. For example, he quotes James Altgens and another witness, Charles Brehm, as giving testimony that supported shots coming from behind the wooden fence on the grassy knoll. Well, you've already read what Altgens said. Brehm did not testify before the Warren Commission, but did respond to questions from the FBI. He stood across the street from the grassy knoll as the shots were fired. I asked Brehm—no stranger to gunfire as an army ranger who took part in the Normandy invasion—about the critics who had interpreted his comments about part of the president's skull flying backward and to the left as evidence of gunmen firing from the knoll: "Well, as I say, it was not a number of critics. It was one critic, Mark Lane, who takes very great liberties with adding to my quotation. I never said that . . . any shot came from here [the knoll] like I was quoted by Mr. Lane. Mr. Lane would like me to have positively identified—what I saw fly over here—his [the president's] skull—although I told him I could not. . . . He has added his interpretations to what I said, and consequently that's where the story comes from that I said that the shots come from up there. No shot came from up there at any time during the whole fiasco that afternoon."

Of course, President Kennedy was not the only man to be killed in Dallas that day. Police officer J. D. Tippit was shot and killed near the intersection of Tenth and Patton in a residential section of Oak

Cliff a few minutes after the assassination. A few determined conspiracy buffs even question whether Lee Harvey Oswald killed Tippit. But truck driver Domingo Benavides described how Oswald shot Tippit four times as the policeman got out of his squad car to question the suspicious-seeming young man. Benavides told me how Oswald casually tossed aside the spent shells: "He took the shells up in his hand and, as he took off, he threw them in the bushes more or less like nothing really, trying to get rid of them. I guess he didn't figure he'd get caught anyway, so he just threw them in the bushes. But he—as he started to turn to walk away, well, he stopped and looked back at me, and I don't know if he figured, well, I'll just let this poor guy go, or he had nothing to do with it, or you know, I'm not out to kill everybody."

As Oswald walked away, Benavides went to Tippit's car and tried to use the radio to call the police. Another passerby, T. F. Bowley, actually made the call. When the police arrived, Benavides used a stick to pick up the shells Oswald threw into the bushes and gave them to the officers. He had no doubt the man who shot Tippit was Oswald: "No, sir, there was no doubt at all. I could even tell you how he combed his hair and the clothes he wore and what have you, all the details. And if he had a scar on his face, I could probably have told you about it, but—you don't forget things like that."

Another man, used-car salesman Ted Callaway (ironically, like Oswald, an ex-marine), had a close brush with Oswald after the Tippit shooting. Callaway told me he heard the shots fired from behind his car lot and quickly went to investigate. He saw Oswald running down the street:

I saw right away he had a gun in his hand. And he continued across the street coming in this direction. So when he got right across from me over here, just, oh, about thirty yards or less, why, I called to him and just asked him, "Hey, man, what the hell's goin' on, fella?" . . . And he looked in my direction and paused, almost stopped and said something to me, but I couldn't make out what he said. But he had this pistol in his hand, carrying it in what we used to call in the Marine Corps a raised-pistol position, and then he slowed down and started walking.

Then, I ran to the corner of Tenth and Patton, and when I got there, I saw this squad car parked near the curb. And then I walked around in front of the squad car and this policeman was lying in front of the squad car.

As described elsewhere, police arrested Oswald in the nearby Texas Theatre a short time later.

After sifting through all of the evidence, the CBS series came to the conclusion that, despite its flaws, the Warren Commission's report was essentially accurate. Eric Sevareid acknowledged what many Americans found hard to accept, that such an inconsequential "skinny, weak-chinned little character" as Oswald could bring down the president of the United States: "But this almost unbelievable incongruity has characterized nearly every one of the assassinations and attempted assassinations of American presidents. Deranged little men killed Lincoln, Garfield, McKinley, tried to kill Presidents Theodore and Franklin Roosevelt. Only the Puerto Rican attempt on President Truman represented a real conspiracy. . . . It would be utterly impossible in the American arena of a fierce and free press and politics to conceal a conspiracy among so many individuals who live in the public eye."

Walter Cronkite, "the most trusted man in America," as usual, expressed himself eloquently:

Only in fiction do we find all the loose ends neatly tied. . . . Real life is not all that tidy. In 1943, Lieutenant John F. Kennedy came under enemy fire behind Japanese lines in the Pacific. His PT boat was destroyed. His back, already weak, was reinjured. Yet he swam three miles, towing a wounded shipmate, found shelter on an island, escaped Japanese search, crossed undetected through enemy waters as enemy planes hovered overhead, and survived to become president. The account of his survival is full of improbabilities, coincidences, unknowns. So is the account of his death. So would be the account of your life, or mine, or the life of any one of us. . . . If the demands for certainty that are made upon the commission were applied to its critics, the theory of the second assassin would vanish before it was spoken.

I agree with Eric and Walter. Sorry, I can't go along with the conspiracy theories. Read again what I say in Chapter 5: Lee Harvey Oswald's inability to satisfy Marina's expectations of his manhood had a lot to do with why he killed John F. Kennedy. Remember, he tried to kill Gen. Edwin Walker and then came home and bragged to Marina about it. My opinions have not changed in all this time:

CRONKITE: Are you content with the basic finding of the Warren Commission . . . Eddie?
BARKER: I agree with it, Walter. It's too bad, of course, that Oswald didn't have his day in court. But I felt the night of November 22 that he was the one who had shot the president, and nothing has come to light since then to change my opinion a bit.

References:

[1] "CBS News Inquiry: The Warren Report," Parts 1-4 CBS Television Network script, June 25-28, 1967. Collection of Eddie Barker.

[2] Gerald Posner, *Case Closed: Lee Harvey Oswald and the Assassination of JFK* (New York: Random House, 1993); *Peter Jennings Reporting: The Kennedy Assassination - Beyond Conspiracy*, New York: ABC Television Network, 2003.

[3] Laura Hlavach and Darwin Payne, Eds. *Reporting the Kennedy Assassination: Journalists Who Were There Recall Their Experiences* (Dallas: Three Forks Press, 1996).

[4] Mark Lane, *Rush to Judgment* (New York: Holt, Rinehart & Winston, 1966), 55-56, 353-54.

7

"My Village":
The High and Mighty

When you entered the lobby of the *Dallas Times Herald*, the first thing that caught your eye was the large lettering on the back wall, there for all to see: "The *Times Herald* Stands for Dallas as a Whole." Of course, a few wags had fun with the slogan by leaving the w off of "whole." But the words epitomize what those early builders did for the entire community. It was not the fractionalized Dallas we have today.

A lot of names come to mind as practitioners of that motto, none more so than some of the old bankers in town, like Bob Thornton at Mercantile, Fred Florence at Republic, and Nathan Adams at First National. And while they backed a worthy borrower in hopes of making money off the loan, they also hoped that the success of the business would mean success for Dallas. These men and others looked beyond the immediate to a larger picture of what business leader John Stemmons always referred to as "my village," an affectionate reference to Dallas that mirrors my own fondness for the city. Look at what the Stemmons family (John's father, Leslie, was a very successful property developer) did for Dallas when it donated all the right of way for Stemmons Freeway. That was the old Stemmons farm out there. Sure, Leslie Stemmons became wealthy by developing property along the freeway, but so did Dallas. People like Thornton and Stemmons were paternalistic, and today that's a bad word. But those guys got things done.

A good example of that "Dallas-as-a-Whole" thinking is the Myerson Center. Ross Perot came up with the millions to make it a reality, the only requirement being that the city name it for his long-time associate Mort Myerson. Certainly a gift for everybody, every neighborhood, every age. Another example is Ray Nasher's sharing his world-famous sculptures in the garden constructed near the Myerson.

Not many of the behind-the-scenes group opted for the political arena, one exception being Thornton. Jean Baptiste "Teest" Adoue Jr., of the National Bank of Commerce, also served as mayor, but I never saw him to be in the same class as Bob Thornton.

And speaking of Bob Thornton, several things come to mind when I think of him. For one thing, if it wasn't what Thornton envisioned as being good for Dallas, to him it was "un-Dallas," pure and simple. His great line was, "Keep the dirt flying."

Thornton was an ol' country boy. He never went to college, as far as I know, except for one course at Dallas's old Metropolitan Business College. He was just an old-time banker with a mind like a steel trap. He was mayor from 1953 to 1961. I remember an interview I did with him one time. I asked, "Mayor, do you have a lot of people calling you at night after you get home, or do you have an unlisted number?" He didn't take long to answer: "I've never had an unlisted phone and never will. I answer the phone up to nine o'clock. After that I figure they're drunk, so I just don't answer." Yes, I looked in the phone book. Sure enough, there was his listing.

Of course, I knew all of Dallas's mayors during the time I was at KRLD. Earle Cabell was the colorful mayor in the early '60s, at the time of the Kennedy assassination. He later served in Congress from 1964 to 1972. When he ran for mayor, I don't think he had any earthly idea he would ever run for Congress; he was just doing his civic duty as he saw it. I was very fond of Cabell.

Earle owned a big dairy in Dallas with his brother. I don't know that he ever milked a cow, but generations of children grew up drinking Cabell's milk. The company opened a chain of convenience stores, Cabell's Minit Markets, which was later sold to the Southland Corporation and 7-Eleven.

A lot of people remember Wes Wise, our former sportscaster at KRLD, as the first truly "popular" mayor of Dallas, in that he was a maverick and ran against the old-line establishment and won. But I think Wes has to share that distinction with Earle Cabell. Earle went up against the Citizens Charter Association (CCA), the organization of powerful businesspeople that pretty much called the shots in Dallas politics for a long time. The CCA would choose who was going to run for the city council. They always tried to choose people who had the good of the city—again, "as a whole"—at heart. But times were changing, and Earle won because he was a savvy politician. It shouldn't have been surprising; his father and grandfather had also been mayor of Dallas.

Earle ran against Joe Garry, a sharp lawyer, for mayor. KRLD used to sponsor debates between the candidates on radio and TV. I served as moderator. So the night came for the debate, and Garry showed up on time, but no Earle Cabell. Time went by, and Earle didn't show. And didn't show. And didn't show. I told the Channel 4 crew, "If Earle doesn't show, we're just going to have the empty chair, and Garry's going to do the debate by himself."

About two minutes before we were supposed to start, here comes Earle Cabell, ready to do battle. He knew exactly what he was doing. It totally shook up poor Joe. Cabell ended up "winning" the debate and, of course, the election.

Jane and I had this big old two-story house on University Boulevard, just west of SMU, and for years on New Year's Eve we had a party that was unreal with all the people who showed up, seventy-five or more. We never knew who would be there. Alfred Martínez, my dear friend with the El Fenix Mexican restaurant chain, would bring this huge dish of little tamales. Some of my gumshoe friends would come. They were pretty good parties. All of our kids would sit at the top of the stairs, watching.

One time this guy who worked at the station, a very sweet guy in the art department, came to the party, and the next morning I found him passed out in the flower bed. Once this friend of ours, a very distinguished old-school professor at SMU, got to feeling his oats. He reached down and took off my wife, Jane's, shoe and drank champagne from it, just like in the old movies. His wife saw him doing this, and they made a hasty exit. Cabell and his wife, Dearie, were regulars at the party. But I'll always remember that, right after the JFK assassination, he came to the party with two guys, a couple of burly off-duty cops. Earle said, "They're my bodyguards. I have to have bodyguards now." Things weren't so carefree anymore.

Erik Jonsson succeeded Cabell. I have to say that he was the last of the true heavyweight business leaders to serve as mayor of Dallas, from 1964 to 1971. Erik was one of the founders of Texas Instruments. He was tough and he didn't give in easily. No question, he was a leader.

I remember once the mayor and civil rights leader (later city councilwoman) Juanita Craft were down at the station for some reason. Juanita was a wonderful person who worked within the system. She was a powerful force for the NAACP in Dallas. She was the first black woman to vote in Dallas and started a lot of NAACP chapters in Texas. As Juanita rode around Texas on the train doing her NAACP work, she refused to move from the "whites only" section. She was tough, but she was not a grandstander.

Anyhow, Juanita and Jonsson were discussing some problem or issue on which they didn't agree. The mayor cared not for my being there, as he told Ms. Craft, "Juanita, I don't want to lecture you right here in front of Eddie, but you've just got to see it my way." And I recall he won her over. Juanita was a very strong woman, but Jonsson was persuasive.

I developed a rather close relationship with Jonsson, but in the end, he betrayed me. Remember what I talked about back there on the first pages, feet of clay? Read on.

Jonsson and I had lunch together about once a week in one of the small private dining rooms at the City Club. We would have a drink, eat lunch, and talk for an hour about a variety of subjects. He must have felt comfortable with me. I certainly did with him, so much so that I took him into my confidence, but found it to be something I shouldn't have done.

In 1970, when the *Times Herald* sold out to Times-Mirror, there was an FCC requirement that the new owner sell off either the TV station or the radio station. It couldn't keep them both. A far cry from today's ownership rules. So Times-Mirror opted to keep the cash cow,

Channel 4, and sell the radio station. I got the bright idea that maybe I could figure out a way to buy it. I went to see Jim Chambers at the paper and told him I would like to buy the station if I could raise the money. Jim said, "Eddie, I'd love to see you have it, but $7 million is a lot of money. Keep me posted." I didn't tell Jim whom I had in mind to go to. Okay, you're ahead of me; I would go to Erik Jonsson.

I called the mayor and said I had something I needed to talk to him about. "Fine, usual place, see you there Thursday," he told me. And Thursday at noon we were back in that little private dining room at the City Club.

"What's so important we need to talk about?" he asked

"KRLD radio is going to be sold and I want to buy it," I responded, "but I need financial backing, and that's where you come in."

"Well, that's about the last thing I would be interested in. What's the up side?" he wanted to know. I spent the next hour shooting down every negative he brought up. He was a tough questioner, but I had the right answers.

"Don't you talk to anyone, I mean anyone, about this," he cautioned me. "I'll call you."

The mayor's call didn't come, and I started thinking of that song the old cabaret singer Blossom Dearie used to sing: "I've been waiting for your phone call for eighteen years/Could it be that you've forgotten me?"

Well, the phone call finally came, not from Erik but from Jim Chambers. "Eddie, I've got some good news and some bad news. Someone else has beaten you to the punch and will be buying KRLD. But I know you will be pleased with the new owner. Mayor Jonsson is buying it for his boy, Philip."

That was the end of those luncheons for sure. Erik never called me. Blood runs thicker than friendship, I guess, and a present for his boy won out.

I didn't see the mayor for a long time. His wife, Margaret, became ill. She had some sort of inner-ear problem and lost her sense of balance. I ran into him somewhere. We exchanged cordial greetings, and he then started telling me about his wife and how bad her illness was. I didn't see him again until she died.

There was a place out on Lovers' Lane, a seafood place. Jane and I used to love to go there. We were in there one night, and Erik was in there by himself. I had a long visit with him. We didn't talk about KRLD. I didn't bring it up, but I figured he must have thought about it when he saw me.

Jonsson had his Goals for Dallas program. I don't know how many of the goals were ever achieved, but he did play a big part in getting Dallas–Fort Worth International Airport built as the chairman of the committee that directed the project. There was a lot of talk at the time that he was so influential in building the airport that it would be named for him. Of course, the powers that be in Fort Worth weren't going to let that happen.

The airport matter was a big political issue between Dallas and Fort Worth, with neither wanting to compromise. At one time, Fort Worth had an airport called Amon Carter Field, located on part of the land where DFW Airport stands now and named after the powerful mayor and businessman Amon Carter Sr. Fort Worth renamed it Greater Fort Worth (later Southwest) International Airport. Carter was the principal stockholder in American Airlines. Any American flight that took off from Love Field in Dallas went over and landed at Amon Carter Field, about a ten-minute flight. It was such a joke. Often, nobody would get on or off. Fort Worth had sunk a ton of money into Amon Carter Field, and Dallas was really trying to save Love Field. They both pulled out all the big guns. Of course, Carter had no use for Dallas, anyway. The story goes that he refused to eat in Dallas restaurants and, when he had to be in Big D for business, he took his lunch in a brown bag.

The two biggest supporters of Love Field were Bob Cullum, the Tom Thumb supermarket impresario, and John Stemmons. They were as close as twins joined at the head. Cullum was a little bitty short guy, about five-foot-six, and Stemmons was a great big tall fellow, six-foot-four or so. They were always together, always pushing Love Field. But it was landlocked; you couldn't expand it beyond the boundaries that still exist. They all finally realized that Dallas–Fort Worth was going to be one heck of a population center, and it didn't make sense to have two separate airports.

It was an "interesting" opening for DFW in 1974. They had this big night out there for everyone to come out and see it. They had valet parking, and they got it all screwed up and everyone lost their cars. A terrible, terrible mess, a total disaster. It went on all night. We went out with Jim Mangun, the Texas bureau chief for the Associated Press, and his wife. I was kind of leery of what was going on and conned a parking attendant into letting me park my own car and I took my keys. We got out without any trouble.

Jonsson showed his leadership in moving Dallas toward accepting the new airport, but he really screwed up the stadium deal with the Dallas Cowboys. He and Cowboys owner Clint Murchison didn't get along at all. In the early years, the Cowboys played at the Cotton Bowl in Fair Park. Finally, when the Cowboys' success led to the need for a new stadium, Murchison wanted to build it downtown. But apparently he and Jonsson came at each other in the worst of ways, and Murchison went out to Irving to build Texas Stadium. (Of course, as this is being written, the Cowboys have received the okay of Arlington voters to build a new megastadium there.) But what would downtown Dallas have been like all these years if the Cowboys had built there in the first place?

Of course, my favorite mayor was Wes Wise. Wes was a handsome young man who seemed to have grown up before the eyes of Dallas television viewers. I've already told you how he happened to come to KRLD from WFAA after crossing swords with the Cowboys' general manager, Tex Schramm. He had been at Channel 4 for quite a few years when he decided to get into local politics.

The guy who ran KRLD radio at one point, Bill Roberts, decided he wanted to put a "swap and shop" show on. So I asked Wes, "How'd you like to do it?" And he said he'd like it. We built this thing up as "The Great Garage Sale of the Air," and Wes became very popular with the public. To this day, when I see Wes, he always greets me with, "Swap and shop!" Talking to people on the air every day, he got the idea that he'd like to be on the city council. I can understand this because doing my little talk show on KPLT in Paris, I sometimes I think I'm running a confessional. People get very close to you. So I always credit *Swap and Shop* with getting him into politics.

Wes remembers: "*Swap and Shop* had a certain type of audience, mostly housewives because it was at 3:15 in the afternoon. It got me that whole segment of voters to be familiar with me. The TV sports broadcast that Eddie put me on got me the sports people, who were mostly male at that time. Then I got the audience that was news hounds from my news work at Channel 4."

Wes left the station when he decided to run for council. We couldn't have had him on the air as a political candidate. Jim Underwood, our former weatherman, reporter, and assistant news director, had left the station and was doing political public relations, and he ran Wes's campaign for the council and, later, for mayor.

"After I became mayor, somebody asked, 'Are you kidding that you don't think being on TV and radio helped you become mayor?'" Wes says. "I told him, 'I never said that. What I said was that I took the name identification from TV and radio that Eddie Barker was largely responsible for, and combined it with a full term on the city council, where people could examine what I could and could not do, and how I handled myself and dealt with people."

Wes ran for mayor against Avery Mays, the father of Jerry Mays, the SMU and Dallas Texans/Kansas City Chiefs football star. Avery was a good man, a very fine man, from Oak Cliff. But he was the establishment, the Citizens Charter Association candidate. Wes had decided that he, Wes Wise, was what the city needed.

As it had for the Earle Cabell–Joe Garry mayoral election years before, KRLD sponsored a debate, this time, between Wise and Mays. A political PR man in town named John Van Cronkite (no relation to Walter), with whom I would later work, prepared for Avery Mays a "yardstick of accomplishment": a three-foot-long list of all the things that Avery had done for Dallas. The debate began, but Avery was not a forceful kind of guy at all. It got to his time, and he reached down for the list and said, "I would like to show you my yardstick of accomplishments." Wes said, "What have you got there, Avery? Let me see that!" Wes took it away from him and started reading the items on the list. He said, "Well, I've done this, and I've done that. You say that you did this, Avery? Don't you remember we did this together?" Poor Avery didn't know how to respond, because he just wasn't a fireball politician. It got Avery off target, and he couldn't get back on track.

Wes succeeded Erik Jonsson. It just killed Jonsson to have to give the keys to the mayor's office to Wes Wise. He didn't like Wes at all. Wes wasn't one of the gang. Jonsson stood a little above the hoi polloi, or so he felt.

Wes's political career didn't go as far as it might've. While he was mayor, he accumulated a lot of personal debt. His creditors sued and got a judgment against him. The only thing he owned free and clear was this old Volkswagen Beetle, so they went out and repossessed it. But people liked Wes. A guy who had a bar downtown bought the car and gave it back to him. And then *D* magazine, owned by Ray Hunt, did a gut job on Wes, and he sued. They reached an out-of-court settlement, and I don't think Wes has had to work a day since. He didn't get back into politics after that. I don't care who you are, there's a lot of embarrassment in having your car repossessed and having a big article come out. I think once he got that settlement, he said, "Okay, I'm going to have fun and enjoy it."

Of course, Dallas County government has been just as colorful as city politics over the years. One of the people I knew best was Lew Sterrett, the Dallas County judge, the chief executive officer of the county. He and I just hit it off. Like Bob Thornton, he was a country boy. He came from the little town of Como in Northeast Texas. He was a simple little guy, but a shrewd politician. Don't underestimate the farm boys. In those days, it seems as if it was more common for men from very humble beginnings to reach very high levels of leadership, at least in Texas. LBJ, Sam Rayburn. You talk about a powerful man, Sterrett was a *powerful* man. Of course, in recent years, Lee Jackson, the chancellor of the University of North Texas at the time of this writing, was a pretty darn good county judge, too, but in a totally different way. Lew Sterrett ran Dallas County, period.

Another JFK assassination story. When we were getting ready to make the four-hour-long documentary on the assassination for CBS in 1967, the network very much wanted an interview with Dr. Malcolm Perry, whom, you'll remember, tried to save the president. This is a terribly self-serving statement, but CBS realized they couldn't make the program without me, because I had the keys to so many locks in town. But Dr. Perry was a tough nut; he didn't want to be interviewed and wouldn't return my phone calls. Still, I had to have him. I thought, "How in the heck can I get him to talk? . . . Lew Sterrett!" Sterrett controlled the budget of Parkland Hospital; the county ran it. Sterrett could make life pleasant or unpleasant for the hospital staff and the University of Texas' Southwestern Medical School, which uses Parkland as a teaching hospital.

I called Judge Sterrett and said, "I've got a problem, and I need some help."

He said, "What's the problem?"

I said, "Well, you know Dr. Perry out at Parkland?"

"Oh, fine young man!" he replied.

I said, "Well, we want Dr. Perry on this thing we're doing for CBS, and he won't talk to me."

And Sterrett said, "Oh, you don't have a problem. You just sit there by your phone and I'll be back to you in a little bit." In a few minutes, Sterrett called me back and said, "You go ahead and call Dr. Perry. He'll be glad to talk to you." I know Sterrett talked to Tom Shires, who was the chief surgeon, and Shires told Perry, "Hey, you need to talk to Barker."

Sure enough, I called Dr. Perry, and he gave me a great interview, the only one-on-one interview he ever did. We even got to be good friends. But it shows the power Sterrett had to get things done.

Another legendary Dallas County official I knew well was Sheriff Bill Decker. When Jack Ruby was on trial in 1964 for murdering Lee Oswald, a CBS production assistant named Bobby Wussler (who, as Robert Wussler, became president of CBS Television and started CNN with Ted Turner) was in Dallas for the trial. We had a wireless Vega microphone. Bobby saw we had the mike and he asked, "Does that thing work?" I told him it worked great.

He asked, "Gosh, do you mind if I go out and play with it?"

I said, "Nah, go ahead and take it." And I forgot all about it. We weren't using it for anything.

After the trial was over and Jack Ruby had been found guilty, Decker called me one day and said, "Hey, come over here, I've got something for you." I went into his office, and there he sat wearing his trademark fedora. He reached down and opened up his drawer and pulled out the Vega mike and pitched it to me. I asked him, "Where'd you get that?"

He said, "Well, it's an interesting little story. You know that little Jew boy from New York?" (In those days, Texas sheriffs hadn't learned about political correctness.) "Every time we cleared the courtroom, I had the deputies go in there and they would search the room. We went in there one day and they were feeling under the seats, and here was this mike taped under the seat." The deputies gave the mike to Decker, and he sat back to wait and see what was going to happen when Wussler came back. Decker said Bobby sat down, reached under the chair, and realized the mike was gone. "Then he was down on the floor, on his hands and knees, looking for the mike," Decker said. Wussler never told me about the mike. I don't guess I blame him.

Then there was the great tip Decker gave me when Ruby was dying from cancer at Parkland Hospital. Ruby had been there for some time. I never screen a phone call; a reporter who screens a phone call is a fool. One day in January 1967, the phone rang and a voice said, "He's dead." I instantly knew Decker's voice and I knew he was talking about Ruby.

I said, "What? How do you know?"

Decker just repeated, "I said he's dead."

I said, "Thank you, sir, very much." We went on the air and had about a forty-minute jump on the story.

I immediately gave it to the wire services, and they put it out, saying, "In a copyrighted story, KRLD in Dallas reports . . ." So, very quickly, the other stations were reporting it. But the administrator at Parkland himself did not know that Ruby had died. Everyone was calling him about it. "I've got to find out about this," he told the reporters.

But that was the kind of friend Bill Decker was. He didn't owe me that. There was just something that he liked about me. I never went out of my way to push that friendship. I was asked a hundred times, "How did you find out?" But something else I learned along the way was to never reveal a source. I think the sheriff would forgive me for telling it now.

Decker was an old-time lawman. He was in on the killing of Bonnie and Clyde in 1934. Back in the early '30s, when the Depression was at its worst, guys were trying to get into Dallas riding on freight trains. Decker was a deputy patrolling the railroad yard and wouldn't let them get off the train. But one of the guys on a freight train was W. O. Bankston, who became one of the most successful car dealers in Dallas.

The train stopped, and W. O. was trying to get off. At first, Decker told him he couldn't get off, but something clicked between them. For some reason, Decker let Bankston, out of all these hobos, off the train. They became fast friends for life. Bankston got to be the big Ford dealer in Dallas and he gave Decker a new car every year, the same kind of Ford he drove. And Decker let W. O. put red flashers in the grill of his car, which, I guess, was his way of saying thanks.

If you look at the photos from the time of the Kennedy assassination, you'll see the Dallas police detectives all wearing the "five-gallon," smaller-size Stetson hats. That's because the head of the detectives, Will Fritz, wore a Stetson. In the famous Bob Jackson photo of Ruby shooting Oswald, you see Dallas police detective Jim Leavelle in a Stetson. But down at the sherriff's office, Decker wore a fedora. And so every Dallas County deputy wore a fedora.

Decker smoked constantly, but he never had his own cigarettes. He was always surrounded by deputies, and as you were talking to him, he'd just kind of hold out his hand, and one of the deputies would deliver a fresh cigarette. And then someone would light it. Decker was "god" to them.

The Dallas press liked Decker. In those days, the Dallas Press Club's "Headliner of the Year" was a big thing. The "headliner" was a Dallas person who had been prominent in the news, not a reporter. We'd also award an "All-Time Headliner," and one year, we named Bill Decker. It was a black-tie affair, and he got this big plaque. A couple of weeks after he died, it was just about dark one evening and somebody rang the doorbell. I went to the door and it was Mrs. Decker. She said, "Bill always wanted you to have this." She gave me the All-Time Headliner plaque. He was just that kind of guy.

Yet another of the great characters I found along the way was State District Judge Joe Brown, whom I mention in Chapter 5. Judge Brown was a product of the old Houston Law College, and he had a way of interpreting the law and conducting a trial that was unique, to say the least. He presided over one of three district courts in Dallas at the time, but Judge Brown's courtroom was by far the most interesting.

For example, the trial of the celebrated stripper Candy Barr took place in his courtroom. Candy, a few years ahead of her time, had fallen prey to the evils of marijuana, and the Dallas police were determined to make an example of her. So they brought out the heavyweights to make sure she didn't walk out of that courtroom a free woman. But it was indeed a walk out of the courtroom during the lunch break that I remember. Jim Underwood, our nighttime weatherman, served as a news cameraman during the day, and Judge Brown liked to have Jim in his courtroom. As a matter of fact, he liked for Jim to stand up next to the bench, where they could visit a bit if the proceedings got dull. Well, back to Candy's walk.

Candy started to walk out, and the judge grabbed Jim's camera and filmed away as Candy exited with every bump and grind she knew. Jim got his camera back and headed for the newsroom. He told me what had happened. We quickly processed the film, and the judge turned out to be quite a cameraman. Jim asked me, "What do we do with the film?" I quickly told him to take it back and give it to the judge. I didn't want a mistrial on our conscience. Jim gave him the film, and I have no idea whatever happened to it.

Very much on the Dallas scene in those days was a portrait artist named Dimitri Vail. He was quite good, so good he was often kidded that his paintings were really blown-up photographs. Every celebrity who came to town would more than likely have his or her portrait painted by Dimitri, and he did some locals, too. I rated only a black-

and-white charcoal. My son Ben has it now in Washington, D.C., where he lives and works.

We had Dimitri on *Comment* frequently. He was such a character, a real symbol of Dallas in the '60s. While he was doing the interview, he liked to get down on the floor and stand on his head because he was into yoga. He baked the best bread I ever ate, a kind of nutty fruit bread, very rich. He would bring it down to the station.

Dimitri married a wealthy woman who owned a big mansion out on Armstrong Parkway, and she kind of let him do his thing. Dimitri wanted to paint every star who came to town, and he did a hell of a job. Dimitri used to hold court in the dining room at the "Purple Palace," a Holiday Inn on North Central Expressway. He had a table there with a red telephone. As you came in, you'd see the table with a sign on it: "Reserved for Dimitri Vail." He had all his portraits hanging there, and he'd call people on the phone and have them come have lunch with him.

Dimitri didn't give the paintings to his subjects; he liked to keep them. But he would get a local restaurant to stage an unveiling and hope the subject would be on hand for the event. He painted Judge Brown and got Alfred Martínez of El Fenix to host the event. The judge liked unveilings so much, he ended up being "un-Vailed" three times by Dimitri. Incidentally, as far as I know, the only portrait of a famous person Dimitri ever sold was one of Alabama Governor George Wallace. "The state of Alabama paid me $15,000 for it," Dimitri told me.

You may remember that in the opening of this book I told you that I once dropped a story because of pressure from my higher-ups. Well, I hate to admit it, but the paternalistic position of the *Times Herald* indeed once led me to kill a big story that we were ready to report.

Whenever I hear a mention of the Dallas Crime Commission, I can't help but think back to the time when it was headed by a man whose name we thought to be "John McKee." He was by his own account the city's top crime fighter. He was an arrogant little guy. I got to know him because he liked being a guest on *Comment*. I didn't look forward to John's being on the show because of his bad breath. He never showed up without that cigar.

The Crime Commission job didn't pay a salary. John McKee was an employee of the Ford Motor Company as a government-liaison type. But the other job McKee held was the one that had many Dallasites ready to shine his shoes even if they didn't need a shine. He was a powerhouse in Freemasonry. Yes, Freemasonry, the proud old fraternity. And John McKee could make a Mason's dream come true—a thirty-third degree! I couldn't believe how they wanted that. It was the key to forever. How did he do it? With his strong ties to the Scottish Rite in Texas. He had been the Grand Master of the Grand Lodge of Texas at one time. But John McKee had enemies within the Masonic Order, none stronger than a Dallas attorney, Searcy Lee Johnson. Johnson had heard that John McKee's past was a dark one, and he set out to see just how dark.

In 1968, Johnson hired private investigators to get the dirt on John McKee. Johnson's investigators found information that suggested "John McKee" was really James Zullinger from Pennsylvania, an alleged navy deserter. Searcy Lee Johnson intended to share his findings with the world, and he did. And the walls began tumbling down around James Zullinger, a.k.a. John McKee.[1]

But Searcy Lee was on to something else that involved James Zullinger. Johnson told Bill Ceverha, my able assistant news director, where to look in a certain courthouse in Central Texas for some very interesting transactions. Bill looked and Bill found. Zullinger had strong ties to a very high-ranking member of the Scottish Rite in Texas. We knew we were onto something hot.

The '68 Democratic convention was being held in Chicago, and Bill and I were going to cover it. We rode the special train the Democrats had chartered, and a lot of big Democrat names were on board. Crawford Martin, the Texas attorney general who wore an eye patch just like ill-fated aviator Wiley Post and the Hathaway shirt man, was among them. We thought, this is a stroke of luck; we'll tell the AG what we've found. We assumed he would want to get right on it. Alas, when we mentioned it, Martin shook so badly he almost lost his lapel pin, if you know what I mean. Bill remembers Crawford's exact words: "Eddie, you know we just don't have enough manpower to go after this kind of white-collar crime. We just let these organizations take care of themselves."

It wasn't long before I got the order: "Lay off that story, forget it, *right now!*" And whose voice carried those words? None other than the treasurer and chief spokesman for the *Times Herald*, Robert Jensen. I had never paid much attention to his lapels. It was quite a story, and Ceverha's digging into it was in the best traditions of the business. A few years later, Dallas journalist Hugh Aynesworth wrote an article in *Newsweek* telling the whole tale. It was frustrating, because we really had the story so much earlier. In 1972, Zullinger was convicted of embezzling funds from the Masonic Order.

Okay, you purists, you First Amendment fanatics, get off my back. I know you're asking "Well, why didn't you tell Bob Jensen, the *Times Herald*, and KRLD to take that job and shove it! You're a man of principle!"

Well, offhand, I can think of six reasons: a wife and five children expecting to be put to bed every night with a full stomach. Not to mention a modest savings account due to the rather low salaries paid by my employer, no other job available in town, and a family that didn't want to leave Dallas. As the old Indian saying goes, "Spend some time in my moccasins, Kemo Sabe, before you start telling me how to build the fire."

Here's one I almost forgot to tell you about—the Meadors from Muenster. Where do I start? How about the Saturday afternoon I got a telephone call that set us on the trail of a most unusual family? The caller was a prestigious Dallas photographer at the time, but I had never met him.

"Mr. Barker," he began, "I have a story to tell you that I think you will find very interesting."

I replied, "Please go ahead. I'm listening."

He asked, "Did you ever hear of the Meadors from Muenster?"

I responded, "Not that I recall." But then I remembered that for the past several Christmases and other holidays we had been getting this huge arrangement of bird-of-paradise flowers with a card that said, "Happy Holidays from the Meadors."

"Who are the Meadors?" Jane would ask.

"Darned if I know," was my reply. I suppose they felt they knew me from KRLD-TV and radio. Back to the caller.

The Meadors owed the caller a rather large sum of money for the work he had done for them, including shooting photos on a special train the Meadors had chartered to bring their daughter's classmates from the Hockaday School and other friends to their palatial ranch home outside Muenster, north of Fort Worth. Food, a band, the works on the train. The photographer was at the end of his rope in trying to collect his bill. "I'm coming to you," he told me, "because Channel 4 news can probably help me and some other creditors."

Well, the Muenster Meadors were a story and a half. They were from Indiana, and it was unknown as to how they ended up in Muenster. They supposedly had money and didn't mind that they ran up a six-figure bill with Neiman Marcus, or a caterer, or a florist, a candlestick maker, or what have you. The Meadors were guests of LBJ on *Air Force One* on trips to and from Washington. But the thing that wasn't known was that old Ernest Meador was illiterate and a con man with a con for a wife, Margaret. This was getting juicer by the minute, so I called in our lover of a juicy story, Wes Wise.

In his usual form, Wes was off and running. The stories kept coming. Once, Wes and the late Buster McGregor, our assignments editor and sometime photographer, went to Alabama to find another old codger who had helped Ernest find his pot of gold, a convent of Catholic nuns in Indiana. That's what I said: he got upwards of $5 million from this order of nuns in some sort of phony land deal. Since Ernest Meador was illiterate, he never put anything in writing. The Meadors were finally getting exposed, and Wes helped that exposure considerably in a half-hour documentary we did in prime time. Ernest finally died, as the best and the worst of us must, and Neiman's came a gunning for its money. Not much was left, so Margaret was convicted of fraud and put away for a spell.

I met a lot of Dallas's famous and infamous through *Comment*. One day we received a call, and this little weak voice said, "This is H. L. Hunt. I want to talk to you."

I said, "Well, call me when I get off the air, and we'll talk."

And so the old man called and said, "I want to be on *Comment*."

Of course, I said, "We'd love to have you on *Comment.*" So we set a time for him to come on.

H. L. Hunt was one of Dallas's most colorful and, to some, notorious, businessmen. He had made a fortune in oil, but before that he had been a world-class gambler. In Arkansas, for years after he left there, whenever they'd run a story about him in the newspaper, they'd refer to him as, "Haroldson Lafayette Hunt, former El Dorado, Arkansas, gambler." By the '60s, he was known as (depending on your point of view) a fierce or a nutty anti-Communist. He was a John Birch Society type of guy. But he was never a big figure in Dallas politics.

I was looking out the window while waiting for H. L. Hunt, and here comes this big, black Olds 98, and plastered all over that car were these *Life Line* stickers. Remember the old *Life Line* hard-line conservative radio program that Hunt sponsored? The old man came in, and I said, "Mr. Hunt, this is a real pleasure," and all of this BS. So we go in to do the show. I'm not sure who was doing it that day, whether it was Jim Underwood, Frank Gleiber, Bill Mercer, Dick Wheeler, or someone else. And Mr. Hunt said, "I'd like to read a statement." He brings out this thing, about twenty pages long.

I said gently, "Mr. Hunt, you can't do that. We just want to talk to you." Well, as it turned out, he liked it so much he wanted to come back. It got to where we'd have him on the show about once a month.

One day he called me and said he had something he wanted to film. He asked if I had a photographer he could hire to come out and make some film. I said, yes, we had George "Sandy" Sanderson, an old newsreel cameraman, a great guy, but tough and ornery. He was then in his sixties, and the *Times Herald* wouldn't let me put him on the permanent payroll because it would cost the company too much in benefits. So he worked on an hourly basis. I called Sandy in and told him H. L. Hunt wanted someone to shoot some film. "I don't know what he wants, but I told him it would cost $100," I told Sandy.

So Sandy went out to see H. L. Hunt. He came back and said, "You're not going to believe what I went out there to do." He developed the film. It was old man Hunt's oldest son, Hassie. This is part of a very strange and sad story. Hassie had been successful in his own right as a young oilman. But in his twenties, he was diagnosed as a schizophrenic and had a prefrontal lobotomy. It was the recommended treatment at the time. Remember, one of Joseph and Rose Kennedy's daughters was lobotomized.

In the film, Hassie, then in his forties, is dressed just like his father, in a dark suit and string tie. H. L. is holding him by the hand and leading him around. They had a couple of pet deer, and Hassie goes over and pets the deer. This is what H. L. wanted. He was sentimental about his son. Sandy took the film back to him, and Hunt paid him the $100.

Another time, Mr. Hunt called and wanted my wife, Jane, and me to come out to his estate on White Rock Lake, "Mount Vernon," a replica of George Washington's mansion, only bigger. By then, his first wife had died and he had this other family waiting in Louisiana, whom he moved into this stately manor. We entered Mount Vernon, and Jane noticed these awful, horrible drapes. "They probably were put up when Washington lived here," she cracked.

I never did figure out why we were there. But two of his daughters, in their teens, were going to entertain. We all sat, and the daughters sang various songs, and then they sang this takeoff on "How Much Is That Doggie in the Window?" It had something to do with the "HLH" retail products that he marketed. They sang, we all clapped, and then we left.

In 1968, Bill Ceverha and I were in Miami to cover the Republican convention. Who should we run into but H. L. Hunt. "Mr. Hunt, good to see you. What are you doing down here?" I asked.

He said, "I'm going to get Gerald Ford elected president of the United States." Which came as a shock, because Ford was not running and was not all that nationally prominent at the time. "Come up to my room, I want to show you something," Mr. Hunt said. So we go up to Mr. Hunt's room, just an ordinary hotel room, and he had all this stuff about Gerald Ford.

Of course, nothing came of it. Richard Nixon had it pretty well sewn up. To my knowledge, H. L. Hunt was the only person in Miami working for Gerald Ford. Of course, it turns out Mr. Hunt was ahead of time, at least where Ford was concerned.

A roguish Dallas real-estate man named O. L. Nelms used to buy an ad in the personal column of both papers every day that said, "Thanks for helping O. L. Nelms make another million." He had trailers parked all over town with the same message.

I'm not sure how I got to know him, but one day he called me. His mother had died. Like H. L. Hunt, he wanted to hire a cameraman, this one to come and take pictures of the funeral. So I called Sandy in: "Sandy, got another job for you." He went out to O. L. Nelms's mother's funeral, and O. L. directed what he wanted shot. And again, Sandy came back and said, "Barker, you gotta see this." There's O. L.'s mother's coffin getting ready to be lowered into the grave, and the coffin has this big floral arrangement on it. O. L., apparently on cue from Sandy, comes over, looks at the camera, looks down at his mother, reaches down, breaks a flower off, holds it up to his nose and sniffs it, and puts it back on the coffin.

Bill Sparkman, at Sparkman-Hillcrest Funeral Home, told me this story. O. L. owned the Yello-Belly Drag Strip, which still exists in Grand Prairie. There was a driver out there named Lefty, and Lefty got killed. Sparkman got the body. O. L. wanted to wait till the next Saturday night, when they were racing again, to bury Lefty and told Bill he wanted "the biggest hearse you've got." He wanted to put Lefty's coffin in there so he could have one more trip down the track.

Despite the great years I had in radio and television, I regret that I never worked for a newspaper. The major figures of early television news all came from the newspapers—Cronkite, Edward R. Murrow and all the CBS fellows known as "Murrow's boys," David Brinkley at NBC and, later, ABC. I just have so much respect for newspaper journalism. I have always had this very close relationship with newspaper people. Even when I worked at KMAC, my friends were Harold Scherwitz, who was the sports editor of the *San Antonio Light*; Johnny Janes, who was Harold's number-two guy; Dick Peebles at the

San Antonio Express; Bill Bellamy, who later became publisher of the *Express-News*. I felt very close to those guys. For some reason, they really accepted me, and I was very comfortable with them.

I addressed the journalism class at St. Mark's School in Dallas awhile back and I told those kids, "If you really want to be journalists, forget about television. If you want to be remembered one hundred years from now, it's going to be what you wrote, not what you said."

I was always more interested in beating the newspapers than the other television stations were. Ironically, as a result, I became good friends with all of the editors at the *Dallas Morning News*: Johnny King, Tom Simmons, Bob Miller, and Bill Reeves, who later became the publisher of the *Denton Record Chronicle*. And the same thing with the people at the *Times Herald*, fellows like Bert Holmes, Charlie Dameron, Hal Lewis, and Jim Lehrer (who's gone on to great fame at PBS).

I always liked and admired Felix McKnight, who was the managing editor of the *Morning News* when I came to Dallas and later jumped to the *Times Herald*, as co-publisher and editor. So many of the great newspaper people started out as sports writers. McKnight was the Southwest sports editor for the Associated Press for many years, and he served as president and chairman of the Cotton Bowl Association for a long time. He and I just hit it off for some reason. I always thought Felix was a great newspaperman. He covered the unspeakably terrible 1937 New London, Texas, school explosion for the AP, in which 280 children and 14 teachers died. "Today, a generation died," was Felix's unforgettable, heartbreaking lead sentence.

When the *Morning News* did a "High Profile" article on me several years ago, Felix wrote me a note: "We really ought to get together. I'm going to be 90 years old soon." He gave the date of his birthday, and it fell on a Saturday. At that time, I was reliving my youth by doing Saturday newscasts on KRLD radio. I announced on the air, "A lot of you will remember Felix McKnight, the great newspaperman. He's ninety years old today." And McKnight called me and said, "My God, Barker, what did you do?" He said he was flooded with calls from well-wishers. He repeated, "Why don't we have lunch?" I said I'd love to. So he set it up over at the Dallas Country Club and we had this great lunch, Felix, Jim Chambers, another friend and *Times Herald* publisher, and me. Felix died at the age of ninety-three.

Of the state and national political figures I've known, the Democratic Speaker of the House from the Northeast Texas town of Bonham, Sam Rayburn, was certainly a favorite of mine. Of course, I was not alone in admiring "Mr. Sam." In the Sam Rayburn Library in Bonham, there's an interview with Mr. Sam that you hear when you take the tour. That's me with the Speaker.

For some reason, we just became very friendly. He was gruff on the outside, but he had great character, and I just used to go up and visit with him. So one day I told him, "You know, Mr. Speaker, I'd like to bring a camera crew up here, and the two of us will just sit and talk."

He lowered his bald head, looked at me warily, and said accusingly, "You want to do my obituary."

And I said, "No, no, no, Mr. Speaker, don't even think about that!"

So he said, "All right, I'll make a deal with you. I'll do it if you'll give all the film to my library."

I said, "That's a deal. You've got it." So I brought the cameraman, Jim Murray, and we spent a couple of days with him. We were doing the film outside, and he always had that darn hat on. Finally I said, "Mr. Speaker, would you mind taking that hat off for a little bit?"

And he said, "How long do you want me to have my hat off? You know, my head gets sunburned." Of course, he didn't have a hair on his head.

You know, the saying was he took care of the people in the Fourth District, and he did. All you have to do is look at the Veterans' Hospital in Bonham and everything else that's scattered around Fannin County and the rest of the district. Sometimes you just sense that a person is "in command." There was no doubt that Sam Rayburn was the engineer on this train.

I'll always remember one thing that really hit me about him. One time, I was there in his office, just the two of us, and the lady who worked for him for so many years knocked on the door and came in. "Mr. Speaker," she said, "old [so-and-so] is here and wants to see you."

And he said, "How's he doin'? Whatever happened to that boy of his? The one that was having the trouble?" He turned to me and said, "I've got to take care of this district. We'll do this later." Here was this old farmer sitting out there in his overalls, and Sam Rayburn greeted him like they were brothers and took him into his office.

People in the news business tend to be cynical about politicians, and not without reason. But most of the newspeople in Dallas loved Rayburn. Johnny Runyon was the publisher of the *Dallas Times Herald*. He'd come over to the KRLD newsroom at noon and we'd play dollar poker. In 1960, of course, Lyndon Johnson was on the Democratic ticket with John F. Kennedy. Johnson was Rayburn's protégé, and Mr. Sam had a lot emotionally invested in Lyndon. In those days, the newspaper endorsements were very, very important, but it looked like the *Times Herald* was going to endorse Richard Nixon. It was really getting kind of hairy, because Johnson was from Texas and there was a lot of pressure for the paper to endorse Kennedy-Johnson.

Of course, everyone knew the election was going to be awfully close. One day, Runyon came over and said, "I've got a telegram here that breaks my heart. I want you to read it." And he handed it to me. It was from Sam Rayburn, urging him, "Please support Kennedy and Lyndon." Johnny loved Rayburn, and he said, "It breaks my heart that I can't do this. We can't support Jack Kennedy." Dallas may have been Democratic in those days, but that didn't necessarily mean liberal then.

They used to have a Sam Rayburn Symposium at Texas A&M University–Commerce, formerly East Texas State University, because that's where Rayburn went to school when it was known as Mayo College. Whoever was supposed to be the speaker for the banquet in 1999 called and said he couldn't come. The school turned to H. G. Delaney, the Rayburn Library director, and asked who knew Mr. Rayburn and could speak at the banquet. I feel honored that he said, "Eddie Barker." I went to Commerce, and it was one of the better speeches I ever made, because it was from the heart.

Unlike Rayburn, I did not know Lyndon Johnson well, but here's a story about him. When they got ready to put television on the air in the late '40s, they needed the highest point in Dallas County, Cedar Hill, to put a tower. It was right down at the end of the runway at the Naval Air Station, and the Federal Aviation Administration turned down the positioning of the tower. Well, Johnson was in the U.S. Senate at that time. By the stroke of his pen, or whatever he made strokes with, the tower was done. And to hell with the navy; they just had to curve their flights in and out of the airport.

It's ironic that the *Times Herald* didn't endorse Kennedy and Johnson in '60, because in every other way, the paper treated Johnson like a god. It was really kind of pathetic. If he came to town, the *Times Herald* always wanted KRLD to do an interview with him. And he certainly wanted whatever niceties we could offer him. We didn't have a lot to offer, except we would always get this big, overstuffed leather chair, which looked like a throne, and set it up for him.

I had a meeting with Johnson just before he became president. I was in Washington the week before the JFK assassination for some reason, and I went to see Joe Poole, one of the congressmen from Dallas. Joe Poole Lake is named for him. Poole was really a likable, lovable, roly-poly little guy. In the summertime, he stood down on the street corner and handed out fans like you used to get at a church or a funeral home that said, "Keep cool with Poole." Anyway, Joe and I went to have lunch in the House cafeteria, and when we were through, he said, "Let's go by and see Lyndon."

I said, "Joe, why do you want to go over there?" I didn't want to bother the vice-president of the United States. He said, "Aw, he doesn't have anything to do. Let's go over there and say hi."

Johnson's secretary said, "Stick around, he's having lunch right now." He was meeting with Bobby Kennedy and a couple of other big Democrats. Sure enough, the door opened, Bobby came out, and there was Lyndon. We went in. I had met him before, but he didn't know me from Adam. The first thing he did was to reach under his desk and press a button, and, just like that, here was a photographer. Johnson knew the value of photos with the folks from home. He sent it to me within a couple of weeks.

We chatted for a while, strictly small talk. Joe didn't have anything to talk to Lyndon about. Finally Johnson asked me, "When are you going back to Dallas?"

I said, "Tonight."

And he said, "Well, if you can go tomorrow, come ride down on the plane with me." I couldn't because I had a meeting or something, but it would certainly have been an interesting flight.

I found it hard to like Johnson. He always seemed a little phony to me. But, as everyone knows, he was a brilliant politician. And that means he related well to people. He came through Love Field one time when he was vice-president, and we went out to cover his visit. I had seen a serviceman in the airport. I got to talking to the boy, and he told me he had to get home because his mother or someone had died, a real tragic story.

I went over to Johnson and said, "I thought I'd tell you this. That young serviceman over there—his mother has just died. It's a very tragic time for him, and I thought you'd want to know that." Well, he could have ignored the information, but without hesitation, he went over there. Johnson stayed with that young soldier for a long time and put his arm around him. I thought, well, he did it for a political reason—of course, Johnson knew his photograph would be taken consoling the youngster—but maybe he also did it out of genuine concern. Who knows what's in someone's heart?

Just as Johnson was Rayburn's protégé, John Connally, the governor of Texas, was Johnson's protégé. And while I never really warmed up to Johnson, Connally was my favorite politician. I never had anything but high regard for him. He was a strong leader. Like Sam Rayburn, he was an excellent negotiator. He and his wife, Nellie, were just very nice, charming people. You never felt being around him, the governor of Texas, that he considered himself a big deal. He just took his success in stride, and he was very gracious.

Maybe one reason I liked Connally so much is that we came from the same place. One day I got to talking to a cousin of mine, several years older than me, and she said, "Have you ever met John Connally?"

I said, "Oh, yeah, I know him."

She replied, "Well, do you know where John Connally grew up? Right down the street from where you did." So, as it turned out, Connally, though more than ten years older than me, grew up in the same old San Antonio neighborhood, just a few hundred feet from my family's home. He had been born in Floresville, but spent part of his childhood in the Harlandale section of San Antonio.

Besides the interviews I did with him, other situations brought Connally and me quite close, although not in the happiest of circumstances. These were very personal encounters. Once, I got a call from somebody at CBS. "You know John Connally, don't you?" I said, sure. "Well, you need to know that we're about to do a 'gut job' on him. You need to get a copy of the script to him." My source said he would take it to the airport and ask someone on the flight to carry it. The source then called me, described the person, and I met the flight. This was after Connally's tenure as governor, but he was considered a potential presidential candidate.

I read the script and it was a half-hour piece, probably for the old CBS Reports news program. It got into a lot of things that were nothing but innuendo and rumor. They were trying to make the case that he had his hand in the till at a savings and loan in San Antonio. I called him and said, "John, I've got something here that you really need to see." I briefed him on it, and he knew absolutely nothing about it. I called Pollard Simons, a commercial developer who was a good friend of John's, and said we had to get this script to Connally. He said, "Well, I'll just send my jet down with it." So they flew down and gave it to Connally. I don't know what happened, but CBS never ran the story, which was good, because it was a terrible, poorly researched story.

Because of his East Coast background and style, we don't think of George Bush, the elder, as a Texas president, as we do LBJ and George Bush, the younger. But, of course, he was. I didn't have much contact with him, but I do remember him at the 1968 Republican convention in Miami Beach. He was a congressman from Houston at the time. He had good connections with Richard Nixon, and I think he thought he might have a chance at the vice-presidential nomination. (As it turned out, he'd have been a far better choice than Spiro Agnew.)

We all got to know George at the hotel. He could be kind of off-the-wall at times, and he was a young, athletic fellow. So one day he rented an early version of what we'd today call a Jet-Ski and rode it out into the surf. The motor died on him, and he started floating in. The lifeguard started yelling at him, "Go back! Go back!" He didn't want George bringing that thing in near the beach with the swimmers. But there wasn't much else poor George could do. He couldn't get the engine started again. Finally, he just dived off of it and told the lifeguard, "You can keep the damn thing!" Even future presidents have their clumsy moments.

I loved broadcasting the news on KRLD-TV and radio all those years and getting to know all those eminent people. But the time comes to move on. That time came for me sooner than I expected at KRLD.

References:

[1] Lee H. Latham, *A Survey of the Greater Dallas Crime Commission and Its Effect on the Criminal Justice System* (Master's thesis. University of North Texas, 2001).

8

"I Knew I Had to Do It"

Iworked for only two radio (or radio/television) stations in
my career, except for KPLT in Paris, where I now host a weekday-
morning gabfest. The first was KMAC in San Antonio, and then
it was KRLD. KRLD was everything I could want as a newsman,
because of the tremendous backing I had from the president of
the station, Clyde Rembert. My wife, Jane, says, "He's the only
person you still call 'Mister.'" And then I always got tremendous
backing from Times Herald publishers Jim Chambers and Johnny
Runyon. They were old newspaper reporters and they saw what I
was trying to do. A lot of newspaper people resented television, but
they didn't.

But then, as you know, the Times Herald and KRLD were sold to
the Times Mirror Company, the parent company of the Los Angeles
Times, in 1970. I knew there would be changes. Mr. Rembert had
already retired. Ves Box took over, but he soon retired. So Bill Baker, a
salesman, became the new general manager of KRLD, but he was just
a holdover until Times Mirror brought in its own people.

Leaving KRLD was something I didn't want to do, but I knew I
had to. It was no longer the same. The good old days were gone
forever, and the days ahead were full of storm clouds for me, not
because I wasn't doing a good job, but because the man Times Mirror
brought in to run the station in 1972, John McCrory, wanted no part

of the past. He wanted his own "team," and I realized I wouldn't be on it.

I had lunch with McCrory one day at the Fairmont so he could see whether we were on the "same team," or words to that effect. He brought with him a man I could only liken to the fellow who follows behind the elephants, Wayne Thomas. I first noticed him prowling around the newsroom, reading over my reporters' stories as they wrote them, never coming to ask me anything. I got the clue.

I made a big mistake in telling McCrory that Bill Ceverha, my longtime assistant, would be ideal as my replacement when the time came. Well, that was the end of Bill's time with Channel 4, and he soon joined me in the public-relations business. McCrory named Thomas news director.

John Van Cronkite, the wise old political public-relations practitioner, had been after me for a long time to join him. John was a fascinating character and for years was the advisor to the Citizens Charter Association and okayed every candidate who ran under that banner. Van Cronkite and I had lunch one day. He said, "Political PR is really where you ought to be. You've done the television thing at KRLD." He had already hired Jim Underwood from KRLD, after he saw how effective Jim had been running Wes Wise's campaign. It was time to do it, and I did. I first came into Van Cronkite's organization as his employee, but it was understood that I would soon buy him out, and I did, creating Eddie Barker Associates.

I was not about to give McCrory the word I was leaving. Let it be a surprise, I thought, and it was. I went across the street to the *Times Herald* and told Jim Chambers and Felix McKnight. I asked if one of them would tell McCrory when he got back from out of town. Jim smiled and said, "I'll do the honors." The *Times Herald* board threw a dinner for me at the City Club and gave me a resolution commending my outstanding service to the station. I don't recall ever talking to McCrory again; he certainly didn't attend the farewell party the staff gave me in the newsroom on my last day. It was a wonderful part of my life, and I am thankful for the years we, KRLD and I, had together.

Eddie in the KRLD newsroom, circa 1970. Assistant News Director Bill Ceverha is seated to L

Legendary actor Humphrey Bogart. Eddie remembers that Bogart was a relaxed and friendly guest.

Genial CBS "House Party" host Art Linkletter visits with Jim Underwood, Wes Wise (standing) and Eddie.

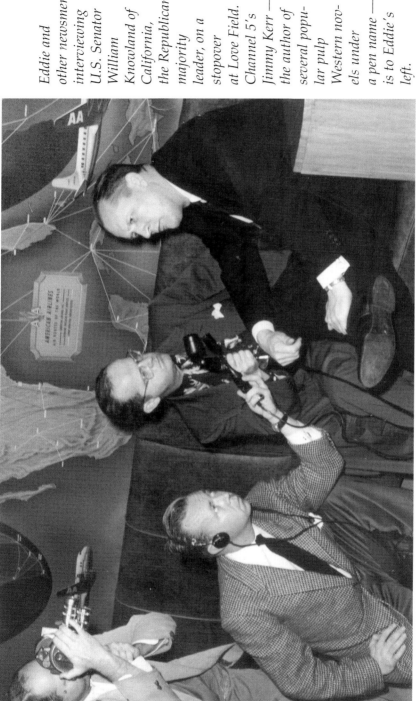

Eddie and other newsmen interviewing U.S. Senator William Knowland of California, the Republican majority leader, on a stopover at Love Field. Channel 5's Jimmy Kerr — the author of several popular pulp Western novels under a pen name — is to Eddie's left.

Dimitri Vail, the flamboyant Dallas portrait artist, speaks on
"Comment." Vail liked to do yoga exercises while being interviewed.

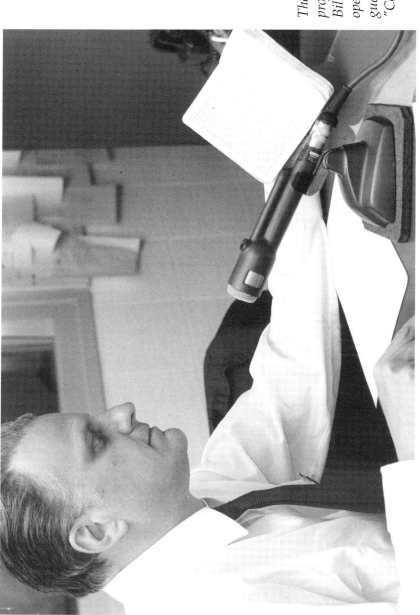

The striking profile of evangelist Billy Graham, Bible open. Graham guested on KRLD's "Comment."

The wondrously talented Steve Allen —talk-show host, comedian, actor, composer, author—visits Dallas. KRLD-TV carried Allen's syndicated talk show in the 1960s. Eddie's wife, Jane, is to Steve's left. On his right is Gloria (Mrs. Ves) Box, and at right is Marilyn (Mrs. Joe Dave) Scott.

Pop singer Frankie Laine, best known for "I Believe," "You Gave Me a Mountain" and the theme to "Rawhide," in the KRLD radio studio.

Hypnotist Franz Polgar casts his spell on the "Comment" audience. The extravagantly dressed woman at left is unidentified.

The winner of two Nobel Prizes, one for chemistry and one for peace, Dr. Linus Pauling, with Underwood, Mercer, Frank Gleiber and Barker. Eddie asked Dr. Pauling to scribble a mathematical formula. He did, and Eddie hung it on the KRLD studio wall.

*Eddie interviews Robert Spears, the man at the
center of the mysterious crash of a jetliner.*

*Eddie interviewing Sen. Joseph McCarthy of Wisconsin,
the pursuer of Communists in government, real and imagined.
While it looks as though they're enjoying themselves,
Eddie remembers that it was a tense interview.*

*Eddie has fond memories of interviewing then-Vice-President Richard
Nixon. He says Nixon was engaging and approachable, not at all like
the image most people have of him.*

In the 1950s, Arthur Godfrey was perhaps the biggest star in television and radio, with the possible exception of Lucille Ball. His CBS programs aired on KRLD.

Eddie with El Fenix restaurant executive Alfred Martinez and the late Dallas-Fort Worth anchorman Chip Moody.

Radio - Television News Directors Association former presidents.
Back row (l to r): Bill Small, Bill Roberts, Chet Castleman, Paul Davis, Jack Shelley, Wayne Vriesman, Jack Hogan, Jay Crouse, Bill Monroe, Wayne Godsey, Chuck Harrison, Ralph Renick, Sig Mickelson.
Front row: John Salsbury, Jack Krueger, Jim Borman, Eddie Barker, Curt Beckman, Hal Baker, Bob Gamble, Ernie Schultz, Bos Johnson.

Barker family (l. to r.) Jeanne, Ben, Eddie, Leslie, Susan, Jane, Allan. The dog is "Sam."

The Barker clan makes an annual trip to Estes Park, Colorado, each summer. Here they have gathered at a favorite spot in town, the Dunraven Inn.

Seems like old times. Eddie and Jane Barker greet Walter Cronkite at a Press Club of Dallas event in 2004.

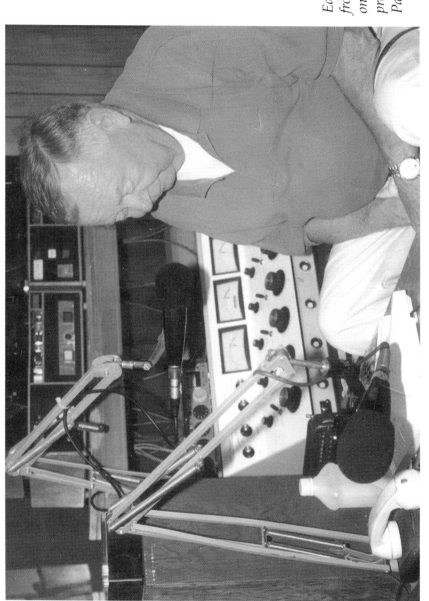

Eddie taking a call from an "associate" on his "Talk of Paris" program on KPLT in Paris, Texas.

When I look back on it now, one of most satisfying things about the years I spent in broadcasting was seeing young people who started out with us at KRLD grow and develop into great professionals, some of them now at the peak of their careers.

Not too long before I left KRLD, I met an ambitious young man named Bob Phillips, the same Bob Phillips who today hosts the wonderful *Texas Country Reporter*, which features well-crafted vignettes of rural Lone Star life. I hired him to the lowest-level job we had short of cleaning the toilets, and he took it from there.

When I was working on this book, I contacted Bob to see if he'd like to contribute a comment or two about starting out at KRLD. He generously responded with a lovely memoir that says more about him than it does about me, although he didn't intend it that way. Here it is:

Eddie Barker changed my life.

I was a poor kid that grew up in Old East Dallas. Daddy managed a full service gas station for Dunlap-Swain Tire Company on the west side of Southern Methodist University and Mama was Executive Housekeeper for The Hilton Inn on the southeast side of SMU. I had my heart set on attending that school some referred to as "The Ivy League School of the South," but SMU also had the highest tuition in our part of the country. After graduation from high school in 1969, I took some courses at El Centro College, part of the Dallas County Community College District, with the hope that a miracle would occur and I would somehow be allowed to go to school "on the Hilltop" with all the rich kids. Eddie Barker walked into my Journalism 101 class and had the miracle in his pocket.

I couldn't imagine why a television legend like Eddie Barker took time to talk to a bunch of first-semester journalism students, but he did and I was very impressed. I had never once in my life thought about a career in television, but his presence, his voice, his self-confidence forced me to reconsider. In my mind, I would go to SMU, study journalism and immediately be snapped up as a writer for *People* magazine. I'm not sure if I really thought any of that would happen to me, but it was a dream I carried around and didn't often mention to other people.

As he finished his speech and left our tiny junior-college journalism classroom, I stopped Eddie ("Mister Barker!") and asked if I could have his business card. I'm not sure that I even knew what a business card was except that important people always seemed to have one and I figured this man's card could help me somehow. I had no idea how much!

"What are you going to do with it?" Eddie asked when I requested the card. "Call you and ask for a job," I replied. "Call me," he said.

I gave him 30 minutes to get back to his office and made the call. The next day, I was sitting across the desk from the King of Dallas Television, the man whose daily 6 p.m. newscast began every day with a message from Walter Cronkite at the end of the "CBS Evening News."

"And now stay tuned for my good friend Eddie Barker and the award-winning Channel 4 Evening News," Cronkite said. (I later learned that the TV station had several "cuts" of Cronkite's personal Barker intro so they could match it every day to the suit Walter was wearing that night.)

He asked me why I should hire him. All I can remember is that I somehow uttered the words "because I'll sweep your floors if they need it." He seemed to be terribly busy during our short interview and barely looked at me, but he almost smiled when I said that, then told me he paid two bucks an hour and to see Buster McGregor about my schedule. I didn't know who Buster was but I was afraid to ask for fear that he might realize he had just hired me and change his mind. Buster, as it turned out, was the long-time assignments editor and he was almost as scary as Eddie Barker. He asked how much I wanted to work, I told him as much as he would let me and that was that. I never looked back.

In the next few months I learned to change the paper in the AP and UPI wire machines. I learned every code the

Dallas Police Department used when talking on their radios (part of my job was to sit in a little room and listen to the police talk, then tell Buster when it sounded like "something was up"). I learned how to drive fast in traffic so I could retrieve 16-millimeter news film and bring it back to the TV station for processing and editing for the news. I eventually learned how to shoot news film so I wouldn't have to sit in that little room. I could drive around in a Channel 4 news unit and listen to the radios. That way, I could look cool and be on the street where I could react quickly when "something was up." And, most importantly, I learned how to stay out of Eddie Barker's way when he was angry.

Eddie Barker was not a mean person. He was not an unreasonable boss. He was *a perfectionist*. He demanded everyone's best and accepted nothing less. When that didn't happen, he would yell. Some people were offended by that and afraid of Eddie, but I had grown up around a bunch of aunts and uncles who loved to yell (my mom and dad did not) and it didn't faze me. So I somehow survived when others didn't and, in return, learned more from Eddie Barker and a few others at Channel 4 than I did in all my years of college. *And I got to go to SMU.* I have Eddie to thank for that, too.

I never saw the letter so I don't know what it said, but Eddie Barker wrote a letter to someone in SMU Chancellor Willis Tate's office and suddenly things started happening. I had applied to attend SMU and somehow was accepted. The problem I had was that I couldn't pay for it. I casually mentioned to Eddie that I had been accepted but didn't have the money to go and he told me to let him see what he could do. After Eddie's letter, a lady in the financial-aid office called me and said she could offer me a combination of scholarships and loans that would allow me to go to school at Southern Methodist University. Though he never took credit for it, I knew Eddie Barker had somehow convinced someone at SMU that they should let in a poor local boy. I went on to get my Bachelor's and Master's degrees there, all while working full-time for Channel 4.

I only worked for Eddie Barker for two-and-a-half years before the station was sold and new management came in. But that short period of time set my life in motion and put me on a path of success that has carried me to this day. It was Eddie who chose me to travel with the Dallas Cowboys and shoot their games for the station when I was only 19 years old. It was Eddie who looked at the first feature story I put together on my own (I even did on-camera stand-ups by starting the camera, then running around in front of it) and made the decision to air it on Channel 4. And it was Eddie who said he thought the idea of an ongoing series similar to Charles Kuralt's "On the Road" was a good one. After Eddie left the station, I was the first photographer on that show, "4 Country Reporter," and soon became the producer and host. I'm still doing that job today, though now I produce the program through my own production company and syndi-cate it to 22 other television markets across Texas.

More than 30 years after he gave me that job, I asked Eddie Barker why he hired an 18-year-old kid in the first place. He told me he figured if I had enough guts to ask him for a job, I just might have enough guts to *do* that job. It's a lesson I shall never forget.

Did I miss television and radio? Not too much. I think I geared myself not to miss it. But then, I stayed close to television through Eddie Barker Associates's production of the Cowboys' preseason games and *The Tom Landry Show*. Also, I had been the president of the Radio-Television News Directors Association (RTNDA) in 1967, and I managed the exhibits at their annual convention for many years after that.

I'm not much of a joiner, but RTNDA was an exception. From the time I joined in 1960 to this day, being a part of RTNDA has had a big role in my life. The members of RTNDA are the men, and now quite a few women, who are responsible for what you hear and whom you watch or listen to on radio and television. News directors are very seldom seen or heard. They don't make the million dollar–plus salaries of those on the air, but they bear the brunt of any mistake the "stars" make. I was both a news director and an anchor. An old and dear friend of mine, the late Ralph Renick of WTVJ in Miami, was another of the handful who did both jobs.

The on-the-air talent often reminds me of a traveling circus, a new town every rating period. The Metroplex has defied that circus for quite a few years with few major changes. Gloria Campos, John McCaa, Troy Dungan, and Dale Hansen at Channel 8 have been there quite a few years, as have Clarice Tinsley at Channel 4 and Jane McGarry and Mike Snyder at Channel 5. Of course, Tracy Rowlett at Channel 11 had a long career at Channel 8 before making the move across town. And Chip Moody had a long Dallas–Fort Worth career with stints at each station. I'll return to Chip later. But back to RTNDA. I became active, served on the board, worked hard, and ended up being honored by my peers when I was elected president in 1969.

RTNDA was a lot smaller then, and it was run by some part-timers who felt a calling that this group was playing a big role in journalism. Rob Downey, who was news director at the Michigan State University radio station, was everything—secretary, treasurer, membership guy. And working just as hard from his professor's office at the University of Iowa was Joe Andrews, a real pro, the editor and producer of *The Communicator*, our monthly newsletter. We had an annual convention, and it got to where a few vendors would show up in the hallways. And that got my attention.

"We ought to start charging them to show their wares," I told the board.

"Well, would you like to take on that job?" they asked. I did, and I would like to take a little credit for changing RTNDA from a small group struggling to stay alive to one that eventually became so successful in its exhibit hall that the National Association of Broadcasters lured it to become part of its annual exhibits convention, now held every year in Las Vegas. The first six years I did it as a labor of love and a first-class plane ticket, covering other expenses myself. It finally got so big it was taking a lot of time and money, so I did it on a commission basis. It launched me into the convention business, but that's another story.

From its humble beginnings to an organization headed by a six figure–income president and a Washington, D.C., staff so large I've lost count, RTNDA has come a long way. And I can't help but pat myself on the back a little for working in the trenches to help make it so.

I'm glad I maintained my television connections through RTNDA after leaving KRLD. It was good for me, and it's also allowed me to help some others along the way.

Like Walter Cronkite and Dan Rather, Bob Schieffer is a Texas product, and a good one. I was moving into public relations as Bob was starting to make his mark at KXAS, Channel 5. I had known him since he was a reporter for the *Fort Worth Star-Telegram*, and I always admired his work, but didn't know him much beyond perfunctory meetings. Still, I liked him.

Then one day I got a call from Bob. (He tells his version of what happened on pages 110 and 111 of *This Just In*, his excellent autobiography, but that's not exactly how I remember it.)

After Bob called and we exchanged the usual pleasantries, he said he wanted to ask a favor of me. "Shoot, Bob, what do you need?" I asked.

"I want to move to Washington and go to work for CBS, but I don't know anyone there. I thought you might have a name and put in a good word for me," he said.

"That's no problem, I'll call Bill Small, the bureau chief, and tell him he needs to talk to you."

I called Small, an old friend from RTNDA, and told him, "Bill, this guy is a winner and somebody will pick him up pronto, but he wants to work for CBS."

Like a lot of newspeople, Small was sarcastic. He replied, "If he's that good, tell him to call me and we'll set up a time. I'll try and move him out of your hair."

Bob called, they did meet, and the rest is history. Small called me back and said, "I owe you one; I'm gonna hire him."

Actually, he told Bob to get a job at a Washington station until he had an opening at CBS. The opening came quickly. Well, like Paul Harvey always says, "Now you know the rest of the story."

Through RTNDA, I met another CBS icon, Charles Kuralt, whose work, as you already know, helped inspire Bob Phillips's career. I met Charles at the RTNDA convention in Dallas in 1967. He was not what you picture as the handsome, fingernails-manicured, every-hair-in-place reader of the evening television news. His hairline receded and he was a bit on the chubby side. But he had a great smile and a warm voice, and his wonderful *On the Road* stories had no need of a guy with a pricey haircut. He was truly the "king of the road," to quote Roger Miller.

After I got into public relations, I had a story that I thought might interest him, the fact that much of the Dallas–Fort Worth airport was still being farmed. Here was the past meeting the future: a jet roaring down a runway next to a tractor and a hay bailer harvesting the field. Ernie Dean was the airport executive at the time and a friend of mine. I don't recall the airport having a full-time public-relations type, and I would counsel Ernie over a drink now and then. I told him I was going to see if I could interest Kuralt in a story.

Charles said he would like to take a look, and he did. We spent the better part of a day at DFW. "I'll keep it on my 'to-do' list," Charles told me, but for one reason or another, the DFW story never made the cut.

Later, a new hospital was opening in Garland and they were looking for someone to give the dedicatory address. They wanted Charles Kuralt to do it, but they had only $2,500 in the budget for a speaker. Would he do it? I said I would ask, and Charles said, sure.

Charles was a letter writer. Every once in a while I'd get a note from him. In light of what happened after his death in 1997, when a woman came forward claiming to have been his secret mistress for nearly thirty years, one letter comes to mind. He wrote me and said a lady whom he had met in Montana wanted to move to Dallas and asked if I had any contacts there who might be of help. "I told her about you, Eddie, and told her that she should contact you when she got to Dallas." I never heard from her but assumed she was the woman who came to light after Charles's death. Who knew? Certainly not me.

When you do a book about yourself you start looking back to see what you've saved through the years, such as pictures. I ran across one of Chip Moody, the late Dallas–Fort Worth anchorman, and me. It was taken at El Fenix, our favorite Mexican restaurant. Our paths crossed there a lot, and as Chip's health started to fail, our mutual friend Alfred Martínez had the kitchen fix Chip something a little milder than the usual fare.

Thinking back about Chip, I remembered the time he called me and wanted some career advice. He was at Channel 5 and I was in the public-relations business. And what did he want? "Eddie, I want to visit with you about a call I've had from Channel 4."

"Great, Chip, come on out." Channel 4 had offered him a job making about four times as much as would ever make at KXAS-TV.

"What should I do?" he asked.

"Take it," I said, "but tell them you want a $25,000 signing bonus." Why not? The ballplayers do it. He made the deal, and Channel 5's loss was Channel 4's gain. But then Channel 8's executives saw what they had missed out on, and he was soon in the Belo stable. After spending a mandatory year in Houston to satisfy the local "noncompete" clause in his contract, Chip came back to Channel 8, and you know what happened with partner Tracy Rowlett: they went all the way to the top of the ratings. Chip got dealt from the bottom of the deck when he was stricken with cancer, that's for sure. A great guy left us all too soon.

My "celebrity" as a television anchorman certainly helped me in making the transition to PR. I never was anxious about it. I just always figured it would work, and it did. We had some great clients. Gifford-Hill, the Republic Bank, Storer Cable. But the meat-and-pota-toes was always political public relations.

John Van Cronkite was a genius at political PR. He advised the Citizens Charter Association and helped it select candidates, everything. We did not have single-member districts then; everyone ran at large. Somebody from South Dallas had to fight for votes in North Dallas, and vice versa. The CCA was a powerful group and pretty much dominated the city managers in those days, Scott McDonald and Elgin Crull, all of those people.

Van Cronkite was an integral part of the CCA's success. I learned a lot of political PR from him. He gave the CCA good advice, whom to run as candidates, where to spend its money. He was the brains who made the CCA successful.

The CCA continued to play a major role in Dallas politics for years after the upstart Wes Wise beat the establishment's Avery Mays. It started losing steam when single-member districts came into being in 1971. Single-member districts made Dallas like any other big city, politically. The city started developing all these little fiefdoms. "Dallas as a whole"? Forget it. I still think you can get a heck of a lot more accomplished when everybody is pulling their share of a single load rather than having fifteen different loads.

Here's an example of how city government gets sidetracked by unrealistic, unproductive objectives. One of my clients was the advertising firm of Foster and Kleiser, which owned a lot of billboards in Dallas. They were just getting slaughtered by the Dallas Planning and Zoning Commission. The city didn't give the sign people a fair break at all. Commission employees used to go out on Lemmon Avenue and use a telephoto lens to take a picture of all the signs; the exaggerated effect was to show the signs lined up like dominoes on a tabletop. Adlene Harrison, who went on to become mayor of Dallas and a regional administrator of the Environmental Protection Agency, was the chair of the commission and led the campaign against billboards.

I agreed to take on the job, even though I was sure we'd lose, and we did. But of course, all the restrictions the city put in have either been revoked or they're ignored, which also was predictable. The way the antisign ordinance was written, Reunion Tower, with all the moving lights, violated it.

A lot of the clients I took on were not going to be easy wins, and some not too popular, like Foster and Kleiser. But those were the ones that paid the best. And some of the best payers were the most fun, and not a lot of trouble. Like Coors Beer. The late Raymond Willie Jr. and Bill Barrett were the distributors, great to work with, even though they were as different as day and night. Raymond was the quiet one of the two, with a bit more sophistication. Bill should have been in the PR business himself, sort of a born press agent.

Bill called me and said they had to have coverage of the first Coors Light trucks rolling into town. He said, "This is big, Eddie. It's a big story."

I told him, "Bill, I'll see if it's as big to some media folks, but a lot of other beers are 'light,' too." He replied firmly, "Well, I'm counting on you."

It turned out I was able to sell the story to Al Altwegg, the *Dallas Morning News* business editor. He sent a photographer out to take a picture of these eight eighteen-wheelers loaded with Coors Light and ran the picture. I don't remember how we did on television coverage, but Bill was more interested in that picture in the paper to send back to the Coors folks in Colorado.

One day, Raymond called me and said we needed to talk about what could be a problem. "Raymond, what is it?" I asked. He told me, "The gay community is upset over those controversial statements Joe Coors is making [the Coors company was accused of making employees take polygraph tests to prove they were straight], and the gay bars are talking about having a big party throwing out all of our beer. I want you to go with me and talk to them."

There were six gay bars in Dallas at the time, and we made a call on all of them. As I remember, one bar did have an emptying party late one Sunday night, too late for any of the television stations to make an appearance, thank goodness.

Cable started out as such a simple thing, designed for folks who lived beyond the reach of the local television stations or over a mountain that blocked the signal. Someone got the idea to run a cable on poles to these outlying regions so that all could share the joy of watching big-city TV.

That went along fine for years. Then came satellites, which carried all kinds of new channels—CNN, TBS, ESPN—but you couldn't get them in the city unless you put a huge, unsightly "dish" in your front yard. The cable folks said, "Let's make these programs available to the city folks as well as those who live out in the country." Great, the cable rush was on, sort of like the "Boomer Sooner" land-rush days in Oklahoma.

But the cities said, "Wait a cotton-pickin' minute, we want some say in who comes into our town." However, the city fathers didn't know any more about cable television than what they read in the paper. They needed someone to tell them what they needed and how to go about getting it. Thus was born a cable-television association and the emergence of Harold Horne, the Answer Man.

The Dallas City Council was soon among the bidders for Mr. Horne's time to tell it what to do. As I recall, there were six cable companies that wanted the lucrative Dallas cable franchise. And I must tell you that the quest for the franchise caused me to lose a lot of confidence in the workings of the city. Yes, I represented one of the six bidders, Storer Broadcasting Company. Every time Mr. Horne came to town to lecture the council, I was in attendance, along with the lobbyists for the other five companies. I say "lobbyists" because, in a sense, that's what we were, as well as public-relations representatives and press agents.

The bidding formula was established, and we were off and running. The formula required that the needs of minorities be paramount and advice be sought from the minority communities. And so we hired, at a very handsome retainer, a member of the black community and, at an equally generous retainer, a member of the Hispanic community. And Storer could proudly show these names in the proposal presented to the city.

You know, sometimes you get a feeling about what is going to happen? Well, I got a feeling early on that Warner was going to get the franchise, despite the efforts of Storer or any of the other bidders. A young woman from Ohio was brought in to run the Warner effort. Her father was a longtime member of Congress.

I felt for the city employees who were directly involved in the project. They were as helpful as they could be. The woman in charge for the city was Camille Cates, assistant city manager. City Manager George Schrader put her in that position instead of overseeing it himself. I always felt that, with the enormity of the project, George should have retained control.

The weeks went by, proposals were put together. Ours was four thick volumes, and the other bidders' about the same size. And there were all kinds of special rules on how the proposals should be packaged.

Finally, presentation day came. John Grubbs, a Storer vice-president who had moved to Dallas to work on the project, would make our presentation. And then something happened. Remember I said I had a feeling about who was going to get the franchise? Well, I was standing in the foyer outside the council chamber when I was approached by a man I had known for years as a political powerhouse; one of his sons was on the council. "Hey, Eddie," he said as he patted me on the back, "Guess where I've been?"

"Tell me," I said.

"Well, I just got off the Warner jet that flew me in from New York."

Of course, when the vote came, Warner got the franchise. Storer got one vote, but to me it was the most principled vote on the council, Joe Haggar of Haggar slacks fame.

I met a lot of public-relations people, the good and the not so good, through the years at KRLD and, later, when I started Eddie Barker Associates. If you asked me who was the best PR person I ever met it would have to be Buck Marryat of American Airlines, with Al Harting of Southwest Airmotive, a Love Field–based business-aviation facility, a real close second. Both of them had worked on newspapers in their early years. Neither Buck nor Al ever pushed you to cover their story. They had the common sense to know that an editor makes the decision if the story is newsworthy, not the PR rep.

I respected and enjoyed working with others, like Hal Copeland, an independent public-relations practitioner, and Bill Aston of Dallas Power and Light. Bill moved up to the president's office to cap his career. And then there were those who drove us nuts at KRLD trying to get us to cover a story. Like who? I'm not going to mention any names.

The role of the PR person is, of course, to tell the story of the client in the most favorable, but straightforward and honest, way possible. If there are obvious warts on the company, deal with them head on and don't pretend they don't exist. And don't duck the call when it comes from the media. Smart reporters are going to figure out a way to get the story, so you may as well tell your side of it.

Offhand, I can't think of any big story we ever got from a public-relations rep, and that's good, because if we had the story alone and it came from a PR agency, an awful lot of folks with the competition would be very unhappy. In the same way, if someone in the news media comes to you, the PR rep, with an idea for a story involving your client, you don't dare pass the idea on to other media. In other words, be a square shooter, as Tom Mix used to say, in dealing with all media types. Unfortunately, we had one PR practitioner who played favorites with the news media a couple of times when I was at KRLD, and that person soon found our door was no longer open. And I notice in the phone book that that practitioner is still in the business.

As these pages are being written in 2005, the City of Dallas is in the throes of redefining itself. But the city council doesn't feel confident enough to do the job, so city funds are being expended by hiring an advertising and public-relations agency, the Richards Group, to tell the city what it really is and wants the world to think it is, if that makes sense.

When Eric Sevareid was in town to cover the Jack Ruby trial in 1964, he described Dallas this way in one of the many masterly commentaries he did on *CBS News*: "In no fundamental sense whatsoever are the people of Dallas, Texas, different from other Americans, though their professional boosters think they are. . . . The 'Big D' is a metropolis in body, but not yet in spirit. . . . Dallas wants the rewards of big city-ness, but it doesn't want to pay the penalties." As I reread Sevareid's analysis, I ask, "Would you please spell out how Dallas has changed since then?"

But the Richards Group isn't the first ad/PR group to get involved in the image molding of Dallas. Tax dollars will help in the new redefining; the first time around, the quiet but powerful Dallas

Citizens Council (DCC) footed the bill. The DCC was smaller in numbers but had even more clout than the CCA. And therein lies a fascinating story of what went on behind the scenes prior to November 22, 1963, which illustrates the often-misunderstood role of public relations and how even the most meticulous of planning can be thwarted by events beyond our control.

The police, the press, and the politicos were not alone in their concern over the impending visit of President Kennedy. The concern of all was well founded. There were the John Birchers, the ultra-right wingers who called themselves Republicans; the incident a few weeks earlier when a woman whacked Adlai Stevenson on the head with a protestor's sign; and Congressman Bruce Alger's tasteless behavior during the 1960 election campaign when he tried to crash the Lyndon Johnson luncheon at the Adolphus Hotel. All combined to give Dallas the image of being the capital of "nut country," in John F. Kennedy's own words. In fact, Stevenson counseled Kennedy to forgo Dallas on his Texas trip.

No group was more concerned about the presidential visit than the Dallas Citizens Council. None of its members held elective office, but they were the "doers" of Dallas, and its defenders. You could probably count on one hand the number of DCC members who voted for President Kennedy and still have a couple of fingers left over. But the president was their president, too, and they wanted nothing to go awry that would bring disgrace or shame to the City of Dallas. And, of course, there was that matter of a new federal building that never seemed to make the cut at budget time, and this might be a good time to get in a word about it to the right folks.

School integration had gone smoothly and nothing happened to make the national headlines, thanks, at least in part, to the help of Sam Bloom and the Bloom Agency. The DCC approached Bloom to help paint a good picture of Dallas and to be prepared to put out any brush fires that might crop up surrounding the president's visit. Sam hired on.

A bit of background on Sam Bloom. Prior to starting his own agency, he was the advertising director and part owner of the *Dallas*

Times Herald. His part ownership in the paper was a gift from one-time owner and publisher Edwin J. Kiest. That city park in Oak Cliff is named for him. Kiest had no family other than a niece who lived in Florida. So he gave her an annual share of the *Times Herald* profits and gave the *Times Herald* Printing Company to seven employees, including Sam Bloom. I remember the annual trip that the brass made to Florida every year to keep the niece up to date on her inheritance.

I don't recall ever officially meeting Sam Bloom. He was a big man, tall, heavyset. The occasional times I would see him I always had the feeling he was looking right past me, looking to someone who carried a bigger stick than I did. You know the type. He was kind of like Lyndon Johnson in that regard. Bottom line: I never thought of him as a "people-to-people" kind of guy. And I think he knew it, too.

Bloom may not have been a "people" person himself, but he scored high marks in plotting, planning, and finding the right lieutenant to carry out his battle plans. The right lieutenant for this job was already in the employ of Bloom's public-relations department — Helen Holmes, then Helen Hankins. Helen was assigned the job of managing the city's public relations for the visit of President Kennedy.

I had known Helen in her earlier career as a reporter for the International News Service, which later melded with United Press to become UPI. I recently asked Helen to remember just what it was that Sam Bloom told her she would be doing. Her tasks included accrediting the local press and all others, save for the press traveling with the president. "No press releases or anything to look like we were doing PR work for the Democratic Party, we were just taking care of the press," Helen told me.

Badges for the press were one thing, but Helen and crew also worked with the welcoming committee. Sam Bloom thought it would be a good idea if prominent Dallasites wrote statements to the press welcoming the president and, at the same time, without using the exact wordage, urging no more Bruce Alger fiascos. In other words: Everyone behave yourself! Helen recalls writing most of the letters herself and hand delivering them to the *Morning News* and the *Times Herald*. Most were published.

A president doesn't come to town every day, and even if you didn't vote for him, he's still the president. An awful lot of folks wanted to see Kennedy. Helen was in the thick of what developed into a bitter struggle over who would get tickets to hear the president speak at the Trade Mart. I've already related the story about Baxton Bryant, the grassroots Dallas Democrat and Methodist minister who complained to the White House about the limited seating for the "regular folks" at the president's appearance. The vast majority of the fourteen hundred seats were going to members of the DCC; several hundred seats went to Democrats hand picked by conservative governor John Connally, which didn't sit well with the supporters of liberal senator Ralph Yarborough, including Baxton Bryant. It became Helen's unenviable task to get more seats, which she did, obtaining eleven hundred seats in the Trade Mart balconies.

Helen did a marvelous job, a model of professional public-relations work. The hall was ready; the luncheon was set to proceed with Erik Jonsson, the DCC stalwart and future mayor, as master of ceremonies; Luther Holcomb, with the Greater Dallas Council of Churches, would say the prayer; and a member of our First Presbyterian Church, Jean Kerr, would sing the national anthem. But it was all for naught because no one thought to keep an eye on an ex-defector to the Soviet Union who had recently returned to Dallas. The best-laid plans . . .

Helen's work did not end after the assassination. The DCC was concerned about what would happen when Jack Ruby went on trial. Judge Joe Brown elected to keep the trial in his courtroom rather than grant the defense's motion for a change of venue. Again, the council turned to Sam Bloom, who turned to Helen. "Judge Brown was a delight to work with and did take a few suggestions I offered, " she said, "but on the most important one, he refused to listen to me." Helen counseled the judge against allowing live television in the courtroom for the jury verdict. "I knew what would happen and it did—chaos," she remembered. After the guilty verdict, Ruby's attorney, Melvin Belli, went berserk, shouting about a "kangaroo railroad," mixing his metaphors in his fury. Reporters climbed all over the room, trying to get photos or sound bites. Helen said she didn't want to see it so she wasn't in the courtroom when the guilty verdict came in.

Here's an example of a lame public-relations stunt. Thankfully, it was not one of my own.

Reporters and editors are a skeptical bunch, as well they should be: "Trust everybody, but cut the cards," in the inscrutable words of the old-time newspaper columnist Finley Peter Dunne. This story involves a good hundred or so elite members of the Dallas–Fort Worth media corps and an airline. It happened on a beautiful spring day.

I might as well go ahead and tell you the airline was Braniff. For a couple of weeks, Braniff had bombarded everybody who was anybody plus a few nobodies with the promise of a great "mystery flight." "Where are we going?" the question was repeatedly asked. "That's the mystery, where we're going to take you. But be sure and bring along your swimsuit. We'll supply everything else."

The appointed day dawned, and out to old Love Field traipsed the elite of local radio, television, newspapers, and the wire services. The Braniff people, no need to name them, played the mystery to the hilt. We flocked on board the Electra and waited wide-eyed, imagining where we might be heading. The Braniff folk suggested we have a guessing game on where the mystery flight was headed. We hadn't been airborne all that long when we started our descent. Somebody on the right side of the plane said, "Hey, we're landing in Houston!"

"Only for lunch, only for lunch," came the response. Buses awaited and whisked us off to the old San Jacinto Inn.

Soon the Braniff people were shouting, "Let's go, let's go on to our destination!" So back on the plane and more of the guessing game. Some of us noted that the plane seemed headed in a westerly direction. Could it be San Diego? Acapulco? No sooner were we airborne than the descent began. Someone on the other side of the plane yelled, "Why, we're landing in San Antonio!" And we were. Now, this was before San Antonio had created a more glamorous image for itself, so it was no great thrill for a planeload of Dallas newspaper and broadcasting people to pay a visit to the Alamo

City. Again we boarded buses, our destination a San Antonio country club pool. That's why the swimsuits.

Now, if you're trying to figure out what the purpose of this little excursion was, join the club. Braniff had no particular new program or service it was trying to promote. If the Braniff PR geniuses were trying to create some general goodwill with the news media, this aimless sojourn was not the way to do it. The feeling of the media corps was, "We've been had!" And we had been. No wonder Braniff went out of business a few years later.

You can meet some fascinating people on a plane. I met Denton Cooley, the first man to perform a heart transplant, when I was on my way to Guam, where I was doing a lot of public-relations business with the Guam Oil Company.

On one of these trips I was at the Los Angeles airport waiting for a Pan Am flight that made a stop in Honolulu. Braniff in those days was flying a daily nonstop between Dallas and Honolulu. I'm standing around the waiting area and up rushes this man I thought looked familiar. It was Dr. Denton Cooley. Our eyes met and I said, "Hello, Dr. Cooley." That was about all I got out before he started telling me that blankety-blank Braniff flight had landed in LA and wasn't going any farther for some reason. He had to be in Honolulu the next day to speak at a professional meeting. What could he do?

"Well, Dr. Cooley, you're in luck. This Pan Am flight here stops in Honolulu," I said. "Maybe they have some open seats." Pan Am did have two first-class seats and would be pleased to accommodate Dr. Cooley and his wife. Turns out the Cooleys were seated right across from me. Pan Am in those days served dinner in the upstairs lounge of its 747s. And they gave you a choice of two seatings. The Cooleys and I were scheduled for the second seating, and when we got upstairs, the nameplates were in place and the bar was open. Dr. Cooley was extremely easy to talk with and we chatted on a variety of subjects. Don't ask me now what we talked about because I don't remember. But I do remember the good doctor liked his scotch, as I did mine, with soda. And I couldn't believe the number of cigarettes he consumed before we landed in Honolulu and said our alohas. I thought, "Good Lord, this guy is the great heart man?" The ironies of life.

Around the same time, I met the equally great heart surgeon Michael DeBakey.

It's not hard to find a heart surgeon these days. Bypasses, replacements, and stents are no longer looked upon as pressing the envelope of can-do. You can't use the word *routine* in describing heart surgeries, but it's safe to say such procedures are certainly more commonplace than a few years ago. But it wasn't too long ago that two names immediately came to mind when you thought of the heart, Cooley and DeBakey: two surgeons from Houston setting the medical world on fire with their inventions and breakthrough procedures. Now this isn't to say they were in concert in these activities; quite the opposite. Stories abound of the rivalry between the two.

I met DeBakey, who's best known for his work on the artificial heart, when he came to speak to a group called the Dallas Assembly, of which I was a member. It was a leadership organization for people in Dallas under fifty. Pete Baldwin, one of my political PR clients, got me to join. Darned if I know exactly what the purpose of it was, but we met about once a month. One weekend we went to a resort and listened to the great architect Buckminster Fuller explain his geodesic dome. That kind of thing.

DeBakey got his airline arrangements all confused and ended up getting to Dallas about four hours early. Somebody asked me if I'd go pick him up, so I did, and had this great afternoon with Michael DeBakey. Unlike Cooley, he was a real straitlaced guy, but he had some great stories.

DeBakey was a frustrated race-car driver. He had driven some and was well on his way to making quite a hobby out of it when, he said, "the insurance people told me I had a choice, being a race-car driver or doing heart surgery without insurance. So I'm not racing anymore."

I had always heard that he stitched up his patients in a particular way, not like other surgeons did. I asked him about this and he told me, "My mother was a seamstress and I was fascinated in how she went about her work, especially how she stitched. She taught me her way and I use it to this day."

Remember citizens band (CB) radios? They were the craze in the '70s until the foul-mouthed louts came along. Then, later, the cell phone really did in the CBs. One thing I remember is we all had a handle, the way the world knew it was you on Channel 19. Remember your handle? I remember mine; actually I had two handles. The first, "The All American Boy," soon gave way to "Mr. Wonderful."

Well, did you know that I once had the "handle" of publisher? I did, and here's how it came about. Bill Ceverha told me about a woman he had met in church who was a solar-energy genius and wanted to talk with us about starting a magazine, since there wasn't one on the market for the fast-growing solar industry. "Bring her in and we'll see what she's talking about," I told Bill.

Her name was Anna Faye Friedlander and, true to Bill's description, she talked a pretty good solar game. She didn't have any money but had contacts with every solar manufacturer in the country and was on a first-name basis with the Solar Energy Industries Association bigwigs. She convinced us that her contacts could bring in advertisers and knowledgeable industry writers. While our talks were going on, Bill was elected to the state legislature and he was out of the magazine picture.

I bit the bullet and took on the burdens of publishing a magazine. Anna Faye produced as she said she would: interesting articles, open doors to advertisers. We became the official publication of the Solar Energy Industries Association. This was not the kind of magazine you sell on the newsstand, as its area of interest was so limited. It had to be sold by subscription and mailed. The magazine caught on, and it wasn't too long before we had subscribers around the world.

Despite the startup costs and monthly expenses, we were keeping our head above water. And then it happened: Ronald Reagan was elected president of the United States. And it was like the Titanic hitting the iceberg: the solar energy industry sank just as fast.

The oil industry didn't then, nor does it now, want anything to do with solar energy. And as government interest and dollars left the solar folks high and dry, the major oil companies came in, bought them out, and quietly put the thriving solar industry out of business. Now the major oil companies own most of the patents for solar energy. Don't hold your breath while this answer to our energy problems gets back on it feet.

I was able to unload the magazine to a plumbing-and-heating publication that felt it could meld the two. No idea what happened after that.

As I said before, I'm glad that I gave Bob Phillips, the *Texas Country Reporter* host, his first job. Another time I was able to help out a couple of guys with a lot more news experience than Bob had: Ken Johnson, the final executive editor of the *Dallas Times Herald* before it went out of business in 1991; and Will Jarrett, the editor. Kinda interesting.

Try this on for size. You don't really want to retire, but the job plays out and the hefty package for your golden years means you can play all the golf you want, sail wherever you want, and pay somebody to cut the grass. Sounds pretty good, eh? Only problem is, you're not old enough to retire and you still have the itch to do something. What do you do?

Well, Ken Johnson found himself in that fix. One day the phone rang and it was Ken. Pleasantries aside, Ken said, "I want to have lunch with you and ask you a question."

I replied, "Great, Ken. Let's do it." And we did.

Ken at one time was a vice-president of the *Washington Post*. The Times Mirror Company, lured him away to the *Times Herald*. And what did Ken tell me at lunch? "I'm going stir crazy with nothing to do, and I need some advice."

Well, I told Ken, the first thing he had to do every morning was to get out of the house and head to an office. "A man with the drive you have will atrophy sitting around the house," I told him. "Tell you what, I've got an extra office and you're welcome to use it."

Ken took me up on the offer and moved in. He's a first-class guy and he decorated the office with some fine furniture and a waterfall. I knew Ken had something in mind for what he wanted to do, but it just hadn't jelled. After a couple of weeks he came in said, "Will

Jarrett is leaving the paper and we'd like to get together. Any problem with him moving in, too?"

No problem, so two of the former top executives of the *Dallas Times Herald* were sharing space with me, but not for long. Their goal was to buy small newspapers around the country. Their first acquisition was the paper in Castle Rock, Colorado. But that was just the beginning. They needed space and a more prestigious address and they soon moved out after forming Westward Communications. One of the terms of their moving was to take a secretary with them that I didn't have the heart to fire.

Ken and Will have been fabulously successful. The last I heard, they owned well over two hundred papers nationwide and were doing a lot of the printing of *USA Today* around the country. Our paths haven't crossed in years, but it's nice to remember the success of a publishing venture that started in my humble little office.

Working in broadcasting and political public relations, naturally, I met a lot of politicians. Some of the most interesting political figures I've known are mostly forgotten today.

Going back to the early days of television, we had to be resourceful. The networks provided a minimum of programming, and we had to create our own local shows to fill time and sell advertising. And so I found myself as the host of a game show. How in the world they picked the panel for the game show, I don't know. Maurice Carlson was pretty much a regular on the show. I'll get a lot of flak from a lot of Republicans for saying this, but, to me, Maurice Carlson was the father of the party in Dallas County. Why? Because he had the *cojones* to make a pitch for all comers to come on in, in an effort to move away from the stigma that still haunts the party, that it's not for you unless you're in the six-figure-and-above salary bracket.

Maurice was a fascinating person, married to Martha Carlson, the highly successful Dallas realtor. He was a Greek scholar with at least a master's degree and deeply involved in LIFT, Literacy Instruction for Texas. He was a frequent *Comment* guest and a fixture on election night. He was president of the Republican Party in Dallas County, but that was it. He never ran for public office, always staying behind the scenes. With some politicos today you have to wonder what they are in it for. You always knew Maurice had the best of intentions.

I've always felt the Republicans dumped on Maurice. He suffered some personal losses, and the party he had worked so hard to see succeed left him hanging out to dry. Maurice then turned to teaching at Arlington State University, now the University of Texas at Arlington. He invited me out to talk to his classes a couple of times, and from seeing him in the classroom, I think he was a quite a teacher.

When Maurice Carlson died, his service was held at the Sparkman Chapel on Northwest Highway. It was a cold, bitter, rainy day, and the pastor of the Parks Cities Baptist Church, Jim Pleitz, delivered the message. We went to bury Maurice, and I looked around: not a big Republican anywhere in sight. Barefoot Sanders, the liberal Democrat federal judge, was there, and several others, but no major figures in the Republican Party. I don't think they even sent a wreath for his coffin.

Steve Bartlett was another trailblazer in the Republican Party in Dallas. He was a very active, civic-minded guy and wanted to run for the council. Of course, he later served in Congress and as mayor of Dallas. In 1977, he ran against Pete Baldwin, and I handled Baldwin's campaign. Ironically, both Steve and Pete were active members of the same Presbyterian church. I thought Pete was a dream candidate until he gave an honest answer about his political beliefs. It cost him the election. The race was really the first time when the Republicans got together and backed a candidate—Bartlett—although he didn't explicitly run as a Republican. It became a real political race. I remember the first time we had a news conference. Dottie Griffith, the food editor of the *Dallas Morning News*, was covering politics at that time. She asked my man Baldwin, "Pete, how about describing your-self politically?" I imagine Baldwin voted Republican a lot more often than he voted Democrat. But he said, "I'm a social liberal and a fiscal conservative." And I thought, "Well, there goes the election."

Pete was a first-rate citizen who had contributed a lot to the city. He was a real-estate executive. To show you what kind of person he was, a *Dallas Business Journal* article lamenting the vanishing ethics of the real-estate business comments, "Once upon a time, brokers were taught proper manners by pillars of the Dallas real estate community such as . . . Pete Baldwin." He'd been an important member of the board of directors for KERA public TV and radio. But a savvy politician he was not.

In a town where the "L" word was evil, uttering it was like sitting in a deck chair on the aforementioned *Titanic*. Of course, Bartlett won. It was a tough one to lose, but it cured Pete Baldwin, and he never ran for public office again. I was disappointed at the time, but it turned out well for the Barker family. My son Ben ended up working as an aide to Bartlett when he was in Congress.

Steve opted for loftier goals than the House offered; the Senate would be his goal. But he had no statewide power base and felt that, if he served a couple of terms as mayor of Dallas, he would be well known enough to move on. But, alas, the cards said no. Steve got elected mayor all right, but the council was in chaos and being mayor didn't help his image.

Another memory of that election. The only time I ever met Jesse Jackson was during the Baldwin campaign. I think it's bad in campaigns when candidates turn pulpits into political stumps. Of course, a "free-will love offering" is involved, and the minister allows you a few minutes with the faithful at the eleven o'clock service. Nevertheless, as a political PR operative, I played the game.

We arrived at one of the largest black churches in Dallas and were escorted into the minister's office. And who should be there? Jesse Jackson—he was the guest minister for the morning. He was the least friendly man of the cloth I think I ever met. But so be it. We went into the sanctuary, and the minister told my candidate and me where to sit and that he would call on the candidate to come forward. The time came for the call, and the minister couldn't remember Pete's name, but he knew me from television. He said, "I want to introduce to you my old friend Eddie Barker, and he can introduce the man he brought with him." The minister and I embraced and I introduced Pete. Jesse Jackson never broke the cold stare he directed at me.

My path crossed John Connally's again a few years after getting into public relations. I had a call from Peter O'Donnell, a Republican behind-the-scenes fellow, who said he wanted to come out and see me. This was right before the 1976 GOP convention, when Gerald

Ford received the nomination to run for a full term. By that time, Connally had switched from the Democratic Party to the GOP, and President Nixon had named him secretary of the treasury. Nixon reportedly considered nominating Connally for vice-president when Spiro Agnew resigned, but chose Ford instead. Now, Ford was considering Connally for vice-president. O'Donnell said he wanted to hire me to go to Kansas City and work Connally's press room. Because I liked Connally so much, I agreed to take the job.

Connally had tons of charisma. I remember he flew in on a Braniff flight to the new Kansas City airport, which was way out in the country. At the same time, coming into the downtown airport was Nelson Rockefeller, who had been appointed vice-president under Ford. We had a press turnout that you wouldn't believe for Connally, and I don't know if anybody showed up for poor Rockefeller.

Of course, the deck was stacked against Connally. The dyed-in-the-wool Republicans resented him anyway because of his history with the Democratic Party and his close affiliation with Lyndon Johnson. The old delegates from Iowa and North Dakota didn't want any part of him. As the delegates started to come in, it was obvious he was not their type. And the Republicans' uneasiness with John was at least somewhat understandable. He had a big speech to give on prime-time TV. He was anxious about it, and he continually called one of the old LBJ speech writers in Washington. The LBJ aide was a good speech writer, but checking with the other side was not good form.

The morning after Ford was nominated, we were there in the suite at the hotel in Kansas City, waiting for a call from Ford. Finally, the phone rang. Whoever answered the phone said, "It's Mr. Ford." Connally said, "I'll take it in the bedroom." He closed the door. He was only in the bedroom a very short time. He came out and said, "Well, he's going with Bob Dole." It was a real letdown for John, because, of course, the vice-presidency can be a stepping-stone to the White House.

Some time later, Connally had an even greater disappointment, and, again, I was involved, reluctantly. Pollard Simons was one of my clients and he was developing Prestonwood Mall in North Dallas. He gave 25 percent of the mall to Connally—just gave it to him. Connally, I'm sure, thought this was going to be his great nest egg. But one Saturday afternoon, Pollard called me and said, "I've got bad news.

The insurance company for the project has refused to finance the mall as long as John Connally's in it." Connally had been accused of bribery and conspiracy in a milk-price scandal after serving in the Nixon administration. He was tried and acquitted in a Washington, D.C., federal court, but apparently the charges had severely damaged his reputation.

After hearing Simons's bombshell, I exclaimed, "My God, Pollard, what does that mean?" He said, "It means I want you to call him and tell him." So I called John on a Saturday evening to tell him he was out of the deal. He was mad as the dickens at Pollard. He said, "Why didn't he call me?"

I said, "John, I don't know." I know it was bitterly disappointing to Connally. Of course, years later, John had to declare bankruptcy and sell off his ranch after the oil bust of the '80s. I felt very bad for him. I couldn't help but think back to what might have been had that darn insurance company not demanded he be taken out of the Prestonwood Mall deal. His business judgment may not have been the best, but I really felt he was a good man. The only thing I ever questioned about John Connally was some of the people with whom he surrounded himself. I always felt that Connally was so much better than his underlings. My philosophy has always been to hire someone smarter than I am. I don't feel John always did that.

Another story on Pollard Simons and Prestonwood Mall. A high-ranking city official had a relative who owned some land nearby and didn't want the mall built, so the official was blocking the project. Pollard called me one day and said he had finally figured out why the holdup: "It's ———, " he told me, naming a member of the zoning board, "and that land across the road is in the family. They'll fight to keep me from getting my zoning." He continued, "You know what I can do with Prestonwood?"

I said, "No, what?"

"All I have to do is move across the road and I'll be in Addison. I think Addison would like to have my business."

I called Hank Tatum, who was then a reporter for the *Morning News*. I said, "Hank, I'll let you in on something. If Pollard doesn't get a favorable ruling from the city council, he's moving the mall to Addison." Hank ran the story in the Sunday paper, and on Monday we had the ruling Pollard wanted.

I probably knew Bill Clements, twice the Republican governor of Texas in the '80s, as well as any politician. I had gone to Washington, D.C., for some deal at the White House. This was when Gerald Ford was president. Clements was undersecretary of defense. It was a Radio Television News Directors function of some kind. I took my son Ben with me. Clements was present at this talk that Ford made. I had not met him but I knew who he was, and he knew who I was, and we passed some pleasantries.

Sometime later, I got a call from Felix McKnight, the editor of the *Times Herald*, and he said, "Hey, you're about to get a telephone call from Bill Clements. He wants to run for governor. He called me and said he needs some help and I gave him your number." Sure enough, he called and we had a little visit.

"What are you doing for breakfast tomorrow morning?" he asked.

I said, "Well, that depends on what kind of offer I get."

He said, gruffly, "I want you to have breakfast with Rita [his wife] and me in the morning." That's the way he talks. He kind of growls.

So I went over there. He lived in a big mansion on Preston Road that had belonged to Pollard Simons. Simons willed it to SMU, and Clements bought it from the university. I sat down with Bill and Rita, who, let me tell you, is as politically savvy as he is, if not more so. "Rita and I had a little pillow talk," Clements said (everything was always "pillow talk"). "I want to run for governor and I need your help. I want you to take me all over the state, and I want to meet some editors and newspeople. Nobody knows who I am, and I'm not officially running yet. But you know everybody." So I said okay.

Bill had a friend who had an Aero Commander, a prop plane. We went from Brownsville to Amarillo, East Texas to West Texas. I set up meetings with the newspapers. We met the editors and political writers for a lot of papers. After he'd walk out of the room, these people would ask incredulously, "What have you got there?" Because he was wild. He just said whatever he wanted to say and how he wanted to say it.

He, Rita, and I had quite an adventure on a trip to Oklahoma City. He was receiving some honor from Oklahoma Christian University. We went to Love Field and the pilot said, "We're not flying today." It was a cold, cold, icy day. So I called Braniff at DFW and they had a flight to Oklahoma City. As we were landing in Oklahoma City, we hit a wind shear, and the plane almost fell out of the sky. The pilot struggled with it and pulled it back up, and we circled around and finally landed. The university picked us up in a limousine. The wheels started spinning on the ice, and the limousine nearly went in the ditch. So we had to get out and push. Here was the future governor of Texas shoving the car back onto this treacherously slick highway. But we survived it and enjoyed better days together.

In Dallas, especially in the '50s and '60s, it was difficult to separate politics and business. Most of the great political figures were also big-time businessmen. But some of the business leaders whose names we all know did not get into politics, or at least not overtly.

Of course, the prince of all the Dallas business leaders was Stanley Marcus, the Neiman Marcus chairman. I knew him as 100,000 other people knew him—casually. He was an independent thinker. He grew his beard when many people in Dallas were anti–long hair and beards because of the Vietnam War protestors. But he was very gracious to me.

When I got out of television in May 1972, the *Times Herald* made a big thing of it, with a front-page article, and I got a letter from Stanley Marcus. He was in Hong Kong. He wrote me and said, "Alice [Snavely, Marcus's longtime secretary] tells me that you're leaving TV. While I'll miss you on the screen every night, I wish you well in your new endeavors. My regards, Stanley." It was a beautiful letter. I saw him a few times in later years, but it would be very misleading to say, "Oh, yeah. Me and Stanley. Big buddies."

Earlier, I told you about my experiences with H. L. Hunt. Another eccentric Dallas-area businessman was Rex Cauble, a flamboyant rancher who became famous with Cutter Bill Western Wear stores, named after a great cutting horse he owned. Rex became even more famous, or infamous, as the reputed ringleader of the "Cowboy Mafia." He ended up in federal prison for being involved in drug trafficking. I got to know him when he found himself in trouble and he hired me to handle his public relations. I was sad to see that Rex recently passed away.

Someone told Rex he ought to hire another PR man in Dallas. This person approached the PR practitioner and asked him, "Would you be interested in handling Rex Cauble?" And the PR man said, "Heavens, I wouldn't touch him with a ten-foot pole! No way." The people I sometimes handled, like the sign-industry company Foster and Kleiser, were seen as villains by the Dallas establishment. To me, it was a great challenge. And they paid well.

Rex had a major role in the birth of Southwest Airlines. He was the chairman of the Texas Aeronautical Commission. Herb Kelleher and some others got the idea for Southwest Airlines. They needed to get routes, and Rex Cauble was the one who set up routes for them through the commission. The commission didn't have a lot to do; it was pretty much a prestige appointment for Rex. But it could grant intrastate routes, although no one had ever applied for any. But Herb Kelleher and friends found the little-used authority and made the most of it.

Rex wasn't your typical bland government official. He was up in years when I met him, but he always had to have good-looking young gals around, sharing his pillow. And he was paying top dollar for them. But I digress. He got into a big fight with another commission member. Right there in the hearing room, Rex hauls off and coldcocks this guy. He was always looking for a fight. He was mean and tough, but I liked him. One reason I liked him was he paid off like a slot machine. For example, he had a Mercedes-Benz that I liked. He asked me, "You like that?" I said, "Yeah." So he signed it over to me. Just like that.

Somehow, he got caught up in smuggling drugs. I have no idea why someone like Rex Cauble would get involved in that. He had plenty of money, and his wife had plenty of Exxon stock. Before she married Rex, she had been married to one of the founders of Humble Oil, which became Exxon. I gave Rex the benefit of the doubt. I always thought he might be covering up for somebody. He might have thought he could get off where someone else could not. They said he had smuggled 147,000 pounds of marijuana into the country on shrimp boats between 1976 and 1978. Weird.

He called me out of the blue. I had never met Rex Cauble, but he talked to me like he'd known me all my life. Finally, he said, "Hey, did you see in the paper I got into a little trouble?"

I said, "Yeah, I heard about that. Well, are you guilty?"

He said, "Hell, no, I'm not guilty. I need some public-relations help and everybody tells me you're the best. I only go with the best. Would you work for me?"

I told him I'd talk to him about it. I went up to his ranch north of Denton and it was his birthday. We were in his office. Whoever was outside opened the door and said, "Rex, there's somebody here to see you." In burst this stripper. One of his cronies had hired this girl to come out as a birthday present. She did her bit, and he loved it. As I remember, he gave her a very big tip.

In 1982, they tried him in Tyler. We got John Connally and Herb Kelleher to be character witnesses for him. But Rex was hard to advise. I loved ol' Rex, but he had to be flamboyant in everything he did. He wore these $500 western suits. I used to tell him, "Rex, please, please, please. Let's get rid of that 'beautiful' hat. Let's get rid of that darn Rolex, and that bolo tie with the big diamond in it. You know, they're not going to help your case." He'd say, "Well, that's just me!" He didn't kowtow at all to the jury or anybody. And, sure enough, I think that his flashy style was as responsible for his being convicted as anything. And then, I don't think he got his money's worth from his lawyers. The judge actually thought he was going to walk. "He may get a hung jury," the judge told me. But he was wrong. Rex appealed the case, but the appeals court in New Orleans turned him down.

Well, the *Times Herald* did a story about him getting ready to go to prison. They talked him into posing for a picture standing beside his jet. They ran a big front-page photo. The prosecution went ape. They said, "This guy's going to skip the country." They forced the judge to put a million-dollar cash bond on Rex.

You'd be surprised how hard it is to come up with a million bucks. So he told me, "Call John [Connally]. Tell John I really need his help." So again I called Connally. "John, we have a little problem here," I said. "Rex needs a million dollars."

He said, "Eddie, I can't. This is hard for me to tell you, but I'm broke. Tell Rex, if I had it, it would be his, but I don't have it."

Who next to call? Rex asked me to call Jack Binion, out in Las Vegas at the Horseshoe Casino. He knew Jack, and he had known old Benny Binion, Jack's father and a big gambler in Vegas. So I called Jack Binion, trying to get a million dollars. But he didn't come through, either. Finally, Rex and his wife put up enough Exxon stock to get him out.

The time came for him to go to federal prison in Big Spring, which in 1984 was a "country club." He said, "Well, I've got to go. Will you go with me?" He had a jet at the Denton airport. I agreed to go with him, but it got to bothering me. I didn't want it to be just the pilot and me on that plane with him. The feds might get the idea that he was trying to leave the country and take a shot at him. So I called Howard Swindle at the *Morning News,* who had covered Rex in the past, and asked if he'd like to go. "You bet, I'd love to go," he said. Then I called the *Times Herald* and invited another reporter who knew Rex.

When the day came for Rex to go, I told everyone, "We've got to have wheels up at 8:00 a.m. The pilot has told me, 'It isn't very far to Big Spring, but they'll vector me all over the place,'" because of DFW Airport. He was worried about delivering Rex late to prison, and he knew the feds were concerned about Rex making a run for it. We all gathered at the airport, and Rex said his farewells to whoever showed up to see him off. Rex's son came along, too. We got off the ground right on time. I was sitting directly behind the pilot. We were barely airborne when he leaned back, and said, "Come up here." I went up to see him and he told me, "I don't know what's going on, but as soon as I filed a flight plan, they cleared us direct to Big Spring. No vectoring, no nothing. So we'll be there in about forty minutes."

I started looking around and said, "You think there's anybody on our tail?"

He said, "Probably so." I don't know that there was, but they sent us right on through and Rex was early in reporting to prison.

When Rex reported to Big Spring, we all went into the lobby with him. The warden, who was a woman, was there, and Rex, long noted for his ability to charm the opposite sex, found his gentlemanly attitude didn't faze his new keeper. No handshake. No "welcome to your new home away from home." She just walked away.

One of the problems Rex had in prison was his great sex urge. As time went on, he really felt the need to get rid of all this pent-up energy he had. So he made a deal with a guard to find him a gal and rent a room at a motel not too far from the prison. There were no gates out there; they were on the "honor system." Of course, if you ever walked away, you never went back to the "country club." But the time came, the guard gave him the key, and Rex left. The guard told him where the girl was and what motel she was in. He went in the room full of dreams for the night ahead—and it was full of cops. The guard had told his superior what was going on. Poor ol' Rex didn't get to release his lust. And then they transferred him out to El Paso, to a place called La Tuna. It was a pretty rough place out there, but finally he did his time and got out in 1987.

Do you believe timing is everything? Well, I do, and after you read this you'll understand why.

Had my timing been better, you would not be reading a few good yarns from an old reporter, but the autobiography of one of the twentieth century's true entrepreneurs, with stories of the company jet, the wooing by presidential candidates, and ringing the opening bell on Wall Street when the company went public. It would be the true story of one who first wore shoes in the fourth grade, who now frets over the problem of getting decent help to serve at all those soirees. Alas, you will have to be content with the yarns.

Over the years, I made a stab or two at going into the media business for myself, as when I toyed with the idea of buying KRLD. My admiration for the newspaper industry led me to make a bid to buy the *Park Cities News* in the '70s. Richard Curry, who had been the business editor of the *Times Herald* and was part of our team at Eddie Barker Associates, went in with me. He was the newspaper guy and would have been the publisher. The paper was the most mixed up, crazy thing I ever saw. I don't know if they ever kept books on it. I offered $25,000 for that paper, and the lady who owned it said, "I'll take it." I thought we had the *Park Cities News* sewn up. But an SMU journalism professor heard that the paper was for sale and that I was going to buy it. He went to the owner and offered her $35,000 for it, and swept it right out from under me. So much for my long-standing newspaper ambitions.

But my boldest attempt to become a media mogul came when I started what I believe was the first cable-shopping show in the country in the mid-1970s.

I had known the president of Storer Cable. He was an old friend from San Antonio, the former Humble Network football announcer, Bill Michaels. When Storer decided it was going to try to get the cable TV franchise in Dallas, he called me to help with political PR. As you know, Storer didn't get the franchise, but through the association with the company, I got the idea for a shopping program. The more I saw of cable and its possibilities, the more I thought about selling merchandise on cable. No one in the country was doing it, so why not give it a try? I flew to Miami to try to sell the brass at Storer on the idea. They were receptive and we were off and running.

We called it *The Cable Store.* The hostess was Judy Jordan, the first TV anchorwoman in Dallas at Channel 4. Her talent shone through in this format even more than it did when she anchored the Channel 4 news. We didn't have satellites, and we had to "bicycle" half-hour tapes around to the various cities on Storer cable. That was a terrible way to have to do it, but the only way we had at the time. Since I never knew when the various systems would be airing the tapes, it meant always having someone to answer the phones if they did ring. But it was a very well done show.

Unfortunately, Storer started losing money at a fast clip trying to put in cable systems around the country and it became a negative example of trickle-down economics. I knew I had to do something fast. I decided to go for the Big Bucks.

I wrangled a meeting at the World Trade Center in New York with American Express and had all my financial numbers and my aircheck tape locked and loaded. They were very interested in using an 800 number for mass marketing. They told me that American Express had reserved an 800 number — "The Card" — for when they would eventually need it. Of course, they're using it now.

The numbers man came back, said the figures looked in order, no problems. How much did I want? Oh, boy, I thought, I'm in. Five million dollars would get *The Cable Store* into the big time. Sorry, they said, but American Express would be interested when the need was in the $100 million range. Keep in touch.

I really wanted to get that thing going, so I kept trying to get the financing. I had heard of the J. H. Whitney Company, the venture capital firm that had started Minute Maid orange juice. The head of the company was Benno Schmidt, a West Texan by birth. His son, Benno Schmidt Jr., became president of Columbia University and has been involved with the Dallas Independent School District in the "Edison Project," an experimental public-education venture.

I called Benno Sr. on the phone. He took my call, and I guess I made an interesting enough pitch. He asked, "Do you have a tape of it?" Of course! "Well, come to New York and I'll talk to you."

The offices of J. H. Whitney were in Rockefeller Center. My appointment was at 11:00 a.m. I stepped off the elevator and into the most impressive mahogany-walled offices I had ever seen. I went in to meet Benno, a wonderful man. He was one of those people you just instantly felt you knew. We talked about his growing up in Abilene, his meeting J. H. Whitney, and how Mr. Whitney persuaded him to start the venture capital company. It seems a lot of Mr. Whitney's friends were coming to him after the war seeking money to start new businesses, and the venture capital company would take the onus of his having to say yea or nay to old friends. A promising tidbit, or so I thought: it turned out that Benno was old friends with John Connally.

We were talking, and Benno said, "By the way, if it's all right, I sent out to 21 for lunch." Well, the hog doesn't get much higher than the 21 Club, one of New York's swankiest restaurants, so I gulped and replied, "Oh, that's fine," or something like that. And, sure enough, here comes lunch from 21.

Benno was fascinated by the cable-shopping program. "This is the L. L. Bean of television," he said. "I'm interested, but I'm getting along in years and would prefer one of our younger associates take a look at it. He's not here today. We'll just fly down and see you." They came down in the company jet, a four-engine model they used to fly to Australia to look over investments there.

This dear man and his young associate flew down to look at the program. They stayed at the Mansion on Turtle Creek, naturally. I had lunch with Benno twice, the only two times in my life I've had lunch at the Mansion. But I struck out in trying to convince the bright young Harvard MBA that cable shopping had a future.

Well, you can't say I didn't try. Satellite cable TV was still a few years away, and I didn't have the staying power. Channel hopping the other night, I counted eight shopping channels. The old saying is so true: Timing is everything. Ah, what might have been!

9

"Scattershooting" (with Apologies to Blackie)

I use the title of this chapter with apologies to old friend Blackie Sherrod for copping his trademark. But the "scattershooting" on these next few pages, Blackie, doesn't have to do with "whatever happened to," but some thoughts, beliefs, and a story or two that didn't seem to fit in anywhere else. Some odds and ends that the years have honed.

"Ah, 'tis sweet to be remembered," the poet said. And what is it we are remembered for? I always get a chuckle out of the obituaries I read that remind those left behind of the departed's charter membership in Sam's Club and a membership in the National Geographic Society. The latter, of course, comes with being a paid subscriber to the society's magazine. So, that gets to me. I was kicked out of Sam's Club for nonpayment of dues and always found the *National Geographic* in the dentist's office.

When it comes to being remembered, I'm fortunate for the stroke of fate discussed elsewhere in this book that placed me in Dallas on November 22, 1963, and made possible the involvement I had in the coverage of that terrible tragedy.

I suppose I'm associated with covering the John F. Kennedy assassination more than anything else, and so it's natural for me to reflect on JFK.

A lot of the network people and many of my friends in the media are more to the left of center than I am. I like to think of myself as a centrist, but when push comes to shove, I'll tend to go to the conservative side. I didn't vote for Kennedy in the 1960 election when he ran against Richard Nixon. The people Kennedy surrounded himself with, the John Kenneth Galbraiths and Arthur Schlesingers, were too liberal for me.

But even though I didn't favor Kennedy politically, I respected him. When he went before a group of Baptist preachers in the 1960 West Virginia primary campaign and said, "I hope the day I was baptized a Roman Catholic was not the day that deprived me of being the president of the United States," it was a stroke of genius. Brilliant. I admired his ability to express himself and inspire people. I must admit I still get goose pimples when I hear a replay of his 1960 inauguration address—the "Ask not what your country can do for you" speech. It was one of the great political speeches of all time, even though his ghostwriter Ted Sorenson probably had a major hand in writing it. So what? Kennedy was a great orator.

And Kennedy deserves enormous credit for how he handled the Cuban missile crisis in October 1962. You remember that we discovered the Soviet Union was placing nuclear missiles in Cuba, just ninety miles off the tip of Florida and well within range of most American cities. When Kennedy told Khrushchev to get those missiles out of Cuba, that took guts. I have a vivid memory of the night President Kennedy told the Soviets to pack up and get out of Cuba. It was the night of the Miss Teenage America telecast from the State Fair Music Hall in Fair Park. I was the put-on and take-off announcer for the show. We were to go live at eight o'clock. About 7:30, New York called and said the president had requested five minutes at eight o'clock and we wouldn't go on the air until he was through. The president laid down his ultimatum to the Russians, and Miss Teenage America had to wait until he finished.

Kennedy was a powerful supporter of the military and his challenge to go the moon was bold and creative. It didn't matter if he was a liberal or a conservative, he stood strong as the commander-in-chief. If he were around today, he'd probably be considered more of a centrist than a liberal.

Much of President Kennedy's magic was in the words he spoke and how he spoke them. He was to deliver an address at the Dallas luncheon, but the cold steel of an assassin's bullet left the world the poorer for not having these haunting words delivered as only President Kennedy could have done. The undelivered speech is powerful and prophetic. Here is the last paragraph:

> *We in this country, in this generation, are—by destiny rather than choice—the watchmen on the walls of world freedom. We ask, therefore, that we may be worthy of our power and responsibility— that we exercise our strength with wisdom and restraint—and that we may achieve in our time and for all time the ancient vision of peace on earth, goodwill toward all men. That must always be our goal—and the righteousness of our cause must always underlie our strength. For as was written long ago: "Except the Lord keep the city, the watchman waketh but in vain."*

A great political problem today is that we back ourselves into corners. The Democrats take some positions they can't back away from without getting egg all over their faces, and the Republicans do the same thing. The Democrats go way over into one corner and the Republicans go into another corner. Ol' Sam Rayburn used to say, "Go along to get along." You work your way to the middle, where you come together. That's just not happening now.

President George W. Bush has tried to be in the center a lot more than his conservative backers want him to be, for example, on immigration policy. A Web site popped up urging the big-dollar droppers to stop giving to Bush because he's "too liberal."

Although I vote in the Republican primaries, that doesn't mean I agree with everything the party is doing, nor do I have much respect for some of the party leaders. Texas congressman Tom DeLay is a good example. He's not my type and I would just as soon see him go back from whence he came, spraying for bugs. I certainly fault the Republicans on a lot of their environmental positions. But there are fewer flaws for me with the Republicans than with the Democrats. The Democrats of old—the LBJs, the Rayburns, the Allan Shiverses— are no more. The party is about as wild-eyed and out of control as possible. As we went through the presidential campaign in 2004, it was striking to me that a man like Joe Lieberman, the middle-of-the-road Democratic senator, didn't have a chance. I believe it was Howard Fineman of *Newsweek* who said it best: "Lieberman was talking to a Democratic party that no longer existed." And the old-timers who proudly wore that "Democrat" label must be having nightmares in their graves at what is going on.

It's interesting living in rural Northeast Texas and voting Republican. Number one, not many people will admit it. Still a lot of "yellow-dog Democrats" out here. On my Paris radio show, I'm always kidding the conservatives who still call themselves Democrats. My challenge is for them to come out of the closet and 'fess up to really being Republicans in what they believe. We don't have many chances to vote for a local Republican. No one running for office has the nerve to admit to being one. But come general election day, the Republicans are the big state and national winners up here. And who elects them? Why, those closet Republicans, that's who!

It's been a dry year up here in the country where I live. My ponds are low and my farmer neighbors' crops need the rain. The other night came a gully washer, and smiles crossed those farmers' faces. "We needed this," my neighbor said. And it made me feel that the passing of Ronald Reagan in June 2004 and the pageantry that surrounded it was what the country needed, too. A man in his nineties who had been out of the public eye for so long brought the "rainfall" that just might help put us back on track. Or so it seemed at the time.

The first time Ronald Reagan was mentioned to me as someone who should be president some day was when John Leedom, a pillar among city council members and an early Reagan booster, said it to me. It turned out John and a few others were on target, and Reagan provided the kind of leadership that was recognized in his passing.

He believed in the need to "reason together," as Lyndon Johnson used to quote from Isaiah. Who has that ability now? Alas, no such leadership has shown itself, from either side of the aisle. It makes me think back to some lines Damon Runyon penned years ago about a great jockey, Earle Sande:

Maybe there'll be another, maybe in 90 years,
Maybe we'll find his brother, with his brain above his ears.
Maybe, I'll lay a'gin it, a million bucks to a fin. . . .

Here's something I haven't told you. And it would probably be best left untold, but I'm counting on you to let it go no farther: I voted for Bill Clinton his first time around. "You what?!" Yes, I voted for Clinton in '92. But in my mind I did not vote for him, I voted against the possibility of Vice-President Dan Quayle's ever becoming president should George the Elder fall by the wayside in his second term. I had nightmares of a Quayle presidency, so I did what I had to do. I understand that upwards of 5 percent of the Clinton votes were cast for the same reason as mine.

As I've already mentioned, one of JFK's great accomplishments was the space program. Nobody really believed we could put men on the moon before the end of the '60s, the goal that Kennedy set, but, by golly, we did it.

We learned a lot from the space program, and not just the chemical makeup of the dust on the moon. The great leaps forward in communications and satellite technology came about largely because of what NASA did in racing the Russians to the moon. But I think the achievement of reaching the moon in and of itself was worthwhile. I like George Mallory's attitude when he was asked why he climbed Mount Everest: "Because it's there." Now people ask, "Why do you want to go to Mars?" Well, we want to see what's there.

Having said that, I'll immediately contradict myself and say that there's no great hurry to get there. As I told one of my KPLT "associ-ates" the other day, "Mars has been there a long time. It's not going to go away." Also, it's going to be pretty tough to keep the public's interest high in a trip to Mars. The interest in the moon missions nose-dived after the first trip. It's going to take seven months to get to the Red Planet. What are they going to say? "Well, it was a pretty good day today. We made three million miles."

As I write this, President Bush has proposed a manned mission to Mars. I want us to do it, but with no end in sight to the war on terrorism, I think our plate is very full right now. I hate to think our beloved president proposed this for political reasons, considering what a Mars program could do for the work force in Florida or California. And we have so many other things to do. One of these days the darn interstate highway system is going to collapse on us. Let's take a few billion and get the highways fixed. Every time I drive Interstate 30 going into Dallas from the farm, I see firsthand that the highway is in very bad need of repair. Or let's get the Medicare thing straightened out. Or, for God's sake, let's take care of prescription drugs.

Of course, after JFK died, Vietnam soon began to dominate the news. Like a lot of people, I guess, I never really understood the war. I began to be troubled by a gnawing question: "Why did the French leave Vietnam?" The answer became increasingly obvious. After years of getting nowhere, they finally declared, "We won" and said their au revoirs.

I'll never forget. We were camping near Taos, New Mexico, in the summer of 1964 in a tent I had borrowed from Steve Landegran at Parkland Hospital. I turned the radio on one night to hear President Johnson give his Gulf of Tonkin speech. This was the speech to the American people in which Johnson ordered an escalation of the war in Vietnam, claiming that the North Vietnamese had twice attacked U.S. Navy destroyers in the Gulf of Tonkin. It turned out later that our destroyer may have provoked the first "unprovoked" attack and the second attack may never have happened at all. As with any war, you hope your leaders have led you into something we had to get into. But I never really trusted Lyndon Johnson. And the longer the thing went on, I, like everyone else, realized that there was no good way out.

Then Walter Cronkite came back from his visit to Vietnam in 1968 and said, "There's no way we're going to win the war." Johnson supposedly said, "If I've lost Cronkite, I've lost the country." And, certainly, Walter's assessment started to make a lot of the home folks think differently about the war.

LBJ was a gambler, but he didn't heed Kenny Rogers's sage advice: "Know when to hold 'em, know when to fold 'em, know when to walk away, and know when to run." In the end, I think Johnson got his just deserts when he saw the country bitterly divided over the war and decided not to run for reelection. He left Washington a beaten man. I cannot help but feel that he let his enormous ego get in the way, saying to himself, "We're not going to lose a war while I'm president." And so he dug in deeper and deeper.

It was such a strange time in this country, especially following the relative calm of the '50s. The rancor over the war began to permeate everything. In the late '60s, CBS televised the Cotton Bowl parade in downtown Dallas every New Year's Day. One year they had Jack Linkletter, the son of *House Party* and *Kids Say the Darndest Things* host, Art Linkletter, as the host of the parade. Another year they had William Conrad, the actor who played "Cannon" on TV. CBS was very concerned that, at a nationally televised parade, there might be some trouble, with all of the increasingly violent war protests taking place around the country. They did not feel comfortable that Jack Linkletter or William Conrad would be able to handle the situation if something crazy happened. So they hired me to go down there. I stood on the side with a microphone, and if any kind of demonstration happened, Linkletter and Conrad were instructed to throw it to me. Of course, nothing happened, but in those days, even an innocent little parade telecast was affected by the bitterness over the war.

I give President Nixon and his national security advisor Henry Kissinger high marks on getting us out of Vietnam. A lot of people wanted to just pull out overnight, but I don't think the United States, the leader of the free world, in the middle of the cold war, could afford to do that. I think Nixon wound it down relatively quickly.

Still, what a devastating thing for the country. It was not only the number of lives literally lost—the names on that wall in Washington, D.C.—but the number of lives otherwise destroyed. When these poor guys came back after the war, they were treated kind of like Dallas was treated after the Kennedy assassination. People hated the city, and many people hated these guys for having been over there. Some of them never got over it. When you go to the Vietnam Memorial, some of them are still hanging around. They'll never put it behind them.

In the later years of Vietnam, Ross Perot first rose to prominence when he led a mission to get the North Vietnamese to account for our missing-in-action military personnel and prisoners of war, another example of what a true patriot Perot was and continues to be. We sent KRLD's Bill Ceverha over to North Vietnam with Perot and some of the POW/MIA wives on a couple of occasions. Through all of that, I got to know several of the wives, because they were always holding press conferences and so on.

I had one of the wives come out to SMU when I taught a night course there one semester. After the POWs were released, Jane and I went to a Chinese restaurant, and there was this woman with her husband. And he was eating a bowl of rice. Just rice. It was a small thing, but it really brought it home to me how profoundly this man's life had been changed by his terrible experience.

Of course, not long after I arrived at KRLD in 1949, the Korean War began. It was nearly as bad as Vietnam, but somehow, the public outrage was not nearly so great, probably because it didn't last as long, but also because there was no significant television coverage. You didn't know as much about what was going on.

Like Vietnam, it's a war we might have won, except President Truman and General MacArthur got crossways with each other. A lot of the callers to my radio show in Paris are Korean War veterans. They didn't get many welcome-home parades either. Thank goodness, a memorial that honors those who fought in the "forgotten war" now stands, appropriately, near the Vietnam Memorial in Washington, D.C.

The civil rights movement reached its peak during my days at KRLD. In Dallas, we didn't have nearly the upheaval that happened in many other parts of the country, certainly no major race riots.

The civil rights movement never took on the intensity in Dallas that it did in Montgomery, Birmingham, and other southern cities. Birmingham police chief Bull Connors became known through television. He did not have a clone in Dallas law enforcement. And although Juanita Craft was known to defy convention by sitting in the white section on the train, she never sparked the uproar that Rosa Parks did by refusing to give her seat to a white passenger on a Montgomery city bus. Of course, the Dallas black community was aware of what was going on in the civil rights movement, but, for whatever reason, avoided the massive demonstrations their brothers and sisters were staging elsewhere. The fire hoses, the dogs, the beatings and jailings didn't happen in Dallas.

One of the things I remember is a white man — can't remember his name — who drove a big bus with a picture painted on it of a white hand shaking a black hand. He drove it to the old Woolworth's in downtown Dallas, which had a lunch counter, and he went in there with a group of black people. They sat down and, as in Alabama around the same time, the manager of the place wouldn't serve them. It was a story at the time, but nothing much came of it.

You look back and think how awful it was that you had "colored" drinking fountains and "colored" restrooms, and blacks could sit only in the back of the bus. So ridiculous. But you knew it had to change.

I love to see blacks succeed in fields that were closed to them before. For example, Shaun Rabb at Channel 4 is a really fine reporter. Plus, he's got his own style, always wearing an elegant hat. He's my kind of reporter.

In Dallas, we certainly had a lot of bigots. They grew up that way, and it took a few generations to break away from it. But still, somehow, things remained fairly quiet in the city during the civil rights era. I remember when we first integrated, I think they integrated eighteen schools that day, and we were just on needles and pins. But nothing happened. As I've mentioned, I tried to get CBS News interested, but they said no thanks — no trouble, no story.

Of course, U.S. Judge Barefoot Sanders stepped in and took control of desegregation in the Dallas Independent School District in 1970 because it was not progressing to his satisfaction. It was thirty-three years before the federal court order was rescinded.

I grew up in San Antonio, which was a very racially mixed society. San Antonio has always been 50 percent or more Hispanic. I remember in the drugstore where I worked was a young Mexican American who had started as a delivery boy, just as I did. He had gone to college and returned to work at the drugstore as a pharmacist.

The blacks in San Antonio were not treated much better than they were in Dallas, however, or anywhere else in the South. Unlike the Mexican Americans, they were not allowed to use the "white" restrooms in San Antonio. Lots of the Hispanics lived on the poor west side of town, but they could live anywhere if they could afford it, which was not true for the blacks.

Still, I'd like to think that growing up in racially diverse San Antonio helped make me more tolerant and that I've passed that on to my kids. Surely, their mother deserves just as much credit, if not more, for their racial openness. All five went to virtually all-white Highland Park High School. Two of my daughters married Mexican American men. They've all happily and unselfconsciously worked and played with members of all other races. I'm very proud of that.

To my knowledge, Martin Luther King never officially visited Dallas, but I met him once in Chicago in the early days of his crusade. We were planning a Radio Television News Directors Association meeting. One of our members said he had heard of Dr. King and we should consider inviting him to speak. We did. I'll never forget his speech.

He was introduced and moved to the podium. I'll paraphrase his opening remarks: "Gentlemen, I am honored that you have allowed me this opportunity to speak to you. But unfortunately, the speech I had prepared is still on my desk in Atlanta. In my haste to catch the plane that brought me here, I left the speech behind. But in summary, this is what I was prepared to say."

And with that, Martin Luther King launched into a barn burner and received a standing ovation when he concluded some twenty minutes later. I hate to doubt Dr. King's word, but it's hard to believe he ad-libbed such an eloquent and powerful speech. He had a showman's sense of drama, and I'll bet he'd used that "no speech" bit before. That was the only time our paths ever crossed.

I've mentioned my distrust of Lyndon Johnson. But you've got to give him credit for one thing and that's his Great Society, the network of social programs he created working with Congress. Whatever your opinion of the Great Society, I think it's indisputable that Johnson tried to do something good for the country, to take care of people who genuinely need help. It was his high-water mark as president.

On the other hand, as far back as 1965, Daniel Patrick Moynihan, then the Johnson administration's assistant secretary for policy planning and research and later the U.S. senator from New York, warned that greater dependence on welfare programs would have a destructive effect on the family: "There is one unmistakable lesson in American history: A community that allows a large number of young men to grow up in broken families, dominated by women, never acquiring any stable relationship to male authority, never acquiring any rational expectations about the future—that community asks for and gets chaos." And I think his prediction has come true.

I think the big problem the country has more than anything else is the decay of the family unit. Marriage, unfortunately, doesn't mean much anymore to a lot of people. When you read the records at Parkland Hospital, it's unbelievable how many illegitimate births there are. Certainly, federal welfare programs have made it possible for men to shirk their duties as fathers, if not as husbands. What happens to the fathers of all these little illegitimate children? Nothing. They just go and get somebody else pregnant. What really blows my mind are the baby showers given for the unwed mothers, with no husband or father in sight. It doesn't seem the occasion to celebrate.

As I was leaving a memorial service for longtime Channel 8 news director Marty Haag, one of Channel 4's former news directors called out to me, "Eddie, do you have a minute to meet somebody?"

I said, "Sure, who is it?"

He said, "It's Maria Barrs, the news director at Channel 4." We had a great conversation, talking about the old days and the new days at Channel 4. But it reminded me again of how much things have changed. For so many years at KRLD radio and TV, we had no women at all in the newsroom. Now a woman is the news director. As this is written, Kathy Clements is the general manager of WFAA, Keven Ann Willey is the editorial page editor of the *Morning News.* Plenty of other examples.

It used to be that the man was the breadwinner. It's not always the case these days, when six- , sometimes seven-figure salaries are paid to female news anchors. No big deal anymore when the wife gets the big offer to move. What's a husband to do? "Come on, you'll find something to do."

To show how different it is now, when I hired Judy Jordan as the first female television news anchor in Dallas–Fort Worth, I had to sneak her on the air very quietly because I didn't know what kind of reaction I'd get. (All right, I'll grant you, Bobbie Wygant at Channel 5 was on the air long before Judy, but Bobbie was a show-biz interviewer—the best at what she did—but not a newscaster.)

I was afraid of the reaction that, indeed, I did get. I remember Clyde Rembert, the president of KRLD, called me in and nervously asked, "Who is that girl you have on the air?" I reassured him and played to his sense of competition: "Mr. Rembert, we're the *first.* All of the other stations are going to be putting women on the air."

He was very uneasy about it. "You really think they're all going to do it?" he asked.

"Yes, sir."

I originally hired Judy in the mid-'60s as a "girl Friday," to use an old-fashioned phrase. She was my assistant or secretary. I guess I was the first news director in the Dallas market to have a secretary. The first secretary I had left the job, and Judy took her place. I didn't hire her as a reporter at all. But she had such a vivacious personality, an attractive girl with a good voice. A lovely person. So we decided to start using her on the air in some things.

We first started using her on a Saturday morning KRLD radio call-in show called *Teen Comment*, kind of a spin-off of *Comment*. It was supposed to attract a teenage audience. Of course, teens didn't really listen to the show, but that was Judy's start.

Then, as television stations did with their women reporters in those days, we started giving her some schmaltzy, easy-to-do TV feature pieces. I put Bill Ceverha in charge of Judy. When she first started doing TV, she could be a little "out to lunch," and Bill would good-naturedly complain about having to direct this neophyte. But, clearly, she had the raw talent.

One of the light pieces we did with Judy was a feature about the size of the new Dallas telephone book. The city was growing like a bloodhound pup, and we did a piece on how enormous the phone book was getting to be. The idea was, "The book is so big, it would certainly be impossible to tear it in two." But we rigged a phone book by nearly cutting the pages in half except for the cover and then we had petite little Judy tear it in half! A funny sight gag. It took us the better part of a day to shoot it, because even though we cut the pages in half, she still couldn't tear it.

Judy was very comfortable in front of the camera, and so we started using her some as an anchor. But we had a saying: "Nobody ever comes into this newsroom as a star." We had no stars. Nobody at Channel 4 ever got to the point some other Dallas–Fort Worth anchors did of demanding that they be picked up and taken to the studio in a chauffeured limousine. Certainly not Judy.

Looking back, I guess I was guilty of doing what I'm always cussing everyone else out for doing, putting an attractive face on TV. But Judy got better and better as a reporter and as an anchor. People *really* liked her. And you can't overestimate the importance of that in television.

My coauthor, John Mark Dempsey talked to Judy during the process of writing this book:

Judy Jordan did not look upon breaking the barrier for women television reporters in Dallas–Fort Worth as a particularly courageous act on her part. She didn't set out to be a pioneer. She simply hired on as Eddie Barker's "gofer" and soon found herself first behind a microphone at KRLD radio and then in front of the camera at Channel 4.

"I never found it a disadvantage being a woman," Judy, who has lost none of her effervescent charm, says. She remembers getting around security at Love Field when Lady Bird Johnson visited Dallas. "I could usually smile my way through," she recalls.

But she remembers that, in at least one way, Eddie treated her differently from other reporters. "Eddie would not allow a woman to carry a camera," she says. "He thought it would be like having a run in my stockings, not a good image."

Eddie assigned Judy to cover entertainment news, a role that led to some exotic assignments such as covering the Cannes Film Festival in France and a series of reports on pornographic film making in Dallas. "I didn't know anything like that was going on. It turned out to be a big business," she laughs. "Eddie assigned a detective to go with me. He thought I was too sheltered."

When Cary Grant visited Dallas, Judy and many other local reporters tried to interview the screen legend. But Grant was going through a divorce from Dyan Cannon at the time and was not in a happy frame of mind. When Judy tried to interview him, Grant covered her microphone with his hand and said, "No interviews, no interviews."

Judy was hosting *Swap and Shop* on KRLD radio at the time. She had to hustle back for the show. "I'm going to have a hard time concentrating on *Swap and Shop* because I've just been rejected by Cary Grant," she joked on the air. Someone in Grant's circle heard what Judy said and told Grant. He called in to the show and told Judy, with true Cary Grant panache, "I'd like to see you without your microphone."

"It was the greatest education," Judy remembers of her years working for Eddie Barker. "It was fascinating. There was a constant parade of movers and shakers coming into the station because of Eddie Barker. He set the tone and atmosphere. Everyone was welcome."

Judy remembers Eddie for his compassion and kindness. She likens him to the wise Jedi Master of the "Star Wars" movies: "He's my Yoda."

And one thing more: "If Walter Cronkite was the most trusted man in America, Eddie Barker was the most trusted man in Dallas."

Another of the first women we had in the newsroom was Davie Ann Browder. She was a darn good reporter, out on the street, really doing the heavy lifting. As you've read, I'm a big admirer of newspaper journalism, and in doing the research for this book, I was glad to learn that Davie Ann has become the managing editor of the *Castro County News*, in Dimmit, out in West Texas.

It's not just in broadcasting and newspapers in which women are making great strides, of course, but all of business. We're gaining from the talent of these women, whereas, decades ago, they never would have had the chance to show what they can do. Everybody ought to have an opportunity. But, in a way, I do think that the rising status of women in business has hurt the family. So often, their career track really means more to them than the family. That's one reason, I guess, that you see later marriages. The average age of couples entering into their first marriages has gone up about five years in the last two decades.

Some women are luckier than others in being able to balance home and career. My daughter Leslie, for example, goes into the *Morning News* office only two days per week. She writes at home. Not many are so fortunate, but computer technology being what it is, I hope more will be able to do what Leslie does. It's so much better for the family.

As a journalist, this is not easy for me to say: The First Amendment is a curse as well as a blessing. It has been used as a defense for all kinds of terribly destructive things. (I don't believe in book burnings, never have, never will. But when it comes to wanting to burn every last copy of *JFK*, Oliver Stone's conspiratorial movie about the Kennedy assassination, I want to light the first match. What this travesty has fostered for future generations is terrible: a pack of lies in an attempt to create history that doesn't exist.)

I spent many years in television, but even so, I think television has played a big role in tearing down the family. A lot of the programs on television don't support the family unit. In fact, they work directly against it. And, of course, it's available twenty-four hours a day. It's so easy to sit there, stare at the tube, and not take care of your family.

It's not just television. *Playboy* comes along. It seems relatively mild today, but it created a firestorm in the '50s, the first mass-marketed magazine with lots of female nudity. But Hugh Hefner and his supporters argued that it should be allowed on First Amendment grounds. And, of course, as the old bit goes, it did have some great articles. (One of those articles was an interview with president-to-be Jimmy Carter in which the usually straitlaced Carter admitted he had "lusted in his heart." And *Playboy* played the exclusive for all it was worth.) Then comes *Penthouse*, and it's worse than *Playboy*. And then *Hustler*. And now you have all the child porn on the Internet. And how to explain Viagra and Cialis commercials to a ten-year-old? It's too much.

As I was writing this, the chairman of the FCC, Michael Powell, was having to deal with some highly publicized incidents of indecency on television that not too long ago would have been unthinkable. The rock star Bono blurted the "f" word on some awards show. And then Janet Jackson decided it would be a good idea to flash her breast during the Super Bowl halftime show. I guess it's encouraging that a large segment of the population is still outraged when such things happen on broadcast TV.

But even though the influence of the mass media has been increasingly negative, who guards the guards? That always scares me. I don't want some ultraconservative deciding what you can write or not write, or read or not read. So there are no easy answers.

It doesn't guarantee that children will turn out to be good, but we reared our kids in the church. Whatever your faith may be, I think children learn a moral discipline there that they don't get anywhere else. I should say that I'm encouraged by the number of young people coming into our church, First Presbyterian in downtown Dallas. A lot of them are attracted by the church's Stew Pot Program, which provides help for the homeless and other needy people. These young folks simply want to help people less fortunate than themselves and want to teach their kids the same thing. You have to feel good about that.

Glad to say, all of our daughters are busy in their churches, Jeanne at Park Cities Baptist, and Susan and Leslie at First Presbyterian. Jeanne's husband, David, is a deacon at Park Cities. Susan's husband, Carlos, is an elder at First Presbyterian.

Ultimately, I have to believe the answer to cleaning things up must lie with ourselves. What got us started on this downhill slide? It is the philosophy in which nothing is sacred, in which you ought to be able to do whatever you want to do, whatever it is, no matter what. Total freedom. I fear we have lost the old wisdom that everybody must answer to something greater than themselves. As John Milton wrote, "License they mean when they cry, Liberty! For who loves that must first be wise and good."

I spent a big part of my career broadcasting football games, but I don't worship at the altar of sports. We are living in an era of a new breed of snake-oil salesmen, the owners of teams in the NFL. Oh, sure, the baseballers and the roundballers have their gig, too. Both the Rangers and the Astros threatened to move if they didn't get new stadiums. But it's harder for baseball teams to make threats, because it takes a larger population base to support a baseball team (eighty-one home games a season), plus there aren't a lot of vacant fifty thousand–seat baseball stadiums out there ready for occupancy. The NFL teams can do what the Houston Oilers did when they moved to Tennessee and play in a college stadium for a year or two while the new arena is being built. As for basketball, the Mavericks threatened to move to Lewisville before the city built the new American Airlines Center, just twenty years after it built Reunion Arena.

But it's the footballers at whom I direct my venom. You know why? Because they're a bunch of cheapskates. They fast-talk cities and gullible fans into building new palaces for them; well and good, but they want you, the fan, to foot the bill. And if you don't, the threat that they'll up and move makes poor city fathers quake in their tax proceeds. "Oh, Lord in Heaven, whatever it costs to keep them, we'll pay through the nose or whatever, but we can't lose them. Our city will be in shambles." How about Los Angeles? LA lost not one but two teams. The Rams and the Raiders left town, but there's no sign asking the last person out of town to turn out the lights. Somewhere, someday, I hope a city will stand up and say, "Build the damn thing yourself with your own money." Call their bluff. I fear it will never happen. In fact, as I'm writing this, the voters of Arlington, persuaded that the stadium will bring an economic windfall to the city, have agreed to help Jerry Jones build a new football palace.

But the real mark of NFL owners being cheapskates is manifested in what happens following every touchdown or field goal attempt— up goes that big ugly wire fence to keep the cheap-seat fan from getting a football. At the most, how much would it cost these scrooges per ball game? And back to those city-built stadiums: it's doubtful the average fan will ever see a game there because he or she can't afford to pay the ticket price designed for the expense-account crowd only. Ol' P. T. Barnum had a point.

George Allen (not the Redskins coach) was a councilman of the old school, elected with the Citizens Charter Association blessing, the first black elected to the Dallas City Council, in 1969. While George, for whom the county courts building is named, wanted the best for South Dallas and other minority neighborhoods, his pledge was to Dallas as a whole. This was before the individual fiefdoms (single-member districts) that exist today.

George always felt that the R. L. Thornton Freeway (built before he joined the council) should have been built on the south side of Fair Park, so that it did not separate the park from downtown. His concern was that the area surrounding the park would always be considered as being on the "wrong side of the tracks," and not as part of the whole. That thinking made a lot of sense, but like so many things that make a lot of sense, it never made the cut.

Just as surely as the area around Fair Park has declined—as George feared—the Cotton Bowl has crumbled with age. Its lack of luxury suites and ladies' rooms leads to the chilling thought that it might lose the Texas/OU game or a first-class New Year's Day bowl game. What's to happen? Good question.

As much as we may long for "the good old days," they're gone forever, thanks to what happened in Washington and New York. By crashing those airplanes into the World Trade Center and the Pentagon on September 11, 2001, terrorists put us on the defensive from now on. As this is being written, a high-profile committee is desperately trying to nail someone or "someones," other than Osama bin Laden, for what happened. No way that's ever going to happen. What's done is done. Cut the losses and move on.

We used to look at the Israelis and think how awful it would be to live like they have to live. They can never get on a bus, go out to eat, or just be part of a large gathering without thinking about what has happened to countless countrymen before them, victims of terrorists whose mind-set is beyond our comprehension. The Israelis have learned to live that way, and we'd better get used to joining them. Things are different now.

In World War II, some of the bloodiest fighting in the proud history of the Marine Corps took place on the tiny island of Guadalcanal in the South Pacific. A top priority was communication between units. We used a code that the Japanese soon broke. What to do? Improvise and adjust, and that's just what the marines did. Several hundred Navajo Indians served as marines and, of course, they spoke the Navajo language. Long story made short, the Navajo code talkers were born, and history records their effort as a major factor in winning the battle. It's a fascinating story and a good read for you history buffs.

And how, you ask, do the Navajo code talkers fit in with what we're talking about, terrorism? Good question. Communication was vital and the Navajos brilliantly improvised, answering the call for help. Not only was it vital that the marines have the ability to communicate with each other, it was just as vital that the enemy not be able to take advantage of those communications. Secure communications are just as vital today as then. The media may answer today's call for help—by *not* communicating. Here's what I mean.

It's hard to count the number of media outlets today that live and die for a ten-second beat on the competition. Ten seconds! Being Number One! Well, a lot of listeners are tuned in out there, and many of them have something in common: they speak English. A famous World War II poster shows a sinking ship and a sailor saying, "Loose Lips Sink Ships."

Not long after the Columbine massacre (itself a kind of terrorism), *Chicago Tribune* writer Carl Gottlieb criticized the live helicopter shots of students fleeing the school. Gottlieb rightly pointed out that the live pictures could have helped the twisted killers pick off the kids as they were getting away. He calls it "point-and-shoot journalism": "How important was it for those Littleton scenes to air immediately? Should stations have waited for students to reach safety before putting these dramatic escape shots on TV? Why not take the minimum precaution you would take with any videotaped story and verify who and what you're putting on the air? . . . In recent focus groups, conducted by the Project for Excellence in Journalism, viewers told us that being first was not as important as being right. Regular TV news viewers, in two cities, unequivocally said glitzy tools, such as live shots from helicopters, were far less important than reliable, concise information." See where I'm going with this? I'm not advocating censorship; newspapers and broadcasters should not back off in the search for news. But if what you find looks like it might be helpful to terrorists, think before you break the story and think about how you cover the story.

On the other hand, the country was sent reeling by news of how some American military personnel treated Iraqi war prisoners in their care at Abu Ghraib prison. Pictures of American servicemen and women disgracing their country by their actions brought instant outrage from every corner and left the military scurrying to find answers for a seething Congress: "How high in the command chain does this despicable action go?" It is inconceivable that Americans would ever stand accused of the actions that took place in that Baghdad prison.

The furious controversy began when Dan Rather showed the photos on *60 Minutes II*. Should the pictures have been shown? Yes, no doubt about it. The chairman of the Joint Chiefs asked CBS to not run the pictures, at least to hold off for a while, which CBS did. General Richard Myers knew what would happen when the pictures saw daylight, and the reaction was explosive, endangering the jobs and careers of generals and the secretary of defense as well as privates. No doubt, General Myers also feared that the photos would give fuel to the terrorists and Iraqi insurgents, which they did.

Some of us want to play arbiter of what the public should know and when it should know it. We may be our brother's keeper, but not in protecting him from the realities of life. Certainly, if the immediate threat of danger exists for some individuals, the media must carefully consider its actions. And we hope that the media will react that way, but the proliferation of news outlets has too often made the desire to be first dominant over accuracy and responsibility. However, if the military or the government seeks the media's help in a cover-up: no way.

Dan interviewed former Marine Lieutenant Colonel Bill Cowan, who had extensive experience as an interrogator of prisoners. He asked Cowan what he would say to people who opposed the photos being released because it would undermine the war on terror. Here's what he said: "If we don't tell this story, these kinds of things will continue. And we'll end up getting paid back 100 or 1,000 times over. Americans want to be proud of each and every thing that our servicemen and women do in Iraq. We want to be proud. We know they're working hard. None of us, now, later, before or during this conflict, should want to let incidents like this just pass."

Remember, there is no censor reading the reporter's notebook or looking at his tape, nor should there be. Every reporter is on his own. And that's a big responsibility. We must exercise it wisely.

Of course, in early 2005, Dan Rather stepped down as anchor of the *CBS Evening News,* after the furor over his *60 Minutes II* piece that attempted to hurt George W. Bush by showing (with what proved to be forged documents) that the president supposedly received favoritism in getting into the National Guard during the Vietnam War.

Frankly, I had felt for a long time that every piece on the *CBS Evening News* that Dan delivered regarding the president showed his obvious disdain for Bush. It showed not just in the *60 Minutes II* disaster, but in his lead-ins and the copy of any *Evening News* story that pertained to the president. Unfortunately, this all contributed to Dan's rather abrupt "retirement" as the anchor of the *Evening News*.

Dan's done some fine reporting through the years, but he hit a low-water mark on this one. His zeal to let the president have one "pow, right in the kisser" (as Jackie Gleason used to bluster) shone like a beacon in the night. I saw where Don Hewitt, the recently retired *60 Minutes* producer, said the story was old news four years ago (even if it had been true) and it would have never aired under his watch. Dan's would-be torpedo was a bit flaccid and, if anything, just helped to make the map "redder" than ever.

I've always said there are two Dan Rathers: one you are proud to call your friend, and the other who achieves his goal at any cost. And I have known them both.

As I wrote earlier, he asked me to induct him into the Texas Radio Hall of Fame. I felt good that he asked me, and I did so with words, I think you will agree, that spelled out the best in Dan. I've got to say I still really like him, warts and all.

Remember when I gave that sage advice to Chip Moody to ask for a signing bonus if he was going to Channel 4? I imagine Channel 4 considered it peanuts to get Chip away from Channel 5. Well, I've been thinking about the time I should have made a like demand in my own case.

You know how CBS was drooling over getting into the Texas School Book Depository and looking out that infamous window? They knew the only prayer they had was through me, and as I have related elsewhere in this book, I knew the combination that got them in. Of course, Dan Rather broke all speed records in getting into that window and blocking all comers. See where I'm going with this? You're right: I should have told producer Don Hewitt the only way I would get access to the window for CBS was if I was the reporter in the window, not Dan Rather. I imagine that, had I played it tough, ol' Dan would have been where I turned out to be, on the street. Darn!

What has happened to the *CBS Evening News* since Bob Schieffer, my old *Fort Worth Star-Telegram* friend, took over is something to behold. As of this writing, the network says he is interim, but if it were my call, I'd forget any further changes. The way Bob is using his reporters in a conversational way—talking to them one to one about their stories—reminds me of what we did at Channel 4. I hope Bob will forget about any retirement plans for a decade or so.

When I went to KRLD-TV in 1949, we were doing fifteen-minute local newscasts a couple of times per day. Today, besides the expansion of local news into half-hour or hour blocks, seen numerous times per day, we have round-the-clock cable and satellite news channels. It's been a huge change for television news, and it hasn't all been for the good.

I watch MSNBC a lot, more than CNN and the Fox News Network. CNN *Headline News* is so repetitive and visually busy it's hard for me to watch. The cable networks are great if you have a big, breaking story, like 9-11 or the beginning of the Iraq war, although, as I said before, the networks need to use very good judgment in how they cover those stories. They would probably love a Mars mission, because, joking aside, it would be a meaningful, ongoing story they could cover for months.

But how many times in a twenty-four-hour period during the proceedings over the child-abuse charges against Michael Jackson did we see him going into the courthouse and coming out of the courthouse? How many times did we see Martha Stewart coming and going? There is not enough legitimate news to run a news channel twenty-four hours a day. By having all of that time to fill, networks build up stories that don't deserve being built up. To broadcast twenty-four hours on something that's ultimately going to be a blip on history's radar screen, or on the back page of the newspaper, is wrong.

I don't know what the answer is, but how about this? You might liken a news channel to a firehouse. Firefighters go about their routine duties but leave the door to the truck open, and they're ready to go when an alarm goes off. Whenever something big happens, a light on your TV screen would appear, and that would signal that big news was breaking. MSNBC, or whatever, would then spring to life and you could go and check it out. Of course, it'll never happen. But the twenty-four-hour concept definitely needs work.

Those of us who have been around a while, at least if they're like me, must look askance at the big change that lets one company own as many radio or television stations as the bank will finance. 'Tain't good, not for employees, listeners, or advertisers.

What's so bad about it? Let's start with employees. Say you get fired from a station or quit for whatever reason, but want to stay in the business and not leave town. Already in some not-so-small towns, one company or individual holds every broadcast license. The fired employee has nowhere to go.

What happens to the advertiser who doesn't want to pay the hike in the rates that is sure to come in such a monopoly? Either he pays them or he isn't advertising on the air. And as the listener, you must either like it or hope your antenna finds a faraway signal to satisfy your wants. Competition? It's not in the FCC's playbook.

The excellent new book by longtime National Public Radio anchor Bob Edwards on Edward R. Murrow quotes a story from *Forbes* magazine about the most powerful man in radio today—the owner of twelve hundred stations—Lowery Mays. Mays, founder of Clear Channel Communications, is quoted as saying something that should make the blood of any radio newsman run cold: "We're not in the business of providing news and information. We're simply in the business of selling our customers products." I'm glad Mr. Mays and his ilk came on the scene as I was leaving. When you say your prayers tonight, remember those twelve hundred Clear Channel news directors.

One of the issues in the presidential election of 2004 was the "outsourcing" of jobs, hiring lower-cost workers outside the normal company structure. I have a lot of sympathy for those whose jobs have been done in by outsourcing, because I've been a victim of it myself.

I was itching to get back into major-market broadcasting. My thinking process was sound, my tones were still dulcet, I could hear the thunder when it clapped, and I still knew how to write a story. I wasn't as old as Paul Harvey or Andy Rooney or Don Hewitt. With those plusses, I decided to see if I could interest my old station in using all these talents in some way. I called KRLD's then-news director Bob Morrison, whom I barely knew, and said I'd like to see him. "Great," Bob said, "come at noon tomorrow and I'll buy lunch." He couldn't have been more gracious. Before the meeting was over, I had a weekend job.

For several years, I was riding pretty high. In the late '90s and the early 2000s, I'd leave the farm in Delta County every Saturday about five o'clock in the morning and head west to KRLD, a hundred miles or so down the road. And there I had a field day, back in the news-room writing, editing, and airing news on my old alma mater again. Not a Saturday went by that I didn't get some calls from longtime KRLD listeners or their offspring who had listened to me all those years ago.

I kept the Saturday job for five years. And why did it end? Glad you asked. The phone rang and it was the news director. Bob Morrison had long since gone and three or four others had carried the title before the one who called. Pleasantries aside, the clap of thunder I never wanted to hear resounded all too clearly in my ear: Don't bother coming in Saturday; we won't be needing you anymore. Or words to that effect. And I immediately speculated on the reason. "Is it my age?" I asked.

"No, no, no, no," came the reply.

"Have my dulcet tones failed me?"

"No, no, no," again the reply.

"Well, why am I being fired?" I asked. And the answer floored me.

"We want to save money and we've made a deal with the traffic-report people to take over what you've been doing," the news director said.

Outsourcing. It happens everywhere these days. Who would have thought that those Radio Flyer wagons would be built in China, or Levi's, the jeans that helped win the West, would be stitched in Thailand?

An article in the February 2004 issue of *The Communicator*, the official publication of the Radio Television News Directors Association, reports a Kansas City television station, KCTV, has made a deal with the local cable company to outsource the station's local sports news. The article doesn't sound encouraging to sports anchors in general, citing the emergence of all-sports radio stations and ESPN, where the diehard sports fan will go rather than have to wait for the station to get around to sports at the end of the newscast. So I guess I was on the cutting edge of what "cutting" is all about. With the years come changes. You can count on it.

Still, I have a lot of affection for KRLD, and I take a genuine interest in what happens there. Like most other AM radio stations, KRLD has had to scuffle for its listeners in recent years. Formats and talk-show hosts have come and gone. A suggestion? *Swap and Shop*! Wes, are you available?

Recent events in Dallas have not exactly reflected well on the city's leadership. The loss of the Cowboys to Arlington, the decline of convention business, the hiring of a firebrand director for the Convention and Visitors Bureau after the former head resigned in disgrace; the return of Frank Poe to manage the convention center; finally, the realization that the "biggies" would pass the city by without a convention hotel; the ongoing bickering between the mayor and the council; the firing of the city manager and the rumbling among the natives that it was time to permanently dump the city-manager form of government to be replaced with a strong, really strong, mayor, even though voters rejected such a proposal in 2005.

Dallas hasn't had a mayor of the Erik Jonsson mold in a long time.

Recent mayors have used the office as a stepping-stone to further their careers. The real "head" of the city has been the city manager, not responsible to the citizens but only to the council. Some say it is "un-Dallas" to say that the single-member districts fall way short, but they do. A bunch of little fiefdoms ruled by tunnel vision, not that vision of "Dallas as a Whole" imprinted on the *Times Herald* wall. A good, strong mayor with the power to get things done is long overdue, but the idea's time will come, just wait and see. Another burst bubble was the loss of the Cowboys to those upstarts out in Arlington. Two mayors, thirty years apart, each played the wrong hand on that one.

The Convention and Visitors Bureau hired the Richards Group, a local advertising agency, to come up with an $80,000 slogan that would set the city apart. They did and the new tag line for Dallas is "Live Large, Think Big." I wonder what Dr. Phil's reaction to that would be. The city needs to think positively about itself, but it needs some outsider to tell it how to do it.

Fortunately, after my return to KRLD came to an end, I still had an outlet for my broadcast ambitions. Anyone who's met me knows I love to share ideas on the events of the day. It's great to do that with people you meet as you go about your everyday business, but there's nothing like having the platform of a television or radio show to express yourself and let others do the same. So I've been lucky since moving to the country to have my daily talk show on KPLT, *The Talk of Paris*. The farm, the show, and my family keep my days more than full.

10

"And Miles to Go . . ."

Whatever else you've done in your career, unless the warmth of a close family has enriched your life, it seems to me it would all be hollow. Well, when it comes to family, I've been richly blessed.

I met my wife, Jane, when she was a stewardess for American Airlines. She transferred to Dallas from her native New York City to find some warmer weather. We met, became good friends, and soon it was more than friendship. Jane grew up in Brooklyn as Jane Elizabeth Rosebrock. She went to a teacher's college in upstate New York.

Of course, I was an only child; as I've mentioned, my mother was in her mid-40s and my dad in his mid-50s when I came along. Jane had a brother eighteen years older and a sister ten years older, so, in a way, she was an only child with no siblings to grow up with. We married in her home church, Grace Reformed Church in Brooklyn, on February 6, 1954, yes, now more than fifty years ago. In those days, stewardesses (as they were called at the time) had to quit when they got married.

We were not family planners. We just figured that was up to the Good Lord. In a six-year period, He blessed us five times, with Allan, Susan, Leslie, Ben, and Jeanne, the first, Allan, born December 27, 1954.

Allan did not choose the college route, but is a ticketless truck driver. When he was in high school, he started throwing a *Dallas Morning News* route in the Park Cities, and he still does today. He loves watching the sun rise every morning.

Susan went to the University of Kansas and is married to Carlos Munguia, a native Dallasite, who is now a bank president. I've always said that Susan is the next Erma Bombeck. She writes a good deal for a children's publication, and some of her work is in a class by itself. She's also written some guest columns for the *Dallas Morning News*.

Leslie went to Baylor and from there to the *Morning News*. Her husband is Juan Garcia, a photographer for the *News*.

Ben went to the University of Oklahoma. He's the athlete of the family, never overweight, always working out. You know the type. He had a long career with the Secret Service and switched over to the sky marshal program, and, as of this writing, is involved in something he doesn't discuss. Ben finally married at the age of forty-three, much to the delight of his mother and sisters. Meg Steele is from California, but, like Ben, thinks Washington, D.C., is the best place to live. They married on the lawn of the Jefferson Memorial. Meg's great, and a welcome addition to the family. As of this writing, she is with C-Span, the nonprofit cable network that covers government, in its educational department.

Jeanne earned the top award for Latin students at Highland Park High School and went to the University of Oklahoma. She's in *Who's Who in American Universities* and, not wanting to see that honor end with her, she's busy with the PTA and makes sure her four are well prepared for the classroom. She married David Wilgus, a native son of Dallas. David and Susan's husband, Carlos, were roommates in college, at the University of North Texas, and Carlos introduced David to Jeanne. David heads his own advertising agency.

The three girls have given us some terrific grandchildren, the first one, Paul, graduating from high school in 2004, and now at the University of Kansas, his mother, Susan's, alma mater. Then there are Susan's other three—Ben, Julie, and Christian; Jeanne's four—Laura, Jack, Sam, and Claire; and Leslie's Charlie.

What else can I tell you? Five beautiful children, three great sons-in-law, a lovely daughter-in-law, and nine wonderful grandchildren. Doesn't get much better than that.

We lived in several rent houses and then found a little house on Devonshire Street in Richardson in 1957 that we could buy by picking up the payments. It was pleasant enough, but I wanted something more, especially when it came time for the kids to go to school. I knew that the Highland Park district was the best and that I would love it if we could ever afford to move there. But KRLD didn't pay Park Cities salaries, and a move there wouldn't be easy.

Then one day I was looking through the *Times-Herald* classifieds and a little two-line ad caught my eye. Something about an old house in University Park. I called the phone number. A lady answered and I asked about the house. For some reason, we got to talking about a lot of other things. Finally, she said, "I like you and I want you to go look at the house. It is on University Boulevard, just west of Hillcrest." She told me where to find the key. "Call me back," she said.

I called Jane and told her that as soon as I got off the air I would be home to pick her and the kids up and we would go look. She kind of chuckled when I told her where it was. We got there, I found the key, and we went inside. The owner had neglected to tell me the electricity had been turned off. We groped our way downstairs and upstairs and knew it was big, but we couldn't see it, only feel it.

I called the lady and said we would go back the next day and see it. She said fine. We did go back. Five bedrooms, two baths, a basement, a huge yard. But it was in disrepair and needed work. We found out she had used it as a rooming house for SMU students. And at one time, it was the manse of the Highland Park Methodist Church.

I called the lady back and said we were certainly impressed—how much did she want for the house? "Twenty-five thousand," she said. That was a lot of money in those days.

"That's a little beyond what I can afford," I told her. I had barely gotten the words out of my mouth when she said, "If you don't have enough for a down payment, I'll reduce the price to $24,000 and I'll carry a second lien." Remember now, at this juncture I had never met the owner. I knew her only from our phone conversations.

"I want you to have that house," she told me. And then came the real reason she was ready to sell it to me. "There is a Jew who has offered me $26,000 for the house, but I won't sell to a Jew."

The rawness of the woman's prejudice notwithstanding, I saw that this was something I couldn't pass up. I got Cullen Thompson at the old United Fidelity Insurance Company to give me a $19,000 loan and the owner took a five-year, $5,000 second lien, and we moved to the Park Cities. The kids all went through the Highland Park schools, made wonderful friends they keep to this day, and grew up living in a wonderful community—thanks, I'm sorry to say, to bigotry. Later, I met the person the owner wouldn't sell to and developed a friendship with him. He said, "I tried to buy that house, but could never make a deal." I never told him the story of why he couldn't.

Now Jane and I live on our little farm, halfway between Sulphur Springs and Paris, with assorted dogs and a flock of peacocks. At Christmas 2004, daughter Leslie presented me with two donkeys. They live for forty years; I doubt that I'll be around when they pass on, but you never know.

Jane said she always dreamed of living in the country someday. And now she does.

Remember that little two-line *Times Herald* ad that led me to University Park? Well, it was another little two-line ad, this time in the *Dallas Morning News*, that led us to the farm.

Sometimes you think about doing this or that, but the timing of "this" doesn't match with "that," and you do neither. Finally, all of the elements come together and the time is right. For instance? How about this? The kids have all finally cleaned out their bedrooms for good, you're tiring a bit of the daily office grind, someone comes along eager to buy the big house, and, at the same time, you've found a place in the country that you've just got to have. That, in a nutshell, is my story. After thinking of all these things over a long period of time, suddenly the opportunity to do them all is there. Let's do it! And we did. It was time to move on.

We had lived in the same house on University Boulevard in University Park for over thirty years. The kids had all been afforded the excellent education of the Highland Park schools and all had moved out on their own, their college days behind them and the future before them. I had started to wind down the business, and it was a good time to exit. Real estate had started a mercurial climb, and our little investment thirty years before would pay off handsomely. The house sold quickly and we started looking.

One Saturday morning, I was going through the *Morning News*'s classified section and ran across a little two-line ad that caught my eye. The owner wanted to sell this place near Cooper with lots of privacy. Jane said, "Call and see about it." I called and the rather no-nonsense lady who answered gave me the rundown. I stopped her and asked, "Well, is there any privacy there?"

"Honey," she replied, "you could run around buck naked all day up here and never be seen." So we decided to drive up and take a look. Daughter Jeanne and son Ben came along. We saw the place and I thought back to what old Brigham Young said when he saw the Salt Lake Valley: "This is the place." And it was. I told the lady I'd call her back, but we already knew this was the place we wanted. We happily landed in Northeast Texas on a thirty-acre farm ten miles from the nearest loaf of bread after a long, full life in the big city.

Farm life was fine up to a point, but after awhile, I started climbing the walls. I wanted to do something! I decided to call the owner of KPLT radio in Paris, Jeff Methven. I had known Jeff for years, especially when KPLT carried a Humble football broadcast every Saturday. I rang him and he said, "Great to hear from you. Come on down and I'll buy lunch." We talked about a lot of things, including talk shows. He said he had never had a talk show on the station, but was curious enough to see if it would go. And that's how *The Talk of Paris* came to life.

I first did talk radio on the old *Comment* show on KRLD starting in 1960 and I loved it. Now all these forty-plus years later, I'm doing talk radio again and enjoying it even more than the first time around. We talked to a lot of the great and those who thought they were great back then, but none can compare to the "associates," the regular callers to the KPLT show. Most of the regulars have on-the-air nicknames; I don't really want to know their real names.

Nine times out of ten when I'm introduced at the beginning of the show, I don't know what I'm going to talk about. I call the little monologue I do from 8:05 to 8:15 my "homily." The topic of the homily may be anything that has somehow captured my attention. The associates know not to call during that time. Occasionally, someone will call during the homily, but they'll hold on for seven or eight minutes until I'm done. Sometimes, weather is the topic:

How were things out at your place yesterday afternoon? I am hearing all kinds of stories, including that the elementary school at Bogata is closed today. Not the high school, but the elementary school, because something, the wind or a tornado or whatever, lifted half the roof off the elementary school. . . . My wife and I at noon were over in the Dollar General store in Cooper, and the storm came in and you wouldn't believe it. . . . Eventually, the storm moved on out, but it was dark, it was rainy, it was windy! I told my wife, well, when we get back to the place [the farm], I'll bet you we're going to have two or three inches in that rain gauge. So we got back home and I looked at the rain gauge and we had half an inch. Very disappointing. . . . Well, it was the first big storm of the spring. Just think, we'll have three or four months of these great boomers. That's one of the joys, I think, of living here, is that we have this kind of weather. I love it. I love it! Oh, I know I've told you this story, but one day we were having a big thunderstorm down there at the place, and I went out on the front porch and the lightning hit the fence, and my hair just went straight up.

Of course, the thunderstorms and turbulent weather are thrilling as long as they don't turn deadly, as Paris knows too well, because the city was nearly wiped out by a tornado in 1982.

I know a little bit about a lot of things. Very seldom do listeners bring up something that is just completely foreign to me. Very often, the calls that I take after the homily have absolutely nothing to do with what I've just talked about for ten minutes, particularly if I discourse on politics or world events. That's fine with me. The concerns of the associates tend to be heartfelt and closer to home:

BARKER: Hi, you're on The Talk of Paris.
CALLER: Hello, Eddie, this is "Connecticut."
BARKER: How in the world are you?
CALLER: Don't even ask.
BARKER: Oh, it's that bad, huh?
CALLER: Yes, sir. My husband needs prayers real bad today. . . . We had to take him to Plano Medical Center yesterday. . . . [They're going] down with the 'scope, to see where the stones are. He had his gall bladder out about six years ago and there's stones up in the viaduct.

Not to make light of anyone's medical problems, but as Johnny Carson might say, I think we all know how painful those stones in your viaduct can be.

Paris's most famous citizen is surely Gene Stallings, a football legend. Gene—"Bebes" as he was known then—grew up in Paris. He was one of Bear Bryant's "Junction Boys" at Texas A&M in the '50s and later went on to coach the Aggies himself. He was an assistant coach for many years under Tom Landry with the Cowboys and followed in the footsteps of the Bear as the head coach at the University of Alabama, leading the Crimson Tide to a national championship. Not long after that, he hung 'em up and moved back to his ranch outside of town.

One day on the show I had a call from an associate, "The Umbrella Lady," who said she'd been seeing "The Woodchopper," another faithful caller, on a television commercial. Well, this seemed most unlikely, but I went along with it. Then someone else called and told me it was Gene Stallings in the commercial.

Pretty soon, The Woodchopper himself called. He hadn't heard the earlier calls, so I decided to have some fun with him. I said, "I didn't know you were making commercials."

He said, "What are you talking about?"

I said, "Well, The Umbrella Lady called and said she saw you in a commercial."

He said, "Naw, I'm not in any commercials." So then I told him we had found out it was Gene Stallings in the ad.

"Who's he?" asked The Woodchopper.

I replied, "How long have you been living here? Don't you know who Gene Stallings is? He's 'Mr. Paris.'"

And The Woodchopper, unimpressed, calmly asked, "What did he do?"

Well, it goes to show that people in the country have their priorities in order. The things that make a person celebrated and famous in the big-city world don't necessarily make a big impression out here.

I've written about how much I loved broadcasting college football on the Humble network. Getting back into radio with KPLT gave me a chance to once again take a seat in the press box.

Nothing is bigger on small-town Texas radio than high school football. It is the easiest sell of the year by far for the radio stations. KPLT has always broadcast Paris High on AM and North Lamar High on its FM sister station. Then along comes Chisum High. They were pushing Jeff to get on the air, but where would he put them? He then made a deal with the local cable channel, but had no one to announce the games. "How would you like to do high school football again?" he asked.

"I'd love it," I replied, and so for a season I was back to where I started.

It was fun, quite different from the last time I did a game. When I was doing college ball, every school had a sports information director to make sure you had whatever you needed. Today, the SIDs are even more finely honed in their skills than they were then. But remember, Chisum is a 2A high school and it thought "SID" was that fella who used to sell peanuts in the stands. I usually had a spotter, an assistant who helps identify the players, if he didn't have a more important job come up. We broadcast the games via cell phone. I don't know that I'd do it again, but the enthusiasm on a Friday night in a high school football stadium is like nothing else in sports.

For a long time, I never gave a lot of thought to this little two-hour talk show every morning. But my Jane, an ardent listener and critic, started telling me there was something about the show that was going well beyond just a way to spend a couple of hours every morning. She said it had become a vital part of life for many of the listeners. It's hard to describe, but what Jane picked up on was true: *The Talk of Paris* has become a very personal show, with callers sharing their lives in vivid detail. Other listeners call in concerned about the well-being of earlier callers.

To show you how neighborly the listeners are, about halfway into the nine o'clock hour one day, the door opened and here was this dear associate with a present for me, an automatic hard-boiled egg peeler. I had complained that I have trouble peeling hard-boiled eggs, so she simply filled my need.

One day a regular caller asked me on the air if I would be a pallbearer at his funeral, which his failing health told him was not far away. The listeners have become bonded to each other and now have a yearly "birthday party" so they can meet each other. Everyone is an "associate" if they call; if they just listen and don't call, they are our audio "voyeurs." But they all come to the birthday party.

A couple of years ago, "Swiss," one of the faithful callers, said it was his birthday. How was he going to celebrate? "Every year I go down to Braum's and have a banana split; it's really a tradition with me. So at three o'clock this afternoon, I'll go to Braum's." He went to Braum's and so did about a dozen other associates, who decided to come and wish him a happy birthday.

The next morning, "Farmer Rex" called. We talked about Swiss and his banana split, and Rex said, "You know, Eddie, I've never had a birthday party since I was a little boy." Well, that did it. The associates started buzzing, and the next thing I knew, one of the associates called and said, "Tell Farmer Rex to come to Braum's in the morning at eleven o'clock and we'll have a party for him." The next morning at eleven o'clock, after the show, Farmer Rex showed up in a freshly starched pair of striped overalls and was greeted by some forty other listeners (more on these events later).

The next year, over sixty associates, joined by some audio voyeurs, came for the festivities. But it was time to move out of Braum's. The annual party is now held in the local VFW hall. And it all started with Swiss and his banana split.

My friend John Mark Dempsey, who has helped me write this book, went to a "birthday party" for *The Talk of Paris* listeners. This is his impression:

Usually when a broadcasting "celebrity"—Oprah Winfrey, Don Imus, Bill O'Reilly—holds some sort of public event, the listeners or viewers turn out to see and meet the famed personage. But the most striking thing about this party was that Eddie's associates came not so much to see Eddie as to see each other.

The get-together on this sunny, early spring day started before Eddie's daily program on KPLT ended. It had been going nearly an hour when Eddie walked in. No applause, no cheers, no crowding around the "star." Very simply, another one of the "gang" had arrived, no more, no less.

Eddie ambles into the meeting room, and attempts to make an announcement. During that morning's program, an anonymous listener has donated four pricy watches to be given as prizes to the associates. But the radio friends are so deeply engaged in conversation, Eddie has a hard time getting their attention. Finally, Eddie's daughter Jeanne, visiting from Dallas, makes her way to the front of the room and tells her dad, "Nobody can hear you in the back." Eddie replies: "Well, go back and tell 'em what I said."

Eddie has given nicknames to many of the listeners, because, in the beginning, many were shy about identifying themselves on the air. Others are known by their given names. Either way, here at the party, they wear name tags. As they enter the little hall, they spot friends they know only by their voices:

"You're just as cute as you sound!"

"I want to hug you!"

"I want to hug you, too!"

"Did you bring your guitar?" (To "Ginger," a listener known for her musical talent.)

Around 150 people have gathered, crowding every room. It feels like a very large Sunday school party, or perhaps a family Thanksgiving get-together. Husbands and wives arrive together. Cameras flash. The conversation flows easily, while paper plates holding doughnuts and muffins balance precariously on the knees of chatting friends. Most of the people in this VFW hall have memories of Pearl Harbor, V-E Day and V-J Day. They wear caps that read: "U.S. Army Retired," "Retired USMC," and "Life Member VFW 3990." They are white and they are black. Just as in any house, lots of folks congregate in the kitchen.

There, Eddie introduces me to "Cuz." "She's the poet laureate of the show," Eddie says admiringly, "and she's the biggest Avon saleslady in Paris." The outgoing Cuz denies Eddie's acclaim, but clearly enjoys the attention.

The unofficial leader of the associates is "Swiss," a neatly mustachioed man in a brightly striped sweater and chauffeur's cap. His real name is John Guy. He was a real-estate man in Port Aransas until he came to Paris 13 years ago and became a special-education teacher. Now he's retired. Swiss works the room like a politician, but he's not running for anything.

"I want to meet you," one listener tells Swiss. "I always enjoy hearing you call in."

"Oh, I stir up a little dust," Swiss jokes. He says people have asked him to run for local political office from hearing him on *The Talk of Paris*.

"These people come from all walks of life," Swiss says. "Farmers and ranchers. You wouldn't know any of them have money. Some of these guys walking around in coveralls are millionaires."

Swiss says Eddie has brought many fresh ideas to his

listeners. "With his background in radio and television, Eddie has brought such a diversity of ideas and thoughts. He gives us new things to think about. It's a wonderful thing Eddie has put together. If the listeners don't hear from someone, they call up and ask, 'Where is he? Is he in the hospital?'" Swiss says he sometimes gets 20 or 30 calls in a single day from Eddie's listeners, inquiring about one of the others. "I've come to think of him as a friend. It's amazing to think I'm really talking to a guy who was so involved in covering the Kennedy assassination, and who knows Walter Cronkite and Dan Rather. It makes you proud to have him in a little town like this. We're so lucky to have him."

After our most recent associates birthday party, I received this heartwarming e-mail message. I think you can see from it how much the listeners appreciate the show:

Eddie,

Just a note to thank you for being the reason for the party this morning!!! It was fun meeting the people that I've wondered for years what they looked like. The turnout was great and the refreshments were wonderful. It couldn't have been a better party!! As I told everybody, "you" start my day every weekday—I always look forward to listening to the *Talk of Paris* and throughout the years I have learned so much from you and your show. I wouldn't trade anything in the world for it! You are the "perfect" host for a talk show—you really know how to do it.

Thanks, Linda

My daughter Leslie Garcia, as I've told you, is a reporter and columnist for the *Dallas Morning News*. Of course, I'm very proud of all of my children. But Leslie is the only one who has more or less followed in my news footsteps, as a columnist and reporter for the *Morning News*. Her stories and columns have so much heart and depth. One editor told her, "Leslie, you're the soul of this newspaper."

She really is so good. The thing that I value so much is that if she's going to do a certain piece, we'll discuss it and she'll e-mail it to me ahead of time so I can look it over.

When she was in high school, she was a copygirl at the *Morning News*. Ben was a copyboy. Leslie worked there a couple of summers and then went off to Baylor. She worked for the *News* every summer during vacation. In the summer between her junior and senior years, Buster Haas, an editor, told her he wanted to make her an official intern. As soon as she graduated, she went to work for the *News*, and it's the only employer she's ever had.

Leslie wrote a wonderful feature story about my KPLT show and, more important, its listeners. I think Leslie's article captures the spirit of our little show. (I might say that, since Leslie's article, KPLT has moved into shiny, state-of-the-art studios):[1]

PARIS, Texas—This doesn't look like a gathering spot, this all-but-deserted brick radio-station building with its empty offices and "Sauna" sign hung by some long-ago jokester on a storage-room door.

But for two hours every Monday through Friday, voices flow through phone wires into the building and onto the airwaves. And somewhere in spaces nobody can see, the voices connect. They intertwine. They create a haven, a neighborhood, a place to listen and to be heard.

From 8 to 10 a.m., the people behind those voices as well as countless other listeners tune in as they chew their cereal or sip their coffee, as they put on lipstick or pack school lunches, as they feed the birds or kiss a spouse good-bye.

My dad, Eddie Barker, may not know each by sight. But in his eight-year run as host of the radio show that brings them all together, he has learned to recognize their voices.

Every weekday morning, he sits on a stool in his little studio, scribbled notes on a yellow legal pad in front of him. Nearby, producer Jerry Anderson—the only person besides Dad who's ever in the building—has placed a bucket to catch water when the roof leaks.

"Good morning, 'The Talk of Paris,'" Dad begins each conversation. And one at a time, a voice answers.

Maybe it belongs to the Old Timer, who often serenades

the radio audience with a tune on his guitar.

"I play in the key of C," he likes to say. "I play and you 'C' if you can tell what it is."

It might be the woman dubbed Dr. Dotty, giving an update on the number of cardinals in her yard (14 on an early spring day). Or Ol' No. 9, who has programmed the show's phone number into the No. 9 slot of his speed-dial.

The Restaurant Critic (a.k.a. Mrs. Nickerson) calls regularly to fill everybody in on how her latest supper or lunch at Chili's or Applebee's tasted. She's even called from her hospital room to rate the food she'd been served there.

The Cat Lady moved to Pennsylvania, but still calls every week or so.

Janyce Draper, a daily caller, keeps everyone posted on her water exercise classes (which Dad refers to as "walking on water") or which part of her house she'll clean today. Wednesday, as listeners know, is bathroom day and one of her two days to vacuum (Thursday being the other). Sometimes she tells of shopping expeditions to what's now known as "Janyce's favorite store"—Wal-Mart.

And dear ol' Swiss, who calls every day, ends his visit thusly: "Happy trails, Eddie."

And Dad responds: "Happy trails, Swiss."

A Father's Dreams

When "The Talk of Paris" first aired eight years ago, it was the fulfillment of one of my father's dreams. He'd hosted a talk show on KRLD (1080-AM) way back in the '60s and spent years as an on-air TV newsman and news director. But the idea of small-town radio had long charmed him.

So about a year after he and Mom moved to the country outside nearby Cooper, Texas, Dad got the OK from KPLT (1490-AM). He wasn't looking too far into the future; all he knew was that he wanted the show.

He didn't dream he'd become what he calls the show's "shepherd"; that he'd bestow nicknames upon the "regulars" who called; that listeners would present him with baskets of figs, plates of homemade peanut brittle and cookies.

How could he foresee that more than 200 people would one day submit recipes for a cookbook? That when callers he had dubbed The Liberal and The Poet Laureate died, people they'd never met in their lifetimes would attend their funerals? [Eddie eventually recognized Cuz as the new poet laureate.] That those who tuned into KPLT during those two hours would become like each other's family?

"I love it because it's just like sitting in a room talking to someone," says Verlene Bills, 82, who calls herself "the oldest black LVN [licensed vocational nurse] in Lamar County."

"I'm by myself, so lonesome."

But for two hours every day—and longer if she, like many listeners, decides to call Swiss afterwards for more information or for his opinion—she knows people care.

"There was a saying on the show one time: 'This is it; we share,' " Swiss says. "Eddie said that jokingly, but everybody does share. "This is a social addiction. If I miss the program, I feel I've missed something."

Lives Joined

Whenever I visit my parents and listen to the show myself, or hear Dad talk about it over dinner, I am struck by how these people—strangers up till a few short years ago—have become part of each other's lives. If one of the regulars isn't heard from for a while, somebody finds out why, and calls the show to give a report.

"Do you ever stop to think how much you help shut-ins like myself?" a woman asks Dad the day I visit the show. "I . . . am confined to a wheelchair. I don't see the TV that well, but I do keep up with everything going on because of your father."

Audience members swap recipes and remedies, trade ways to get rid of squirrels in the attic or bobcats on the front porch. They share opinions on politics, and tricks to distinguishing between a female and a male chicken. When a woman named Emma called to find a recipe for big, fat, soft gingerbread men, the replies came for days.

During the war in Iraq, a listener called to say he'd decided to hang the British flag alongside his American one. For the next few days, others called to report where they'd bought a Union Jack, and that they, too, had raised it with Old Glory. Someone even gave Dad one.

On days when the phone rings only sporadically, Dad might recite poems he learned during his childhood, or ask Bible trivia questions. He offers updates on his and my mom's peacocks, or the duck eggs in their incubator.

He's forever designating somebody to chair one of his made-up "committees"—investigating everything from firefighters' salaries to gasoline prices.

At one point, Dad and Swiss headed up a push to find a wife for Farmer Rex (so named for the vegetables he grows and sells at the local farmers market.)

"I met a couple of women I liked," says Farmer Rex (who does have a last name—Bolton). "But they were looking for a younger man with a lot more money."

No matter, he says. He's made a lot of friends since listening to the show. People stop by the farmers market to meet him and buy his peas, beans, turnips and tomatoes.

"When I got something I feel like is important to say, I always call in," Rex says. "I don't call just to chitchat."

Some do, and that's fine. Others comment on news of the day, or make an announcement. Swiss calls the show "a community bulletin board."

One day, Dad tells me, the water commissioner called to ask listeners to cut back on water usage until a leak was fixed. The day I was there, he called back to say thank-you, that the conservation methods had greatly helped.

John Kelley, pastor of Faith Presbyterian Church of Paris, has a voice rich as the Yum-Yum Pie recipe that Inez Shawhart submitted to the cookbook. You find yourself hoping he talks longer, just so you can revel in the deep resonance. (And yes, people have recognized him by voice at restaurants and at Janyce's favorite store.)

"Edward," he begins.

"Johnnnnn," Dad drawls out in answer.

On this day, the pastor is calling to remind everyone that

Agape House is scheduled for this weekend. The free monthly medical clinic is sponsored by his and other area churches.

"As I drive around, his show is my priority," John tells me later. "It gets the pulse of things. I know your dad has a listening audience in the community. It helps to raise awareness on issues."

During a fund-raiser for Agape, Dad encouraged listeners to send in $5, $10, whatever they could spare. They came through, donating $400 to the church.

Swiss' own generosity earned him his nickname. One day, he was just a man named John Guy calling the show to talk about his garden, its dirt brimming with Swiss chard.

Dad had never heard of the vegetable. So the next day, John brought him a basketful. In return, Dad gave him a new name.

Now, he signs letters to the editor of *The Paris News* "John 'Swiss' Guy." Everybody calls him Swiss.

"I have been recognized at Braum's, at Brookshire's several times, at the car wash, the hardware store," says Swiss, 54. "There are people I've met in the past who say, 'I just found out you're Swiss.' "

Loyal Listeners

A slew of listeners gathered at Braum's last year for Swiss' annual birthday banana split. Swiss, a diabetic, had told Dad that he allowed himself the yearly treat "so he wouldn't forget what it tasted like."

One listener decided to go to Braum's, wait for him and introduce herself. She encouraged listeners to join her; several dozen showed up.

She also organized a birthday party for Farmer Rex, who told Dad last year he hadn't had one since he was a little boy. He's now had two, the most recent in mid-March.

At the party, "We'd go up to each other and say, 'Who are you?' 'Who are you?' " because we wanted to see what each other looked like," a listener says. "The ones who don't call . . . are almost apologetic. We had to get the point across that a listener is very valuable."

Some listeners are better known by their nicknames. For example, Dessie Nickerson is the Restaurant Critic. Dad bestowed the moniker when Mrs. Nickerson called to say how good her meal at Applebee's had been. That was one of her first calls; now, she's considered a regular. And her voice, like that of her compatriots, has been recognized.

"I went to Clarksville one Sunday to church and this lady came up and said, 'Are you Mrs. Nickerson?' " she says, "and I said, 'Yes, who are you?' And she said, 'I'm Detroit Dorothy!' [another listener]

"In the hospital, it was like being a celebrity. People came to my room and said, 'Aren't you on the air?' and, 'I want my mother to meet you.' I just love it."

After her hospital stay, two listeners called to ask Mrs. Nickerson if she needed a ride to the doctor. She did. When she realized she'd forgotten her insurance card, they drove back to her house to retrieve it.

"They treated me full of love," she says.

On the way home, they stopped at the grocery store. She waited in the car, thinking they'd just grab a few items. But the Jurys came out with bags brimming with fresh fruits and vegetables, bread, milk, coffee, soup. When Ken presented her with a dozen red carnations, she cried.

They care and they share, these wonderful listeners. And at the end of two hours, you find yourself wanting more. But no. Jerry the Producer (whom some suspect — correctly or incorrectly, I cannot say—as being the mysterious Movie Critic) is playing the send-out music: "Happy Trails."

And Dad's giving his daily goodbye:

"I hope today is a wonderful day for you. In the morning, after the 8 o'clock news, we'll find you here. On 'The Talk of Paris.'"

At this point, I am sorry to add that our old friend Swiss died in early 2005, a real loss for *The Talk of Paris*. We miss him.

Anyone who has known me for any length of time or who has listened to me on the radio has heard me quote lines of poetry that seem appropriate for the occasion, whatever it may be. One of the lines I like to recite gravely when something terrible has happened is, "The young recruits will want their beer today," from Rudyard Kipling's "Danny Deever," about the hanging of a British soldier. It ends:

For they're done with Danny Deever,
you can 'ear the quickstep play,
The regiment's in column, an' they're marchin' us away;
Ho! the young recruits are shakin', an' they'll want their beer today,
After hangin' Danny Deever in the mornin'.

My love of poetry came from my mother, who recited it to me when I was a babe in arms. One of the first poems I memorized was "A Psalm of Life," by Longfellow. You remember, a few lines from the poem kick off Chapter 1. It's an inspirational exhortation to dream big and do great things. It begins:

Tell me not in mournful numbers,
"Life is but an empty dream!"
For the soul is dead that slumbers,
And things are not what they seem.
Life is real! Life is earnest!
And the grave is not its goal;
"Dust thou art, to dust returnest,"
Was not spoken of the soul.

My mother just had this love of poetry that I've passed along to my kids, Susan especially. But not long ago, we were in Washington, D.C., having dinner with Ben and his then-fiancée, Meg, and something came up about "The Midnight Ride of Paul Revere," also by Longfellow. Ben recited the first line of it : "Listen my children and you shall hear, of the midnight ride of Paul Revere"; then the second:

"On the eighteenth of April, in Seventy-five; hardly a man is now alive, who remembers that famous day and year"; and then he recited the whole darn poem. He was amazed at himself: "Look at me remembering that."

All of the grandkids know "The Cremation of Sam McGee," an epic poem by Robert W. Service:

There are strange things done in the midnight sun
By the men who moil for gold;
The Arctic trails have their secret tales
That would make your blood run cold;
The Northern Lights have seen queer sights,
But the queerest they ever did see
Was that night on the marge of Lake Lebarge
I cremated Sam McGee.

It's about a gold prospector in Alaska who suffers so much from the cold that he tells his partner to cremate his body when he dies. And so the old prospector leaves his friend in the wreckage of an abandoned boat and sets it on fire. But he looks inside and is astonished to see Sam McGee alive and well:

Please close that door.
It's fine in here, but I greatly fear you'll let in the cold and storm—
Since I left Plumtree, down in Tennessee,
It's the first time I've been warm.

Of course, Service also wrote "The Shooting of Dan McGrew" and a lot of other great poems, tales of the Yukon. Every schoolkid used to learn them. A couple of years ago, Ben found a leather-bound book of Service's poetry and sent it to me, which of course, I greatly prize.

Here's one I quite often quote. It was in a book my mother had, which I've looked for for years and never found. The poem is "Dr. John Goodfellow, Office Upstairs," and I'm sorry to say I don't know who wrote it. Whenever I hear of someone's passing I usually say:

He died as the best and the worst of us must,
No gold had he gathered, no gear had he won,

His wealth was the memory of noble deeds done.

When asked to do a eulogy, you can bet I'll find a spot for these lines. It's a beautiful poem, the story of a simple life, greatly told.

One of my favorite poets is Robert Frost. I could read him all day. "Stopping by Woods on a Snowy Evening" is a favorite, a meditation on pausing to appreciate the beauty in a moment before moving on, something we all should do a lot more. And so, as we all gaze to the horizon, I could do no better than to leave you with Frost's famous lines:

The woods are lovely, dark and deep.
But I have promises to keep,
And miles to go before I sleep,
And miles to go before I sleep.

References:
[1] Leslie Garcia "Talk of the Town," *Dallas Morning News* (May 10, 2003): 2-E.

ABOUT THE AUTHORS

Eddie Barker is a pioneer of local television broadcasting. He joined KRLD-TV, Channel 4, in Dallas as an announcer on the first day the station signed on, December 3, 1949. He later became news director of both Channel 4 and KRLD radio. His work with CBS in covering the John F. Kennedy assassination is legendary. He is known as the first television reporter to announce the president's death. He remained with KRLD (now KDFW-TV) until 1972, when he left to form his own public-relations firm, Eddie Barker Associates. He is a past president of the Radio Television News Directors Association. Today, Eddie lives on a farm in Northeast Texas and hosts a daily talk show, *The Talk of Paris*, on KPLT radio in Paris. He is a charter member of the Texas Radio Hall of Fame.

John Mark Dempsey is an associate professor of radio-television at Texas A&M University–Commerce. He has published two other books, *The Jack Ruby Trial Revisited: The Diary of Jury Foreman Max Causey*, and *The Light Crust Doughboys Are on the Air!* He holds bachelor's and master's degrees from East Texas State University (now Texas A&M–Commerce) and a Ph.D. from Texas A&M University. He has served on the faculties of the Texas A&M University and University of North Texas journalism departments. He also works as a radio news announcer and producer for the Texas State Network.

Major Sources

Aynesworth, Hugh. "The Strangest Story I Ever Covered." *D Magazine* 10, no. 8 (August 1983): 86-89, 137-43.

Bliss, Edward. *Now the News: The Story of Broadcast Journalism.* New York: Columbia University Press, 1991.

"CBS News Extra: November 22 and the Warren Report." CBS Television Network script, September 27, 1964. Collection of Eddie Barker.

"CBS News Inquiry: The Warren Report." Parts 1-4. CBS Television Network script, June 25-28, 1967. Collection of Eddie Barker.

Chappell, Frank. "KRLD-TV Program to Combine Best Radio, Theater Technique." *Dallas Times-Herald* (December 4, 1949).

"Closeup of a Twister." *Time* (April 15, 1957).

Cronkite, Walter. *A Reporter's Life.* New York: Alfred A. Knopf, 1996.

"Demo Ranks Split on JFK Luncheon." *Dallas Times-Herald* (November 15, 1963).

Doherty, Thomas. "Assassination and Funeral of John F. Kennedy." In Les Brown, ed., *Les Brown's Encyclopedia of Television*, vol. 2, 880-83. Detroit, Mich.: Gale, 1992.

"Education Needs JFK Topic Here." *Dallas Times-Herald* (November 14, 1963).

Edwards, Douglas. "News Coverage Keeping Pace with Industry." *Dallas Times-Herald* (December 4, 1949).

"Epochal Stride Taken in KRLD-TV's Opening." *Dallas Times-Herald* (December 4, 1949).

"A Far Out, Far Up Mystery." *Life* (February 1, 1960).

Garcia, Leslie. "Talk of the Town." *Dallas Morning News* (May 10, 2003).

Hlavach, Laura, and Darwin Payne, eds. *Reporting the Kennedy Assassination: Journalists Who Were There Recall Their Experiences.* Dallas: Three Forks Press, 1996.

Isaacs, Stan. "Once Around the Bases of the National Pastime." http://www.thecolumnists.com/isaacs/isaacs/166.html. Accessed July 20, 2005.

"KRLD-TV Takes to Air in Official Ceremonies." *Dallas Times-Herald* (December 3, 1949).

Lane, Mark. *Rush to Judgment.* New York: Holt, Rinehart & Winston, 1966.

Latham, H. Lee. "A Survey of the Greater Dallas Crime Commission and Its Effect on the Criminal Justice System." Master's thesis, University of North Texas, 2001.

"News Beat in Dallas." *Time* (February 1, 1960).

"On-Sport News Broadcasts Set as Daily Feature of KRLD-TV." *Dallas Times-Herald* (December 4, 1949).

Oxley, Billy B. "A Descriptive Analysis of the Radio Sportscasting Techniques of Kern Tips." Master's thesis, University of Texas, 1965.

"Politics and Presidential Protection: The Motorcade." Staff Report of the Select Committee on Assassinations. United States House of Representatives. Ninety-fifth Congress, Second Session, March 1979.

Posner, Gerald. *Case Closed: Lee Harvey Oswald and the Assassination of JFK.* New York: Random House, 1993.

Rather, Dan. *The Camera Never Blinks.* New York: Ballantine, 1977.

Report of the President's Commission on the Assassination of President John F. Kennedy. United States. Warren Commission. Garden City, N.Y.: Doubleday, 1964.

Sherrod, Blackie. "Erudition Erupts Where Some Least Expect It." *Dallas Morning News* (April 5, 2001).

"Timely, Fresh News Coverage Set on KRLD-TV." *Dallas Times-Herald* (December 4, 1949).

Van der Karr, Richard K. "How Dallas TV Stations Covered Kennedy Shooting." *Journalism Quarterly* 42 (Winter 1965): 646-47.

"A World Listened and Watched." *Broadcasting* (December 2, 1963): 40.

Zelizer, Barbie. *Covering the Body: The Kennedy Assassination, the Media and the Shaping of Collective Memory.* Chicago: University of Chicago Press, 1992.

Index